Knowledge of God

Great Debates in Philosophy
Series Editor: Ernest Sosa

Dialogue has always been a powerful means of philosophical exploration and exposition. By presenting important current issues in philosophy in the form of a debate, this series attempts to capture the flavor of philosophical argument and to convey the excitement generated by the exchange of ideas. Each author contributes a major, original essay. When these essays have been completed, the authors are each given the opportunity to respond to the opposing view.

Knowledge of God

Alvin Plantinga
and
Michael Tooley

Blackwell
Publishing

BLACKWELL PUBLISHING

350 Main Street, Malden, MA 02148-5020, USA
9600 Garsington Road, Oxford OX4 2DQ, UK
550 Swanston Street, Carlton, Victoria 3053, Australia

First published 2008 by Blackwell Publishing Ltd

2   2009

Library of Congress Cataloging-in-Publication Data

Plantinga, Alvin
  Knowledge of God / Alvin Plantinga and Michael Tooley
    p. cm.
  Includes bibliographical references and index.
  ISBN 978-0-631-19363-0 (hardcover : alk. paper)
  ISBN 978-0-631-19364-7 (pbk. : alk. paper)
  1. God (Christianity)—Knowableness. I. Tooley, M. J. II. Title.

BT103.P58 2008
212'.6—dc22

                                                    2007033954

A catalogue record for this title is available from the British Library.

Set in 10/12.5 pt Adobe Caslon Pro
by Newgen Imaging Systems (P) Ltd, Chennai, India
Printed and bound in Singapore
by C.O.S. Printers Pte Ltd.

For further information on
Blackwell Publishing, visit our website at
www.blackwellpublishing.com

To my children and their spouses – Carl, Cindy, Jane, Jack, Harry, Pam, Ann, and Ray – sources of pride and great joy.

Alvin Plantinga

To the memory of my teacher, Walter Kaufmann, for whose works on religion I have the very greatest admiration, and to Anthony Tooley, my oldest grandson, who, at the age of seven, and not knowing that anyone had ever even entertained any doubts about religion, discovered, entirely on his own, a version of the argument from evil.

Michael Tooley

Contents

Acknowledgements

Alvin Plantinga
I wish to record my gratitude for good advice and wise counsel to many, including Brian Boeninger, E.J. Coffman, Chris Green, Jeff Green, Marcin Iwanicki, Nathan King, Dan McKaughan, Dolores Morris, Brian Pitts, Luke Potter, and especially Mikes Bergmann and Rea. I also ask forgiveness from those I have inadvertently overlooked.

Michael Tooley
During the early, initial research that preceded the actual writing for this volume, I was fortunate to have the help of two excellent graduate students who served as research assistants: Jessica Wilson (now at the University of Toronto) and Rich Geenen (now at Westminster College). I had many stimulating conversations with each of them concerning a number of relevant issues.

Many people provided me with excellent and very detailed comments on my opening statement: Dennis Earl, Michael Huemer, Daniel Korman, Wes Morriston, Graham Oddie, Graham Oppy, Robert Pasnau, Quentin Smith, and Eric Vogelstein. Then Evan Fales, Scott Hagaman, Christian Lee, and Wes Morriston all provided me with extremely helpful feedback on my response to Plantinga's opening statement, while Christian also offered many very incisive comments on my closing statement. I very much appreciate this very extensive input from people who were interested in this debate, and all three of my contributions to this volume have been strengthened significantly by the excellent suggestions and incisive criticisms that I received.

Finally, it is not often that one has a chance to engage in a very extended conversation about a central philosophical question with a philosopher whose views are very different from one's own, and who has thought very deeply about the issues. I am therefore very grateful to Alvin Plantinga for inviting me to join him in this debate.

1

Against Naturalism

Alvin Plantinga

I Theism

Our topic is theistic belief, i.e., belief in God, and, more particularly, the epistemology of theistic belief. Now the main part of my initial contribution will be an epistemological attack on one of the two principal alternatives to theism: philosophical naturalism. First, however, I must say something to characterize theism. Following that, I'll argue that theism has a significant epistemic virtue: if it is true, it is (very likely) warranted; this is a virtue naturalism most emphatically lacks. Then I'll deliver a three-part indictment against philosophical naturalism. I'll argue that (1) if naturalism were true, there would be no such thing as *proper function*, and therefore also no such thing as malfunction or dysfunction. Hence there would be no such thing as health or sickness, sanity or madness; further, and in this epistemological context crucial, there would be no such thing as knowledge. That's bad enough, but there's worse to follow: I'll argue (2) that the naturalist is committed to the sort of deep and debilitating skepticism according to which he can't trust his cognitive faculties to furnish him with mainly true beliefs; he has a *defeater* for whatever he believes, including naturalism itself. And (3) I'll argue that naturalism, insofar as it implies materialism about human beings, has no room for the essential features of our mental life, including in particular *belief*.

A. *Theistic belief: what is it?*

According to classical theistic belief—classical Muslim and Jewish as well as Christian belief—first of all there is God, the chief being of the universe, who has neither beginning nor end. Most important, God is *personal*. That is,

God is the kind of being who is conscious and enjoys some kind of awareness of his surroundings (in God's case, that would be everything). Second (though not second in importance), a person has loves and hates, wishes and desires; she approves of some things and disapproves of others; she wants things to be a certain way. We might put this by saying that persons have *affections*. A person, third, is a being who has *beliefs* and, if fortunate, knowledge. We human beings, for example, believe a host of things. At the moment I believe that I am typing on my computer, that I just had breakfast, that outside it is bright and sunny, that I recently went rock climbing, that I live in Indiana, and so on. I also have a host of beliefs about things more distant from myself: that Beijing is larger than Chicago, that scientists seem to believe that quantum mechanics is highly confirmed, that there once was a war between the Athenians and the Spartans, that even the simplest forms of life are enormously complex, that there is such a person as God, and a thousand other things.

Persons, therefore, have beliefs and affections. Further, a person is a being who has *aims* and *intentions*; a person aims to bring it about that things should be a certain way, intends to act so that things will be the way he wants them to be. Thus I intend to bring it about that my part of this book is written, and written by me. (Put less pedantically, I intend to write my part of this book.) Finally, persons can often act to fulfill their intentions; they can bring it about that things are a certain way; they can cause things to happen. To be more technical (though not more insightful or more clear), we might say that a person is a being who can actualize states of affairs. Persons can often act on the basis of what they believe in order to bring about states of affairs whose actuality they desire.

So a person is conscious, has affections, beliefs, and intentions, and can act. Of course this would be a well-formed, paradigmatic person. Disease or malfunction can deprive a person of one or another of the above characteristics. Due to malfunction a person may lose affect, so that nothing seems either good or bad, desirable or undesirable. A person in a coma is not conscious and cannot act; perhaps a person in a coma also lacks belief or knowledge. The point is that a properly functioning well-formed person will display these properties, not that every person must display them at every time at which she exists.

First, therefore, God is a person. But second, unlike human persons, God is a person without a body.[1] He acts, and acts in the world, as human beings do, but, unlike human beings, not by way of a body. Rather, God acts just by *willing*: he wills that things be a certain way, and they are that way. (God said "Let there

---

[1] The Christian doctrine of the Trinity introduces complications here: the second person of the Trinity had, and indeed *has*, a body. Here I propose to avoid these complications; I'll use the word 'God' as a name of the first person of the Trinity.

be light"; and there was light.) You and I can move our limbs just by willing;[2] but we can't just by willing cause it to be the case that Lake Michigan warms up by 10 degrees, or that it's sunny and pleasant at the top of Mt. Rainier. God isn't subject to any such limitations; whatever he wills must necessarily come to pass. God is all-powerful ('omnipotent'). Of course he can't cause something logically impossible. He can't bring it about that there is a married bachelor, or that $7 + 5 = 14$. And he also can't cause a person to do something or other *freely*: if God *causes* me to do something, then I don't do that thing freely. So God can act, and we can act, but God can act in ways that we can't.

Something similar goes for knowledge: we human beings know a few things (maybe fewer than we ordinarily think), but there is much beyond our ken. Again, not so for God: given that he is all-knowing ('omniscient') as well as all-powerful, he knows everything, whatever can be known. Of course there are disputes in this area. Theists argue about whether God knows the future; they also argue about whether, even if he knows much about the future, he knows what free beings will in fact do. There is also dispute about whether God knows *counterfactuals of freedom*—propositions that specify what free creatures—you and I, for example, if in fact we are free creatures—would do in situations they will never be in. (Propositions like *If Mike were offered $15,000 for his old van, he would [freely] sell it*.) These are really arguments about what can be known; the basic idea is that God knows whatever can be known, even if it isn't clear, in every case, just what can be known. Still further, God is perfectly good. We human beings are a mixture of good and bad; there is evil in the best of us and good in the worst. Not so for God: there is no evil in him at all, and nothing bad about him. It is of course this combination of perfect goodness with omnipotence and omniscience that leads to the traditional problem of evil: it isn't easy to see why there would be so much suffering and evil in a world created by an all-knowing, all-powerful, and perfectly good God.[3]

Finally, God has created the world—from the largest things it contains to the smallest. He has created all the stars and planets, all the galaxies and black holes, all the quarks and gluons and electrons (assuming that there really are such things). He has created all living things—plants and animals and human beings—either directly, or by employing other beings and processes. From the perspective of classical theists—Jewish, Muslim, and Christian theists—human beings are special. From this perspective, God has created human beings "in his

---

[2] Although it is extraordinarily hard to say in detail what goes on when we will to move an arm, and how it is that as a result of that willing, the arm moves.

[3] For interesting recent work on the problem of evil, see, e.g., *God and the Problem of Evil*, ed. William Rowe (Oxford: Blackwell, 2002), *The Evidential Argument from Evil*, ed. Daniel Howard-Snyder (Bloomington: Indiana Press, 1996), and *The Problem of Evil*, ed. Marilyn and Robert Adams (Oxford: Oxford University Press, 1990).

own image"—i.e., in such a way that in certain crucial respects they resemble him. Perhaps the central focus here is *personhood*: we human beings resemble God in being persons. Like God, we human beings have knowledge and affection; we too form intentions and are able to act on the basis of what we know in order to accomplish ends we seek. Of course there are enormous differences between human persons and God (a point some people tend to overlook, at least in their own case): he is an unlimited person and we are decidedly limited. Nonetheless the properties that make us persons—intellect, will, and affection, to use an old triumvirate—are ones we share with God.

God has created the world, but he also sustains it in existence; without this sustenance, the world would disappear like a candle flame in a high wind. Further, God governs the world in such a way that it displays a certain constancy and regularity. These regularities are everywhere: heavier-than-air objects dropped near the surface of the earth ordinarily fall down rather than up; bread is nourishing but mud is not; there is breathable air near the surface of the earth, though not at 35,000 feet or under water. Unlike rocks, seeds planted in soil sprout and take root; heavy steel beams will hold a lot of weight for a long time; a confined explosion will exert pressure on the walls of its container. It is by virtue of these regularities that human beings can act in the world, can learn about it, and act on what they have learned.

These regularities, of course, are what make science and technology possible. From the theistic point of view, the world God has designed and created is something like a vast machine, although that is perhaps too mechanical a term. (Perhaps it should also be thought of as something like a vast organism, or perhaps some amalgam of machine and organism.) In any event it is a structure of enormous complexity. (Think of the incredible complexity of a living cell, with its own hundreds of substructures in the form of molecular machines.) From a theistic point of view, one task of science is to come to know something about this wonderful structure—to learn about it in the systematic and communal way that is characteristic of science. Theism is thus, as such, not only hospitable to science, but enthusiastic about it. It is because God has created the world with these regularities and structures that it can be apprehended and known (to a significant degree) by creatures such as we are. It is because God has created us human beings in his image that we are able to apprehend and know the world.

A particularly interesting feature of the theistic view of the world, in this context, is that God created the various structures of the world *freely*. First, God wasn't obliged, by his nature or by some antecedent structure, or by anything else, to create anything at all. And given that he does create, he wasn't obliged to create just the things he did create. He has created horses, anacondas, and paramecia; he wasn't obliged to create any of them. And given that he creates the things—horses, for example—that we do in fact find, he wasn't obliged to create them with just the properties they do in fact have. It's not a necessary truth that horses have the number of teeth they do have, or a stomach that works just the way an equine stomach does work. Further, given that he has created the creatures the world displays, he wasn't obliged to create them in any particular manner; he could have created them all specially, or, as presently seems more likely, by way of some evolutionary process. These things are all contingent; God could have done things differently. We ordinarily think that it is by *reason* that we know necessary truths; we know these things *a priori*, prior to or in some way independent of experience. Our knowledge of contingent truths, on the other hand, is (at least in part) by *experience*. Now the theistic idea is that what laws or regularities the world displays is a contingent matter; the same goes for the sorts of structures and organisms the world contains, and the properties of those structures and organisms. This suggests that science, as a systematic effort to come to knowledge of the world God has created, will have to be significantly *empirical*. From a theistic point of view, we can perhaps see this as the root of the empirical nature of science.[4]

There are stories about early opponents of modern science refusing to count the number of a horse's teeth or look through a telescope to see how many moons Jupiter has. These stories may or may not be true; nevertheless they illustrate a point. If you think you can figure out the number of teeth in a horse's mouth *a priori*, you won't feel obliged to open that horse's mouth and actually count them. If you think you know just by reasoning that Jupiter has no moons, you won't feel compelled to actually take a look through a telescope to see how many there are. (If the result of looking agrees with reason, the looking is unnecessary; if it doesn't, it is misleading.) On the other hand, if you think the world and its structures are contingent—contingent on God's freely choosing to make them one way as opposed to other possibilities—you'll think looking to see is the appropriate way to find out. In this way the empirical nature of science, as well as its basic charter, arise out of a theistic way of looking at the world and fit in well with it.

---

[4]This thought goes back to the beginning of modern science; thus John Brook and Geoffrey Canton in *Reconstructing Nature: the Engagement of Science and Religion* (Edinburgh: T&T Clarke, 1998), p. 20:

> Marin Mersenne, who was at the nerve-centre of one of the first scientific correspondence networks, objected to Aristotle's claim that the earth must be at the centre of the cosmos. For Mersenne there was no "must" about it. It was wrong to say that the centre was the earth's *natural* place. God had been free to put it where he liked. It was incumbent on us to find where this was.

See also Peter Dear, *Mersenne and the Learning of the Schools* (Ithaca, NY: Cornell University Press, 1988).

B. *Why do people believe theism?*

Most of the world's population endorse and accept some form of theism. Why do they do so? Why do they believe that there is such a person as God, that he is all-powerful, all-knowing, wholly good; and that he has created the world? How do they think they know these things? How do they know there is such a person as God; how do they know he is all-powerful, all-knowing, all-good; how do they know that he has created the world? Well, of course there are the famous theistic proofs, the classical arguments for the existence of God. For example, there are the traditional big three: the cosmological or first cause argument, going back to the ancient world and in particular Aristotle; the so-called ontological argument, first stated by Anselm of Canterbury in the eleventh century; and the argument from apparent design, sometimes also called the teleological argument. Although opinions vary widely as to their cogency, each of these arguments is of great interest and each is under intense contemporary discussion; each also has contemporary exponents.[5] In addition to the traditional big three, there are a host of other theistic arguments—arguments from the nature of propositions, numbers, properties, from colors and flavors, from counterfactuals, and even a couple of arguments from the nature of evil.[6] None of these arguments, nor even all of them taken together, I think, can sensibly be called a proof, if a proof is an argument such that it isn't possible to reject it without irrationality. Of course that's not saying much; there aren't arguments of that level of stringency for much of anything in philosophy.

But believers in God haven't traditionally relied upon proofs or arguments for their belief in God; most of the world's believers, I suppose, have barely heard of these theistic arguments. Why, then, *do* they believe? That question seems to presuppose that the natural or usual or expected way to believe in God would be on the basis of proof or argument. But why think a thing like that? Most of what we believe, we don't believe on the basis of proof or argument; so why think one can properly believe in God, or the essentials of the Christian faith, only on the basis of argument? On the other hand, if theists don't believe

---

[5] For contemporary defense of the cosmological argument, see, e.g., William Craig, *The Cosmological Kaalam Argument* (London: Macmillan, 1979); for the ontological argument, see my *God, Freedom, and Evil* (Grand Rapids, MI: Eerdmans, 1977), pp. 85ff.; for the argument from design, particularly in its 'fine-tuning' version, see Robin Collins, "A Scientific Argument for the Existence of God: The Fine-Tuning Argument," in *Reason for the Hope Within*, ed. Michael Murray (Grand Rapids, MI: Eerdmans, 1999) and Robin Collins, "Evidence for Fine-Tuning," in *God and Design: the Teleological and Modern Science*, ed. Neil A. Manson (London: Routledge, 2003).

[6] See my "Two Dozen (or So) Theistic Arguments" on the web at *http://philofreligion.homestead.com/files/Theisticarguments.html*.

in God on the basis of argument, what *is* the basis on which they believe? If there is no basis, wouldn't belief in God be just arbitrary?

To answer, we must ascend (or descend) into epistemology. Let's think briefly about our whole cognitive establishment, our whole set of cognitive faculties, the set of faculties or processes whereby we form beliefs, reject beliefs, and revise and change beliefs. From a natural and pre-philosophical position, these faculties seem designed to enable us to achieve true belief with respect to a wide variety of propositions—about our immediate environment (by perception), about our own interior life (introspection), about our past (memory), about the thoughts and experiences of other persons, about our universe at large, about right and wrong, about the whole realm of *abstracta* (properties, propositions, states of affairs, numbers, and the like), about modality (what's necessary and possible), and about God himself. These faculties work in such a way that under the appropriate circumstances we form the appropriate belief. More exactly, the appropriate belief is *formed in us*. In the typical case we do not *decide* to hold or form the belief in question, but simply find ourselves with it. Upon considering an instance of *modus ponens*, I find myself believing that it is a valid argument. I look into the backyard and have a certain visual experience; I find myself believing that the trees in the backyard are covered with snow. Upon being asked what I had for breakfast, I reflect for a moment and then find myself with the belief that what I had was eggs on toast. In these and other cases I do not *decide* what to believe; I don't total up the evidence (I'm being appeared to redly; on most occasions when thus appeared to I am in the presence of something red; so most probably in this case I am) and make a decision as to what seems best supported; I simply believe. In other sorts of cases I take a more active role in the formation of my beliefs; I look for evidence, or carefully sift and consider the evidence I have, or evaluate arguments, or consult people in the know. On the (or a) natural theistic view of the cognitive enterprise, God has created us with a complex, subtle, highly articulated establishment of faculties enabling us to achieve true beliefs on a wide variety of topics.

But how does belief in God fit into this picture? As follows.[7] God created human beings originally with something like what John Calvin called a "Sensus Divinitatis"—a sense of divinity, a faculty, a set of cognitive processes whereby we come to know about God. The idea is that the *Sensus Divinitatis* is a faculty analogous, in some ways, to sense perception. By way of this faculty we human beings could know of the presence and properties of God. More important, by way of this faculty we could have the sort of relationship with God that

---

[7] Here what I'm presenting is a widely accepted Christian view of the epistemology of theistic belief; Jews and Muslims will think about the matter in a similar but somewhat different manner.

we have with other persons; there was to be communication and conversation, closeness, mutual love, and affection. Through the greatest catastrophe ever to befall the human race, however, we human beings somehow fell into sin, a ruinous condition in which we turned our backs upon God and rejected him. This condition is one all human beings share. Sin is a sort of madness of the will, a condition in which we love and hate the wrong things. Instead of loving God above all and our neighbor as ourselves, we tend to love ourselves above all, God and our neighbor coming in at best a very distant second. Indeed, according to the Heidelberg Catechism, we human beings are inclined to hate God and our neighbor; we resent the second as in competition with us, and the first as interfering with our own projects and autonomy.

The Christian story continues, however. God wasn't content to leave us in this appalling state. Instead, he proposed a scheme by which we human beings could be rescued from this sea of sin, and restored to our original condition of fellowship with God. The principal feature of this scheme is the incarnation, suffering, death, and resurrection of the divine Word, the second person of the Trinity, the Son of God. According to the Christian story, Jesus Christ, the second person of the Trinity, became a human being, took on our nature and our flesh. During his life and especially at its end he underwent enormous suffering, suffering of a depth and magnitude of which we have no understanding, suffering including not just crucifixion, but also that of feeling abandoned and forsaken by God the Father himself. He was crucified, and died (and rose from the dead); in this way he assumed the burden of human sin, redeeming us human beings from sin and its consequences. This salvation from sin is available to everyone; all that is required is to accept the proffered gift.

But, of course, God needed a way of informing people of every sort and condition, in all sorts of times and places, of the availability of the gift. No doubt he could have done this in many different ways. According to a classical Christian view I'll adopt here, God chose a three-part process. First, he arranged for the production of the Bible, a library of books or writings, each of which has a human author (or authors). These human authors, however, are inspired by God in a special way, a way in virtue of which God himself is the principal author of these books. The central theme and focus of the library is the gospel, the scheme of salvation God has offered. By virtue of this central theme and focus, the library is itself a book.

Second, there is the presence and activity of the Holy Spirit, the third member of Trinity, whose presence and action was promised by Christ himself before his death and resurrection, and invoked and celebrated in the epistles of the apostle Paul. On the classical Christian view, a person hears of God's scheme of salvation—in a sermon, from her parents, by reading the Bible, from a friend, or in some other way. The invitation of the Holy Spirit then enables her to see that the offer of salvation is a live option—not just for others, but also for herself. If the person accepts the offer of salvation, the Holy Spirit produces *faith* (the third part of the three-part process) in the mind and heart of the believer—a deep conviction that the main lines of the Christian story are in fact true. This work of the Holy Spirit also repairs the ravages of sin, including the damage to the *Sensus Divinitatis*. This whole process may go on gradually, over a period of years, or it may happen suddenly, with a shattering impact. The resulting belief can be of maximal firmness; it can also be much more tentative and fragile. What is central to the process is this work of the Holy Spirit in producing faith, whereby Christians come to grasp and believe, endorse and rejoice in the main lines of the Christian gospel.

C. Theistic belief and knowledge

According to Mark Twain, "faith is believing what you know ain't true"; but from a Christian point of view that's a whopping mistake. On the present way of thinking, faith is instead a way of coming to *know* the main elements of Christian teaching.[8] One hears the phrase 'leap of faith,' which suggests something like a leap in the dark. On the present way of thinking, however, Christian faith is not at all like a leap in the dark. It is not a matter of believing something on the basis of scanty evidence. Faith is not to be contrasted with knowledge; rather, if things go properly, it just *is* a certain kind of knowledge, and knowledge of truths of the greatest importance.

But how can faith be a form of knowledge? In order to understand this, we'll have to descend even further into the depths of epistemology. The first question to ask, here, is this: what is the difference between knowledge and mere true belief? I believe the Detroit Tigers will win the pennant this year, and that despite the fact that they finished last in their division last year, and during the off-season they dealt away most of their best talent. Now suppose they do in fact win the pennant: would that show that I knew all along that they would? Certainly not: the fact is I didn't know at all, but merely made a lucky guess. So the question is: what is the difference between knowledge and a lucky guess? What is it that distinguishes knowledge from mere true belief? Suppose we name that quantity, whatever it is, warrant. Warrant is the quantity enough of which distinguishes knowledge from true belief. But what exactly is warrant? That is one of the chief questions of epistemology.

Naturally enough there are several theories of warrant. The most successful, I think, crucially involves the idea of *proper function*, the notion of our cognitive faculties working properly, being subject to no dysfunction or malfunction.

---

[8] See my *Warranted Christian Belief* (New York: Oxford University Press, 2000; hereafter 'WCB'), pp. 256ff.

Any successful theory of warrant, I think, must involve reference to the proper function of our cognitive faculties. I don't have the space here to argue for this thesis properly;[9] let me just give a couple of examples. First example: one very popular theory of warrant is process reliabilism, according to which a belief has warrant for me if it is produced by cognitive faculties or processes that are reliable.[10] We needn't spend a lot of time, here, trying to say just what it is for a faculty or process to be reliable; the basic idea is that a reliable process produces a suitable preponderance of true beliefs over false beliefs. Of course that's not sufficient; a thermometer stuck on 75° F in a place where it is always 75° F (San Diego?) isn't reliable, even though it always correctly registers the current temperature. What it *would* register if the temperature were different is also relevant. To be reliable, a mechanism like a thermometer must produce mainly true readings, not only in the actual world, but in other nearby possible worlds as well. The same goes for a cognitive process like my vision: it is reliable only if it produces mainly true beliefs, and would have done so even if I had been in different surroundings looking at different things. But being produced by a reliable cognitive process isn't enough for warrant. Suppose my vision is in fact a reliable process, but I've been drinking; I'm now seeing double. Maybe I form the belief that there are two policemen looking disapprovingly at me; that belief doesn't have much warrant for me, even though it is produced by a reliable belief-producing process. So process reliabilism won't be satisfactory without a reference to proper function.

Second example: another theory of warrant is coherentism, according to which a belief has warrant for me if it is coherent with the total set of my beliefs.[11] This, too, however, won't work unless it is supplemented by a clause specifying proper function. We can see this by considering the Case of the Epistemically Inflexible Climber. Ric is climbing Guide's Wall, on Storm Point in the Grand Tetons; having just led the classic next to last pitch, he is seated on a comfortable ledge, bringing his partner up. He believes that Cascade Canyon is down to his left, that the cliffs of Mt. Owen are directly in front of him, that there is a hawk gliding in lazy circles 200 feet below him, that he is wearing his new Mythos rock shoes, and so on. His beliefs, we may stipulate, are coherent. Now add that Ric is struck by a wayward burst of high-energy cosmic radiation. This induces a cognitive malfunction; his beliefs become fixed,

---

[9] For a fuller account, see my book *Warrant: the Current Debate,* hereafter WCD (New York: Oxford University Press, 1993).

[10] See Alvin Goldman, "What Is Justified Belief?," in *Justification and Knowledge: New Studies in Epistemology,* ed. George Pappas (Dordrecht: D. Reidel, 1979), p. 10.

[11] See Laurence BonJour, *The Structure of Knowledge* (Cambridge, MA: Harvard University Press, 1985). (BonJour apparently no longer accepts coherentism.)

no longer responsive to changes in experience. No matter what his experience, his beliefs remain the same. At the cost of considerable effort his partner gets him down and, in a desperate last-ditch attempt at therapy, takes him to the opera in nearby Jackson, where the New York Metropolitan Opera on tour is performing *La Traviata*. Ric is appeared to in the same way as everyone else there; he is inundated by wave after wave of golden sound. Sadly enough, the effort at therapy fails: Ric's beliefs remain fixed and wholly unresponsive to his experience; he still believes that he is on the belay ledge at the top of the next to last pitch of Guide's Wall, that Cascade Canyon is down to his left, that there is a hawk sailing in lazy circles 200 feet below him, that he is wearing his new Mythos rock shoes, and so on. Furthermore, since he believes the very same things he believed when seated on the ledge, his beliefs are coherent. But surely they have little or no warrant for him. The reason is cognitive malfunction; his beliefs are not appropriately responsive to his experience. Coherentism, too, then, requires a reference to proper function.

The correct account of warrant, I believe, is as follows.[12] First, a belief is warranted only if it is produced by cognitive faculties that are functioning properly, working the way they are supposed to work, subject to no dysfunction or malfunction. But, second, they must be in an appropriate cognitive environment. Imagine that you take a space voyage to a planet circling a nearby star; as it turns out, a subtle gas is pervading the atmosphere there—one that causes human beings to believe there are elephants present, even when there aren't any within miles. You form the belief that there is an elephant present; this belief has no warrant for you, even though your cognitive faculties are functioning perfectly properly. So we must add that the cognitive environment is appropriate for the faculties in question; from a theistic point of view, that would be an environment similar to the one for which God created our faculties.

But these two aren't enough. To see this, note that people stricken by serious disease often estimate their chances of recovery as greater than they actually are; we may call this process 'the optimistic overrider.' So suppose I fall victim to a life-threatening disease and form the belief that my chances of recovery are excellent. Would this be a matter of cognitive malfunction? Probably not. The fact is someone is more likely to recover if he adopts an optimistic attitude and thinks he'll recover; the cognitive process producing the belief in question, we may suppose, is directed towards recovery and survival. So the belief in question is produced by properly functioning epistemic processes. The purpose or function of this process, however, isn't to produce true belief, but belief with a different virtue: conducivity to survival. But then it doesn't have warrant.

---

[12] For a fuller account, see my book *Warrant and Proper Function* (New York: Oxford University Press, 1993; hereafter 'WPF'), ch. 2 and *passim*.

So we must add, as a third condition, that the purpose or function of the belief-producing processes or faculties is the production of true belief.

There is still another condition we must add. For suppose our cognitive faculties were designed by a junior deity, one with very little competence or experience.[13] His design is unsuccessful. His heart is in the right place and he intends that they produce mainly true beliefs, but (due to his incompetence) when these faculties work properly, i.e., the way he designed them to work, they produce mainly false beliefs. So suppose I form a certain belief *B*, and suppose the conditions so far mentioned are all met: this belief is formed by faculties functioning properly according to a design plan aimed at truth in the right kind of environment. But *B* still has little or no warrant; the problem is that the design plan isn't *successfully* aimed at truth. We must therefore add a clause to that effect. The way to put it, then, is that a belief *B* has warrant for a person *S* if and only if *B* is produced by properly functioning faculties in an appropriate environment according to a design plan successfully aimed at truth.[14]

Now we can return to the question that precipitated this excursus into the nature of warrant: how can it be that faith—belief in the great things of the gospel, as Jonathan Edwards called them—is *knowledge*? The answer is simplicity itself. According to the above story (p. 9), faith, belief in the central features of the Christian message, is produced in the believer by the activity of the Holy Spirit. This is a belief-producing process; it is not part of our natural and original epistemic endowment, but it is still a belief-producing process. When it operates, clearly enough, it functions properly (works the way it was designed to work) in an appropriate epistemic environment (the one for which it was designed) according to a design plan successfully aimed at truth. It therefore meets the central conditions for warrant; if it is held with sufficient firmness (and assuming that it is true) it will constitute knowledge.[15]

So faith is really a special case of knowledge. But isn't this assuming that the Christian story is in fact true? Those who don't think that story true will not be inclined to think that it constitutes knowledge! That is certainly true, but not presently relevant. We have been looking into the question why Christians believe as they do, and how they think they know these things. The above account is one classical Christian answer to that question. This account presupposes the truth of Christian belief, but of course Christians think Christian belief *is* true. But isn't it somehow objectionably circular to answer the

---

[13] See David Hume's *Dialogues Concerning Natural Religion*, ed. Richard Popkin (Indianapolis: Hackett Publishing Co., 1980), p. 37.

[14] Actually, these conditions are not quite sufficient; for nuance and qualification and an additional condition, see WPF, ch. 2, and WCB, pp. 156ff.

[15] See WCB, pp. 256–8.

question 'how do you know *p*?' in a way that assumes that *p* is in fact true? No. An epistemologist might try to give an account of perceptual knowledge: how is it that our vision, for example, provides us with knowledge of our immediate surroundings? Here the account may proceed in terms of light from objects striking the retina and activating photo-receptor cells, signals being propagated along the optic nerve to the brain, neural activity in the vision centers of the brain, and all the rest. This account, however, will clearly presuppose that perceptual beliefs are in fact true; the very idea that there *is* such a thing as the retina presupposes that certain perceptually obtained beliefs are true. But there is nothing objectionably circular in this process. Similarly, there is nothing objectionably circular in an epistemological account of Christian belief that presupposes the truth of such belief. Of course there would be something viciously circular in using such an account to argue for the *truth* of Christian belief.

Finally, by way of concluding this account of the epistemology of Christian belief, it is worth noting that if Christian belief is true, then very likely it does have warrant—if not in the way proposed here, then in some other similar way. For if it is true, then indeed there is such a person as God, who has created us in his image; we have fallen into sin and require salvation; and the means to such restoral and renewal have been provided in the incarnation, suffering, death, and resurrection of Jesus Christ, the second person of the Trinity. Furthermore, the typical way of appropriating this restoral is by way of faith, which of course involves belief in these things, i.e., belief in the great things of the gospel. If so, however, God would of course intend that we be able to be aware of these truths. And if *that* is so, the natural thing to think is that the cognitive processes that do indeed produce belief in the central elements of the Christian faith are aimed by their designer at producing that belief. But then these beliefs will be produced by cognitive processes functioning properly according to a design plan successfully aimed at truth; they will therefore have warrant.

Well, you say, OK, if Christian theism is true, it is probably also warranted. But so what? Isn't that a pretty piddling conclusion? Why should that be thought important? Two reasons. First, a common objection to Christian belief (at least since the Enlightenment) has been not to its *truth*, but to its *rationality* or *reasonableness*. The objection goes something like this: "I don't know whether Christian belief is *true* (who could know a thing like that?), but I do know that it is irrational, or unreasonable, or such that a sensible person couldn't accept it." But what is this 'irrationality' or 'unreasonability' the objector speaks of? In *Warranted Christian Belief* I argued that the only plausible way to construe this objection is in terms of warrant: the objector must be arguing that Christian belief is not in fact *warranted* for those who hold it. This objection, furthermore, is supposed to hold whether or not Christian belief is *true*; the idea is that even if it happens, somehow to be true, it still doesn't have warrant for those who accept it. But that can't be right if, as I claim, Christian belief is true, if it is warranted. So sensible objections to Christian belief will really have to be to its truth, not to its rationality or sensibleness or warrant; the whole class of *de jure* objections—objections that are supposed to be independent of its truth or falsehood—can't sensibly be made.

But isn't the same true for nearly everything? Isn't most any belief such that if it is true, then (very likely) it is warranted? Certainly not; there are plenty of beliefs for which this isn't true. On page 9 I referred to my belief that the Tigers will win the pennant; that is certainly not such that if it is true, then it is probably warranted. It's a lucky guess: even if it does turn out to be true, I was right, so to speak, just by accident; that means that I don't know that the Tigers will win, and hence the belief does not have warrant for me. The same goes, I'd say, for beliefs formed in the process of inquiry or investigations which are at or near the limit of our powers, as in parts of contemporary physics. Perhaps current theories about what happened during the first 10^{-32} seconds after the Big Bang are correct (and then again perhaps not); but even if they are correct, these theories don't have much warrant for us. That is because in thinking about these things, we are close to the limits of our cognitive powers; it is then very easy for us to make mistakes. More to the present point, this isn't true for naturalism either; it isn't true that if naturalism is true, then very likely it has warrant for us. In fact in section B I'll argue that if naturalism is true, then it *doesn't* have warrant for those who believe it. But that means (for someone who sees the soundness of the argument) that naturalism can't rationally be believed.

II   Alternatives to Theism

My focus is on naturalism as a main alternative to theism. We should first note, however, that it isn't the only main alternative. There are at present, and in the Western world, fundamentally three worldviews vying for supremacy: three fundamental perspectives or ways of thinking about what the world is like, what we ourselves are like, what is most important about the world, what our place in it is, and what we must do to live the good life. The first of these perspectives is theism; I've already said a bit about that. In addition to that perspective, however, there are fundamentally two others. Both of them have been with us since the ancient world; but each has received much more powerful expression in modern times. According to the first perspective, *philosophical naturalism*, there is no God, and we human beings are insignificant parts of a giant cosmic machine that proceeds in majestic indifference to us, our hopes and aspirations, our needs and desires, and our sense of right and wrong. This picture goes back to Epicurus, Democritus, and others in the Ancient world and finds magnificent expression in Lucretius' poem, *De Rerum Natura*; it is also extremely popular in the contemporary (Western) world.

According to the second perspective, it is we ourselves—we human beings—who are somehow responsible for the basic structure of the world. *We* somehow bring it about that the world has the structure and nature it displays; it is we who are somehow responsible for the truth of those propositions that *are* true. Call this *creative anti-realism*. This notion, too, goes back to the ancient world, in particular to Protagoras, with his claim that man is the measure of all things, but it has been developed with much greater power and detail in the modern world. Creative anti-realism begins (in the modern world) with the publication of Immanuel Kant's *Critique of Pure Reason*; it is especially popular in continental Europe. Kant's basic idea, at least in that book, is that, in some deep and important way, we human beings confer upon the world its fundamental structure—its spatio-temporal structure, its thing-property structure, and so on. We do this, he says, by our conceptual activity. Exactly how this is supposed to go, according to Kant, is both obscure, and (like nearly everything else about Kant's thought) a subject of great controversy. This much is clear, however: as Kant thought of it, we all do this world formation or structuring *together*, and we all live in the *same* world.

But if you follow Kant in thinking our world is in some mysterious way created or structured by human beings, you may note that human beings do not all seem to live in the *same* world. The world of Jerry Falwell seems quite different from that of Richard Dawkins; which one, then (if either), corresponds to the world as it really is? Here it is an easy step to a characteristic thought of contemporary forms of Creative Anti-Realism: the thought that there simply *isn't* any such thing as an objective way the world is, a way the world is that is the same for all of us. Rather, there is my version of reality, the way I've somehow structured things, and your version, the way *you've* structured things; and many other versions. As Marlowe's Dr. Faustus in effect says, "Man is the measure of all things; I am a man; therefore I am the measure of all things." Call this way of thinking *postmodern anti-realism*.

Now the existence of *truth* is intimately connected with there being a way things really are, a way the world really is. For it is *true* that there are horses (for example) if and only if there being horses is part of the way things are. What lies at the heart of postmodern anti-realism (and is responsible for some of its astonishing excesses) is the idea that there really *isn't* any such thing as the way the world is, and therefore no such thing as truth. That is, there isn't any such thing as truth as we ordinarily think of it. Usually something else is proposed as a replacement for truth—typically, something that somehow depends upon what we (we humans, or our society, or the scientists of our culture circle, or the speakers of our language) do or say or think. For example, there is Richard Rorty's idea that truth is "what our peers will let us get away with saying." This suggestion seems initially unpromising; after all, *your* peers may let *you* get away with saying something my peers won't let *me* get away with saying: are we to suppose that some things are true for you but not for me? Furthermore, if that's what truth is, wouldn't there be a much easier way of dealing with all the ills flesh is heir to, for example cancer? If we all let each other get away with saying that there just isn't any such thing a cancer, or AIDS, then, on this Rortyesque view, it would be *true* that there isn't any such thing as cancer; and if it were *true* that there isn't any such thing as cancer, then there wouldn't *be* any such thing. So all we have to do to get rid of cancer, or poverty, or war, or other nasty things is to let each other get away with saying there aren't any such things. That seems much easier than the more conventional methods, with their substantial cost in time, energy, and money. Second, if you have done something bad, lie about it—try to get your peers to let you get away with saying that you didn't do it. If you succeed, then it will be true that you haven't done it, in which case you won't have done it. Indeed, as an added bonus, you won't even have lied about it! On the face of it, then, this way of thinking doesn't seem at all plausible. Of course I don't mean to suggest that there isn't a serious and sensible view somewhere in the neighborhood; but (as it stands) this isn't it.

Perhaps you will object that I'm just belaboring a straw man: Rorty couldn't really mean that truth is what our peers will let us get away with saying. You may be right. What Rorty actually says is:

> For philosophers like Chisholm and Bergmann, such explanations *must* be attempted if the realism of common sense is to be preserved. The aim of all such explanations is to make truth something more than what Dewey called "warranted assertability": more than what our peers will, *ceteris paribus*, let us get away with saying.[16]

(It is clear from the context here (and elsewhere) that Rorty sides with Dewey against Chisholm and Bergmann). Perhaps you will say that this is just a rough and ready conversational version of his real opinion. Rorty scorns the usual analytic philosopher's necessary and sufficient conditions, principles, analyses, attempts at rigor, and argumentation (maybe taking to these the same playful attitude Derrida takes towards that obsessive concern with quotation marks he ascribes to Oxford philosophers[17]). Philosophy, he thinks, should be conversational; and this is his conversational way of putting his point; but then, of course, it's not fair to hold him to the letter of what he says. Well, perhaps so. A person certainly has a right to write conversationally even on such an austere subject as philosophy; it's a free country. Still, this does complicate matters.

---

[16] *Philosophy and the Mirror of Nature* (Princeton: Princeton University Press, 1979), pp. 175–6.

[17] *The Post Card: From Socrates to Freud and Beyond*, tr. Alan Bass (Chicago: University of Chicago Press, 1987), p. 98.

If we want to take Rorty's alleged anti-realism seriously, we need a relatively clear and serious way of stating what this view amounts to; that's just what we don't have.

III   Naturalism and Its Woes

There is a great deal more to be said about postmodern anti-realism, but this isn't the place to say it;[18] our focus is the other of the two main alternatives to theism, namely naturalism. As you may have noticed, naturalism is all the rage these days; naturalist philosophers spend a great deal of time and energy trying to work out and develop naturalistic accounts of the sorts of problems and topics philosophers ordinarily work on. Thus, for example, they try to develop naturalistic accounts of epistemology; the idea is to develop an epistemology that is purged of any of the elements a proper naturalist would regard with suspicion. They also try to develop naturalistic accounts of personhood, of what it is to *believe* something, of consciousness, of language and meaning, of mathematics, of abstract objects such as universals, of ethics and morality, of religion, and much more. In each case, the idea is to develop an adequate account of the area in question while appealing only to entities—for example, concrete objects and perhaps sets of them—that won't bring a blush to the cheek of even the tenderest naturalist.

But what sorts of entities *are* those—what *is* it for an account to be properly naturalistic? To answer that question, we must first ask another: what is naturalism? Of course the word is used in many different ways. There is naturalism in art and literature, for example, which may have little to do with naturalism in philosophy. There is methodological naturalism in science. In philosophy, there is the sort of naturalism in ethics G. E. Moore objected to when he spoke of the naturalistic fallacy; there is the naturalism of John Dewey and Willard van Orman Quine. What is the basic idea of naturalism, the core notion in terms of which all these others can be understood, perhaps as analogically related to it? This is by no means an easy question; naturalism is not at all easy to characterize.[19] (In this regard it is a little like pornography: as Justice Potter Stewart said, maybe you can't say what it is, but you can tell it when you see it.) Indeed, some who think about naturalism believe that it isn't a *doctrine* at all; it isn't a belief,

---

[18] For a fuller characterization and criticism of postmodern anti-realism, see chapter 13 of WCB; see also my "The Twin Pillars of Christian Scholarship," in *Seeking Understanding: the Stob Lectures 1986–1998, ed. Calvin College* (Grand Rapids, MI: William B. Eerdmans, 2001), pp. 128–32.

[19] Chapters 2 and 3 of Michael Rea's *World without Design* (New York: Oxford University Press, 2002) contain an excellent discussion of some of the ways of characterizing or defining naturalism.

or a proposition. According to Bas van Fraassen, for example, to be a naturalist is not to *believe* anything special—e.g., that there aren't any fairies, or angels, or gods; to be a naturalist is to adopt a certain *attitude*, an attitude involving among other things an exclusive commitment to science in guiding one's opinions.[20] And according to Mike Rea (*World without Design*) naturalism is really, at bottom, a *research program*, a way of conducting inquiry; and what it centrally involves is a commitment or determination, in conducting inquiry, to use only the methods and techniques employed in the empirical sciences.[21]

Without taking a position on this question of the essence or basic idea of naturalism, I'd like to think of it, for present purposes, as fundamentally a way of looking at the world, a high-level belief about the world. There certainly *is* this way of looking at the world, even if naturalism itself is really an attitude or research program; I'll use the term 'philosophical naturalism' to refer to this way of thinking. Here is Bertrand Russell's famous statement of it:

> That man is the product of causes which had no prevision of the end they were achieving; that his origin, his growth, his hopes and fears, his loves and his beliefs are but the outcome of accidental collocations of atoms; that no fire, no heroism, no intensity of thought and feeling, can preserve an individual life beyond the grave, that all the labors of the ages, all the devotion, all the inspiration, all the noonday brightness of human genius, are destined to extinction in the vast death of the solar system, and that the whole temple of man's achievement must inevitably be buried beneath the debris of a universe in ruins—all of these things, if not quite beyond dispute, are yet so nearly certain that no philosophy which rejects them can hope to stand. Only within the scaffolding of these truths, only on the firm foundation of unyielding despair, can the soul's habitation henceforth be safely built.[22]

This may sound a bit florid and overheated, but it does serve to give the flavor of the view I mean to attack.[23]

Following Quentin Smith, we could characterize the perspective Russell expresses as "the thesis that there exist inanimate or animate bodies, with animate bodies being either intelligent organisms or non-intelligent organisms, but there exists nothing supernatural."[24] Of course, as it stands that definition isn't terribly informative; it contains the word 'supernatural,' which presumably

[20] *The Empirical Stance* (New Haven: Yale University Press, 2002), pp. 49ff.

[21] *World without Design* (New York: Oxford University Press, 2002).

[22] *Mysticism and Logic* (New York: Barnes & Noble, 1917), pp. 47–8.

[23] A comprehensive and enthusiastic contemporary book-length exposition of naturalism is Daniel Dennett's *Darwin's Dangerous Idea* (New York: Simon and Schuster, 1995). For critical animadversions on this book, see my "Dennett's Dangerous Idea: Darwin, Mind and Meaning," *Books and Culture*, May–June 1996, pp. 16–18, 35.

[24] "The Metaphilosophy of Naturalism," *Philo* 4:2 (fall–winter 2001), p. 202.

needs just as much by way of definition as does 'naturalism' itself. Perhaps the best way to get at naturalism, taken as a philosophical doctrine, is to contrast it with theism. I outlined the theistic perspective above: there is God, with his special and unique properties, and then there is the world he has created. The basic idea of philosophical naturalism (which from now on I'll just call 'naturalism') is that there is no such person as God, or anything at all like him. So first, a naturalist (as I'm using the term) will be an atheist. But not every atheist is a naturalist. Naturalism is *stronger* than atheism, in the sense that it is possible to be an atheist but not a naturalist, but not possible to be a naturalist but not an atheist. After proposing the above account of naturalism, Quentin Smith goes on:

> The example of something supernatural of most interest to contemporary analytic philosophers is an unembodied mind that is the original and/or continuous creator of the universe, and has the omniattributes described in perfect being theology. Other examples of hypothesized supernatural realities that govern or create in some sense the universe are the governing mind posited by the Stoics or the "Absolute I" posited by the early Fichte.

So naturalism includes atheism, and more. If you are a naturalist, you don't believe in God, but you also don't believe in the Stoics' *Mind*, or Fichte's Absolute I, or Plato's Idea of the Good, or Aristotle's Unmoved Mover, or Hegel's Absolute. This account of naturalism suffers a certain vagueness (nothing at all *similar to* God, but just *how* similar?), but in practice I doubt that there is much of a problem here.

So much for a characterization of naturalism and for the contrast between theism and naturalism. What I want to argue next is that naturalism is an unacceptable belief. As I said above, naturalism should be rejected, and for at least three different reasons. First, naturalism cannot accommodate the idea of *proper function*, for such organisms as plants and animals and human beings. It therefore cannot accommodate the notions of health, sanity, sickness, disease, and the like. Further, as I argued above, warrant, the quality or quantity that makes true belief into knowledge, essentially involves proper function. This means, then, that if naturalism were true, there would be no such thing as knowledge, as well as no such thing as health, sanity, illness, or any other condition that entails these. Second, and more devastating, naturalism leads directly to Humean skepticism, the condition in which you have a defeater for whatever you believe and cannot sensibly trust your cognitive faculties. In this connection I'll also argue that naturalism is self-defeating, in that if it is true, it is irrational to believe it. Third, and perhaps most devastating, naturalism cannot accommodate *belief*; if naturalism is true, no one believes anything.

A. Naturalism vs. proper function

First, then, if naturalism were true (so I shall argue), neither human beings nor their component organs and systems would function properly (or, for that matter, improperly). Fundamentally, *that* is because the notion of proper function really applies only to things that have been designed by conscious, purposeful intelligent agents; the basic notion of proper function is that of working in a way the designer(s) intended. Of course this requires modification and nuance. My refrigerator was designed to keep things cool; it starts malfunctioning, its interior temperature a constant 150° F. I give it to you, and you use it for a warming oven. Is it malfunctioning or not? My grill rusts out and can no longer be used for the purpose for which it was designed (i.e., grilling); my grandchildren paint attractive designs on it, and it is now a very nice planter: is it malfunctioning? In these and other cases qualification and nuance are required.[25] But the basic idea is still that proper function requires intelligent design.

It is this that gives trouble for the naturalist bent on explaining the notion of proper function in naturalistic terms. Proper function requires design; but the only plausible designer for us human beings and our systems and organs would be God, or something very much like God. (Conceivably God himself didn't design human beings, but delegated the task to a high-ranking angel.) Of course a naturalist might maintain that we have been designed and brought into existence by extraterrestrial beings of great intellectual accomplishments. Perhaps these extraterrestrials brought us into being by taking a hand in the course of terrestrial evolution, causing the right mutations to arise at the right times, adjusting the environment so that the right organisms survived, and the like. This is a bit farfetched, perhaps, but not clearly impossible. But it won't help the naturalist. For the same sorts of questions will arise about those talented extraterrestrials: presumably the notion of proper function will apply to *them*, but *they* weren't designed. (Or, if they were, the question will arise with respect to their designers, or to the designers of their designers, ...)

Note that this is not a problem for the theist. She believes that human beings have been designed and created by God, and created in the image of God. As she sees it, God could have created us human beings in many different ways. Perhaps he directly and immediately created a first human pair or group of humans; or perhaps he orchestrated the course of evolution so that we came to be; or perhaps he directly modified an earlier primate form of life in such a way that the result was us human beings; or perhaps our bodies have evolved, but, as is part of Catholic doctrine, God directly creates a new human soul or self every time a human being comes into existence; or perhaps . . . . Clearly there are many different possibilities here. What they all have in common is

---

[25] See WPF, pp. 21–31.

that God designs us human beings, so that it makes sense to say that we and our systems and organs can function in the way God designed us to function. When a system or organ functions the way God intended, then it functions properly; when it functions in a way incompatible with the way God intended, then it malfunctions.

I say the naturalist can't accommodate the notion of proper function; but you may not be inclined simply to take my word for that. Can't a naturalist, just as well as anyone else, see that a bird's wing is damaged and incapable of proper function? Can't a naturalist, just as much as anyone else, see that someone who thinks he's Jesus Christ (and isn't) is suffering from a cognitive disorder? Well yes, of course. The point is not that naturalists can't sometimes see that a part of an organism isn't functioning properly; the point is that the naturalist can't give an account of proper function that is compatible with his naturalism. Naturalism can't accommodate proper function. Let's look into this a bit further; just what is this 'accommodating'? One way to argue that naturalism *can* accommodate proper function would be to give an *analysis* of proper function in terms of properties that are naturalistically acceptable. What properties are *those*? Naturalistically acceptable properties are properties that could be instantiated, (even) if naturalism is true. Such properties as *weighing 200 lbs*, *living in Boston*, and *liking strawberries* are naturalistically acceptable; such properties as *being designed by God*, or *created by God*, or *approved or commanded by God* are not naturalistically acceptable. That is because they could be instantiated only if there is such a person as God; and according to naturalism there is no such person.

So one way to argue that proper function can be accommodated by naturalism is to give an analysis of proper function in terms of properties that are naturalistically acceptable. To give an analysis of a concept or property (or relation), furthermore, is at least to give necessary and sufficient conditions for it.[26] Suppose P is the property in question: to give an analysis of P is first of all to suggest some other (possibly complex) property Q, such that it is necessary in the broadly logical sense that a thing has that property P if it has the property Q, and necessary that it has P only if it has Q. That is, the *analyzans* (the analysis) must be necessary and sufficient for the *analyzandum* (the property or relation to be analyzed). Consider, for example, the traditional analysis of knowledge as justified true belief:

A person S knows a proposition P if and only if S believes P, P is true, and S is justified in believing P.

---

[26] Actually more than this is required, but the more isn't relevant to our present concerns.

This analysis may or, more likely, may not[27] be correct; the point is that it proposes necessary and sufficient conditions for the property *knowing P*. It also gives necessary and sufficient conditions for the relation that holds between a person *S* and a proposition *P* when the former knows the latter. The idea is that if a person knows *P*, then she must believe *P*, *P* must be true, and she must be justified in believing *P*; conversely, if she believes *P*, *P* is true, and she is justified in believing *P*, then she must know *P*. If the analysis is successful, it isn't so much as possible that the *analyzandum* hold but the *analyzans* fail to hold; and it is equally impossible that the *analyzans* hold but the *analyzandum* fail to hold.

Returning to our present concern, proper function can be accommodated by naturalism if and only if there are necessary and sufficient conditions for proper function in terms of naturalistically acceptable properties—properties that could be instantiated even if naturalism were true. Often, however, when naturalists talk about proper function they give an account not of proper function itself, but of some other notion in the neighborhood, one that perhaps, as they think, can nicely *replace* our notion of proper function. (Perhaps they do this partly because it is clear to them that one can't give a naturalistic account of proper function itself.) Most of these accounts—both those of proper function itself, and those of other nearby notions—invoke evolution, in particular natural selection.

Karen Neander, for example, gives the following account of 'proper function':

> It is the proper function of an item X of an organism O to do that which items of X's type did to contribute to the inclusive fitness of O's ancestors, and which caused the genotype, of which X is the phenotypic expression, to be selected by natural selection.[28]

So consider a heart: it is the proper function of your heart to do what previous hearts did to contribute to the inclusive fitness of your ancestors: i.e., circulate your blood (and circulate it in a certain way); and when it does that, it is functioning properly. It is not part of its function to make that thumpa-thumpa sound; your ancestors' hearts presumably made that sound, but that was just a byproduct of their function and did not itself contribute to your ancestors' fitness.[29] Now, despite her use of the term 'proper function,' Neander doesn't propose her

---

[27] See my *Warrant: the Current Debate* (New York: Oxford University Press, 1993; hereafter 'WCD'), chs 1–3.

[28] "Functions as Selected Effects: the Conceptual Analyst's Defense", *Philosophy of Science* 58 (1991): 174.

[29] Well, some people speculate that this sound *does* contribute to fitness: human infants may be quieted or comforted upon being held by mothers (or fathers) whose hearts make that sound. If this is a problem for you, move to a different example of the distinction between function and byproduct.

account as an analysis of the notion of proper function, i.e., the notion we all have and use in ordinary life. What she says is that the concept *she* is analyzing is a *scientific* concept, and one that may significantly differ from the ordinary one. This is an important point, because it is the everyday ordinary concept of proper function that is involved in the notions of warrant, sanity, health, and the like—not some *other* concept in the neighborhood, no matter how scientifically respectable that other concept may be. It is *proper function* (not some other concept) that is entailed by the notion of warrant; and it is proper function, I say, that can't be given a naturalistically acceptable analysis. The fact that we can construct *other* concepts out of naturalistically acceptable elements is perhaps of interest in some contexts, but doesn't cut any ice in *this* context.

So Neander isn't offering an analysis of the ordinary everyday concept of proper function. Still, it could serendipitously happen that the analysis she proposes really is a good analysis of that everyday concept, even if she doesn't intend it as such. But it isn't. It is instructive to see why not, because we can thereby see that no analysis involving natural selection or evolution can work as an account of the ordinary notion of proper function. As we recall, where *proper function* is the *analyzandum*, the *analyzans* must be a property Q such that necessarily, whatever has the property of proper function also has Q, and, necessarily, whatever has Q also has the property of proper function. If the analysis is successful, it won't be possible (in the broadly logical sense) that there be an object that falls under the *analyzandum* but not the *analyzans*, or falls under the latter but not the former.

This condition isn't met by any analysis of proper function that invokes the notion of evolution, i.e., any analysis where the *analyzans* includes the property of having been produced by some process of evolution. Any such analysis will be too strong: it isn't necessary that all biological organs or systems capable of proper function be produced by such a process. That is because even if it is a truth, it is not a *necessary* truth that organisms have come to be by way of evolution. Evolution is a dandy idea (Daniel Dennett exuberantly declares it the best idea human beings have come up with[30]); the idea that we come to be by such a process has currently achieved the status of orthodoxy;[31] still, the proposition that we have come to be by some such process is at most *contingently* true. It is *possible*, in the broadly logical sense, that the view is flatly false. It is possible, for example, that each of the main forms of life was created by

[30] *Darwin's Dangerous Idea*, p. 21.
[31] According to the 1979 edition of the *New Encyclopedia Britannica*, "evolution is accepted by all biologists and natural selection is recognized as its cause. . . . . Objections . . . have come from theological and, for a time, from political standpoints" (Vol. 7, article on Evolution).

God (or by some other powerful and knowledgeable being) *ex nihilo*, or by instantaneous modification of previous life forms, or in some other way incompatible with mechanisms proposed by contemporary evolutionary theory. If that is possible, however, no correct account of proper function can *presuppose* the truth of contemporary evolutionary theory. In particular, then, the account Neander presents, while it may serve *other* purposes, won't serve as an analysis of proper function. For clearly it is logically possible that a thing *X*—a heart, for example—display a proper function even if it is not the case that it is doing "that which items of *X*'s type did to contribute to the inclusive fitness of *O*'s ancestors"; indeed, it is logically possible that *O* doesn't even *have* any ancestors. Whether or not God directly and immediately created Adam and Eve, clearly he *could* have—and if he had, they would have had no ancestors. Still, their hearts would have had proper functions: the very functions performed by yours and mine.

In my book *Warrant and Proper Function* I examined a number of naturalistic accounts of proper function, arguing in each case that they fail. I won't repeat what I said there; what I'll do instead is briefly mention the most important and widely cited kinds of accounts and explain how they fail; then I'll look more closely at a couple of accounts I didn't examine in *Warrant and Proper Function*. One of the most widely discussed and endorsed accounts of proper function is that offered by Ruth Millikan in her book *Language, Thought, and Other Biological Categories*.[32] That account is difficult and complex and hard to get really clear about;[33] fortunately she has since offered a simplified version:

> Putting things very roughly, for an item *A* to have function *F* as a "proper function" it is necessary (and close to sufficient) that one of these two conditions should hold. (1) *A* originated as a "reproduction" (to give one example, as a copy, or a copy of a copy) of some prior item or items that, *due* in part to possession of the properties reproduced, have actually performed *F* in the past, and *A* exists because (causally historically because) of this or these performances. (2) *A* originated as the product of some prior device that, given its circumstances, had performance of *F* as a proper function and that, under these circumstances normally causes *F* to be performed by means of producing an item like *A*. Items that fall under condition (2) have "derived proper functions", functions derived from the devices that produce them.[34]

So consider, once more, a human heart; it would presumably fall under condition (1) above. Your heart has the function of pumping blood because it

[32] Cambridge, MA: MIT Press, 1984, p. 17.
[33] See WPF, pp. 201–2.
[34] "In Defense of Proper Functions," *Philosophy of Science* 56 (1989): 288–302.

originated as a reproduction or copy of a prior heart which also pumped blood, and your heart exists because that prior item performed that function.

Like Neander, Millikan proposes her account as a "theoretical definition" of a "technical term," not as an analysis of proper function itself; and far be it from me to say otherwise.[35] Again, however, it is of interest to see whether her account does in fact provide the materials for an adequate or accurate analysis of our ordinary concept or understanding of proper function. And clearly it doesn't. First, there is the same problem as with Neander: Millikan's account entails that anything that functions properly has ancestors. Now even if it were in fact true that everything that functions properly had ancestors, it is certainly *possible* that something (a telephone, Adam's heart) be the first of its kind and still function properly. The condition proposed, therefore, taken as an analysis, is too strong; it isn't *necessary*.

It's not sufficient either, as the following shows.[36] Imagine that a Hitler-like madman gains control: as part of his Nietzschean plan to play God, he orders his minions to induce a genetic mutation in selected non-Aryan victims. Those born with this mutation can't see at all well (their visual field is a uniform shade of light green with little more than a few shadowy shapes projected on it). When they open their eyes and use them, furthermore, the result is constant pain. As a result, they are unable to listen to music, or read (or write) poetry or literature; they can't do mathematics or philosophy or evolutionary biology; they can't enjoy humor, play, adventure, friendship, or any of the other things that make for human flourishing. Their lives are nasty, poor, brutish, and short. By way of amusing themselves, this Hitler and his henchmen also begin a program of weeding out the non-Aryan non-mutants before they reach reproductive maturity. Contrary to their intention, however, the mutation spreads; it gets out of control; after a few generations the bulk of the world's population, including many of the Aryans themselves, display it; the number of non-mutants dwindles.

But now take some nth-generation non-Aryan mutant m and consider his visual system A and its way of working F. In accordance with Millikan's definition, A originated as a reproduction or copy of some prior item, i.e., the visual

---

[35] This has proven a hard point to communicate. In WPF (p. 201) I said the very same thing and quoted Millikan's disclaimer: "'Proper function is intended as a technical term. It is of interest because it can be used to unravel certain problems, not because it does or doesn't accord with common notions such as 'purpose' or the ordinary notion of 'function'.'" John Post, however, comments as follows: "Plantinga ... badly misreads [Millikan] as attempting an analysis, then tries to counterexample accordingly" ("Critical notice of Ruth Millikan's *White Queen Psychology and Other Essays for Alice*," *Philosophy and Phenomenological Research* 58, p. 233).

[36] Here I return to an example offered in WPF.

system of his ancestors. Those earlier visual systems worked in way F, the same way m's visual system works, and they worked that way due to the possession of the properties reproduced. Further, m's visual system A exists in part because his ancestors' visual systems worked that way; that way of functioning conferred a survival advantage, in that this Hitler, his thugs, and their successors were selectively eliminating those who didn't display it, allowing those who did to live. So working in way F, for m's visual system, meets Millikan's conditions for functioning properly. But wouldn't it be wrong (not to mention crazy) to say that m's visual system is functioning properly? Or that its function is to produce both pain and a visual field that is uniformly green? Or that the resistance medical technicians who desperately try to repair the damage are interfering with the proper function of the visual system? So Millikan's conditions are neither necessary nor sufficient. Let me repeat: she wasn't *trying* to give necessary and sufficient conditions for the notion of proper function, but for some other notion she thinks will be useful in solving certain problems; so this isn't a problem for her project. But it does show that her account doesn't contain the resources for an accurate account of the notion of proper function.

One prominent account I didn't consider in *Warrant and Proper Function* is that of Larry Wright,[37] who, according to Michael Levin, held that "an effect F of S is a function of S just in case S exists or persists because it F's; i.e., a thing's functions are those of its effects that explain it."[38] A heart does many things; its functions are those things it does that explain its existence or persistence: pumping in such a way as to circulate the blood would be an example. Unlike Neander and Millikan, Wright does propose this as an analysis of function, i.e., our concept of function. It's easy to see, however, that this condition is neither necessary nor sufficient. It's not sufficient: a thing might persist because of some feature that wasn't its function or one of its functions, as in the Hitler case I described above. There, a given visual system might continue to exist because it (mal)functions in the way intended by the Nazis; but of course that way of working is not among its functions. The definition has another unhappy feature: it restricts the functions of a thing to the *actual effects* of a thing. But the function of a smoke detector is to detect smoke and sound the alarm; that is its function, even if it never actually detects any smoke or gives an alarm and (therefore) never has smoke detection or sounding the alarm as an actual effect. A diseased heart still has the function of pumping blood in a certain fashion, even if the pumping of blood in that fashion is (because of its diseased condition) not among its effects.

---

[37] In "Functions," *The Philosophical Review* 82 (1973): 139–68.
[38] "Plantinga on Functions and the Theory of Evolution," *Australasian Journal of Philosophy* 75 (1997): 86. Page references hereafter given in the text.

Levin notes some *other* difficulties with Wright's analysis and, in the course of an interesting and useful discussion of functions, attempts to repair it as follows:

> *F* is a function of *S* if and only if "*S* is explained by its leading to *F and* the efficient cause *S'* of *S* is explained by its leading to *S*." (p. 89)

This is a *strengthening* of Wright's analysis: Levin adds the second clause of the *analyzans* in order to deal with the difficulties he mentions in Wright's analysis as it stands (Levin, pp. 88–9). By way of example, pumping blood is a function of a human heart in that the existence of the heart is explained by its 'leading to' the pumping of blood (there are such things as hearts because they pump blood); and the existence of the efficient cause of the heart—whatever mechanism it is in human beings that causes the existence of hearts—is explained by its 'leading to' or in this case causing hearts.

I propose to argue that this attempt is as unsuccessful as the rest. Note first that it is a little vague: when does a thing *S lead to* something *S'*? What is this 'leading to'? Causing? Being part of a cause? Making probable or making more probable? Being an element in a causal chain resulting in? Being followed by? Can it be that something *A* leads to something *B*, and *B* also leads to *A*, as with drinking and depression? Note second that *explanation* is also a slippery customer. What explains what is relative to context and interests. What explains the way the visual system of that mutant works? The cruelty of the Nazis, or the technological excellence of their minions, or the nature of the gene involved in the mutation, or the fact that one of *m*'s parents had the gene, or that the gene is dominant, or . . . . In one context an event or state of affairs *A* can be explained by a state of affairs *B*, and in another *B* can be explained by *A*. What explains the fact that the porch is shady? The position of that big shade tree. What explains the position of that shade tree? It was planted there so that it can shade the porch. This fact about explanations introduces a certain flexibility (not to mention flaccidity) into Levin's analysis. Further, it's not immediately obvious how Levin's analysis applies to individual organs or systems, like a heart. Is the existence or persistence of my heart to be explained by its 'leading to' the pumping of my blood in the relevant way? But what if it is defective, and doesn't pump blood in that way, perhaps only beating at the rate of twenty-five beats per minute? Wouldn't it still be its function to pump blood in that relevant way? In response to this problem Levin says we should think instead about *other* hearts: "my heart exists (in part) because of the blood-pumping of the hearts of my ancestors" (p. 87).

Even with this nuance it is not hard to see that Levin's condition too is neither necessary nor sufficient. First, it isn't necessary: it is possible that *F* is a function of *S* even if Levin's condition isn't met. Consider again the fact that God could have created Adam (or Eve) directly; if he had, the function of Adam's heart would have been just what the function of our hearts is, namely to circulate the blood in a certain way. But (the second clause of) Levin's condition isn't met in this case: it is not the case that, under these conditions, the efficient cause of Adam (namely God) is explained by his 'leading to' Adam's heart. God isn't explained by anything at all, and in particular isn't explained by his being the cause of Adam and Eve.

It is equally easy to see, I think, that the condition isn't sufficient. Consider again that Hitler scenario. Take a given mutant m and his visual system S, which works in that unfortunate way. The existence of S is explained by its working in that way: working in that miserable way kept m (or m's ancestors) from being killed by the Nazis. The efficient cause of S—whatever system it is, in human beings, that causes the existence of visual systems—furthermore, is explained by its leading to S. In this case, then, the proposed necessary and sufficient condition is met; but it is not the function of m's visual system to cause pain and display only a uniform green visual field with a few shadowy figures projected on it.

Now here Levin protests. Speaking of my example, he says that the non-Aryans wouldn't be able to get around and reproduce with a visual system as defective as all that, unless the Nazis let them: "They would be unable to find their way around by themselves in a world full of hostile Nazis, and their constant discomfort would presumably dull their sex drive. There would *be* no non-Aryans after the first generation . . ." (p. 91). Under these conditions, says Levin, "non-Aryans would have to be *grown* by Nazis, much as exotic plants and animals are grown by human breeders now" (p. 91). What this means, he says, is that the mutant's visual systems *really are* working properly, because these traits are purposely bred in by the Nazis. In the same way, we might breed a line of dogs with very small and very dull teeth suitable only for eating oatmeal and jello; such dental systems would be working properly, fulfilling their function, even if they couldn't fulfill the functions fulfilled by their ancestors' teeth a few generations back.

What do I have to say for myself? The first thing to say is that Levin is apparently trying to hijack my example. It's my example, after all, and I get to decide on its details. The fact is that in my example the mutants manage to get around very well, partly because of the help of non-mutant non-Aryans and also anti-Nazi Aryans. Their sex drives, furthermore, are not dulled; in fact their only consolation, in their miserable condition, is sex (during which they keep their eyes tightly closed). It is therefore not the case that in my example the mutants are being "grown" by the Nazis. Still, we needn't argue about that. That is because, as you recall, in my example the mutation gets out of control: it spreads to many of the *Aryans*. So consider some *Aryan* mutant m^*: the way his visual system works also meets Levin's two-part condition for being its function.

The second condition is obviously met. The first condition is also met: why does this visual system, with its peculiar way of working, exist? There will be several explanations (for example, that one of his ancestors mated with a non-Aryan mutant); but among them is the fact ancestors of this visual system functioned in that way, thus escaping the wrath of the Nazis.

There are plenty of simpler examples. Why does my car continue to exist? Because it spun out and landed in the ditch just moments before it would have been destroyed by that onrushing passenger train I didn't see. *Spinning out and landing in the ditch* seems to meet Levin's conditions for being the function of my car. The first condition is obviously satisfied: the (an) explanation of my car's (still) existing is that it spun out and landed in the ditch. But so, clearly, is the second: consider whatever mechanism *m* it is (in a GM plant somewhere) that is the efficient cause of my car's existing (whereby my car came to exist): an explanation of *m* is that it 'leads to' the existence of cars, including mine. Should we conclude that it is the or a function of my car to spin out and land in the ditch? Hardly. I am about to drive my old car to the junkyard, where it would have been destroyed; unfortunately, it won't start. *Not starting* meets Levin's conditions. The second condition is clearly fulfilled; but so is the first: an explanation of my old car's (still) existing is its failure to start. But failing to start (one hopes) is hardly a function of my car. Next week my garage will run a contest to see whose car takes the most oil; the winner gets a three-day trip to Philadelphia. (Second prize, as you undoubtedly know, is a weeklong trip to Philadelphia.) I would have destroyed my oil-guzzling junker a month ago, except that it occurred to me I might win that contest. So my junker exists now because it takes a lot of oil; that is hardly one of its functions. Levin's proposed necessary and sufficient condition is neither necessary nor sufficient.

As far as I know, no one has been able to come up with a naturalistic analysis of proper function that is anywhere nearly adequate or accurate, and by now the project is beginning to look unhopeful. The fundamental reason, I suggest, is that this notion, the notion of function or proper function, essentially involves the aims and intentions of one or more conscious and intelligent designers. The notion of proper function really implies the idea of design by conscious, intentional, and intelligent designers. But that means that the organs and parts of plants, animals, and human beings can function properly (or improperly) only if they are designed and caused to be by one or more conscious, intelligent agents. Of course that is no problem for theism. According to theism—Jewish, Muslim, and Christian theism anyway—God has designed and created human beings and other creatures. But there *is* a serious problem here for naturalists. Naturalists, of course, can't think of human beings as being designed and created by a being like God, they can't think of human beings or their systems or organs as functioning properly (or, for that matter improperly). This means that naturalism has no place for proper function and other allied properties such as health, sickness, sanity, insanity, and the like: if naturalism were true, nothing would display any of these properties. Nor would anyone know anything, if I am correct in thinking that the anaysis of warrant crucially involves proper function. This is my first complaint about naturalism.

B. Naturalism, skepticism, self-defeat

It is unfair to Descartes to call his appeal to God's credibility frivolous.
Indeed, only if we assume a God who is morally our like can "truth" and the search for
truth be at all something meaningful and promising of success.
This God left aside, the question is permitted whether being deceived is not one of the
conditions of life.

—*Friedrich Nietzsche*[39]

Much of what Nietzsche says doesn't inspire confidence, but here he may be on to something. For suppose you are a naturalist: what I'll argue is that you have a good and sufficient reason for doubting that your beliefs are mostly true. More exactly, you have a good reason for doubting that your cognitive faculties—your perception, memory, rational intuition, and the like—are reliable, provide you with mostly true beliefs. I'll argue that the probability that your beliefs are reliable, given what you believe about how they come to be, is low. But if that is so, then (so I'll argue) you have a *defeater* for the natural belief that your cognitive faculties are in fact reliable. This defeater is one that can't itself be defeated; therefore you have an undefeated defeater for that belief. But in that case the rational thing to do is to reject that belief, to give it up. Rationality doesn't require that you believe that your faculties are not in fact reliable; but it does require that you not believe them to be reliable. Further, if you have a defeater for the belief that your faculties are reliable, then you also have a defeater for each of the beliefs produced by those faculties; you therefore have a defeater for each of your beliefs. That means that you have a defeater for your belief in naturalism itself; hence naturalism is self-defeating.

Still further: if you have a defeater for each of your beliefs, then you are enmeshed in a particularly virulent sort of skepticism. Let me explain. One kind of skepticism—a less virulent kind—would be the position that as a matter of fact we don't really *know* much, or don't know what we think we know, or even don't really know anything. Here the emphasis is on the word 'know' or 'really know.' Now it is perfectly possible to think you don't know a given thing you believe, and still be in no particular distress about that fact. You can still

---

[39] *Nietzsche: Writings from the Late Notebooks* (Cambridge Texts in the History of Philosophy), ed. Rüdiger Bittner, tr. Kate Sturge (Cambridge: Cambridge University Press, 2003), Notebook 36, June–July 1885, p. 26.

think that the belief in question is perfectly sensible and appropriate. Skeptics tell me that I don't really know that I am not dreaming, or a brain in a vat, or a victim of a deceitful Cartesian evil demon. Well, perhaps they're right; perhaps we don't know the things we think we know. But that need not cause much distress. Perhaps the standards for knowledge are very high: perhaps I know only what is self-evident, or self-evidently follows from what is self-evident. Then I don't really know that there's been a past, or that there are other people, or that there are trees in my backyard. That needn't cause me much epistemic pain, however. It still certainly seems right and sensible to believe those things; even if those beliefs don't constitute knowledge, they are perfectly sensible, and are the right ones to hold.

But there is also a much more profound kind of skepticism; this is the sort expressed by David Hume in the early sections of his *A Treatise of Human Nature*. When he follows out what seem to be the promptings and leading of reason, when he does his intellectual best, he winds up time after time in an intellectual black hole, not knowing which way to turn:

> Where am I, or what? From what causes do I derive my existence, and to what condition shall I return? Whose favour shall I court, and whose anger must I dread? What beings surround me? and on whom have I any influence, or who have any influence on me? I am confounded with all these questions, and begin to fancy myself in the most deplorable condition imaginable, invirон'd with the deepest darkness, and utterly depriv'd of the use of every member and faculty.[40]

That is a much more serious kind of skepticism. Here it's not merely that you don't know the things we ordinarily think we do know; you don't know what to believe about anything. You don't even believe that your cognitive faculties are reliable. You also don't believe that they are not reliable; you simply don't know what to think—about anything.

I propose to argue first that naturalism, construed as including materialism, implies this peculiarly virulent form of skepticism. I'll go on to argue briefly that naturalism implies skepticism even if not construed as including materialism.

1.   Materialistic naturalism

Most naturalists accept *materialism* with respect to human beings: the claim that human beings are material objects. On this view human beings have no immaterial parts—no immaterial soul, or mind, or self, for example. From this perspective it is not the case that a human person is an immaterial substance or thing that is connected with or joined to (has?) a material body; nor is it

---

[40] *Treatise*, Selby Bigge edition (Oxford: Clarendon Press, 1888), p. 269.

the case that a human being *has* an immaterial soul or mind. Instead, so the materialist thinks, a person *just is* her body, or perhaps some part of her body,[41] so that talk about 'my body' is misleading. I *am* my body (or perhaps my brain, or some part of it, or some other part of my body). Nearly all naturalists would agree. They give at least three sorts of reasons for materialism. First, naturalists often argue that dualism (the thought that a human being is an immaterial self or substance intimately related to a human body) is incoherent or subject to crushing philosophical difficulties; hence, so they say, we are rationally compelled to be materialists. You can find a typical set of such objections to dualism in Daniel Dennett's book *Consciousness Explained*.[42] Most of these objections (including Dennett's versions) are astonishingly weak;[43] no one not already convinced of materialism would find them persuasive. Still, they are often trotted out as showing that we are obliged to be materialists.

A second and better reason is this: many naturalists think it is just part of naturalism as such to have no truck with immaterial souls or selves or minds. It may not be completely easy to see or say precisely what naturalism is, but, so goes the thought, at any rate it excludes things like immaterial selves or souls. Naturalism is the idea that there is no such person as God, or anything like him; immaterial selves would be too much like God, who, after all, is himself an immaterial self. This reason is really quite persuasive, but it isn't conclusive. That is because of the vagueness of the concept of naturalism. If naturalism is true, there isn't anything *like* God in the world; but just how much similarity to God is tolerable, from a naturalistic perspective? After all, everything resembles God in *some* respect (if only in being something or other); how much similarity to God can a reasonably sensitive naturalist manage to put up with? Plato's idea of the good and Aristotle's Unmoved Mover (who is also immaterial) clearly won't pass muster, but what about immaterial soul substances? Can a proper naturalist countenance such a thing? That's not entirely easy to say, and I will leave naturalists to decide this issue for themselves.

---

[41] A somewhat different materialist view is that a human person is a material object distinct from but *constituted by* her body, or by the same matter that constitutes her body: see, e.g., Lynne Rudder Baker, *Persons and Bodies* (Cambridge: Cambridge University Press, 2000). My argument, I believe, will also hold for materialist views of this sort.

[42] Boston: Little, Brown and Co., 1991. Some who don't admire the book have complained that a better title would be *Consciousness Explained Away*. Dennett's book illustrates, I think, the problem for one who accepts materialism but also (like the rest of us) can't help thinking that there is such a thing as consciousness.

[43] See, e.g., Charles Taliaferro, "Incorporeality," in *A Companion to Philosophy of Religion*, ed. Philip L. Quinn and Charles Taliaferro (Oxford: Blackwell, 1997), pp. 271ff., who does a nice job of exposing some of these weaknesses.

A third reason is as follows. Naturalists will ordinarily endorse Darwinian evolution; but how could an immaterial soul or self have come to exist by way of the processes that evolutionary science posits? Thus Richard Dawkins: "Catholic Morality demands the presence of a great gulf between *Homo Sapiens* and the rest of the animal kingdom. Such a gulf is fundamentally anti-evolutionary. The sudden injection of an immortal soul in the timeline is an anti-evolutionary intrusion into the domain of science."[44] According to contemporary evolutionary theory, new forms of life arise (for the most part) by way of natural selection working on some form of genetic variation—the usual candidate is random genetic mutation. Most mutations of this sort are lethal; but a few are advantageous in the struggle for survival. Those lucky organisms that sport them have a reproductive advantage over those that do not, and eventually the new feature comes to dominate the population; then the process can start over. But how could an *immaterial self* or soul evolve this way? What sort of genetic mutation would result in an immaterial soul? Could there be a section of DNA that codes not for the production of proteins of a certain sort, but for an immaterial self? That seems unlikely. These reasons clearly aren't conclusive, but most naturalists find them (or perhaps other arguments for materialism) at least reasonably compelling.

Now what sort of thing will a belief *be*, from this materialist perspective? Suppose you are a materialist, and also think, as we ordinarily do, that there are such things as beliefs. For example, you believe that Proust is more subtle than Louis L'Amour. What kind of a thing is this belief? Well, from a materialist perspective, it looks as if it would have to be something like a long-standing event or structure in your brain or nervous system. Presumably this event will involve many neurons connected to each other in various ways. There are plenty of neurons to go around: a normal human brain contains some 100 billion neurons. These neurons, furthermore, are connected with other neurons at synapses; a single neuron can be involved in many synapses. The total number of possible brain states, then, is absolutely enormous, much greater than the number of electrons in the universe. Under certain conditions, a neuron fires, i.e., produces an electrical impulse; by virtue of its connection with other neurons, this impulse can be transmitted (with appropriate modification from other neurons) down the cables of neurons that constitute effector nerves to muscles or glands, causing, e.g., muscular contraction and thus behavior.

So (from the materialist's point of view) a belief will be a neuronal event or structure of this sort, with input from other parts of the nervous system and output to still other parts. But if this is the sort of thing beliefs are, if they are neuronal events or structures, they will have two quite different sorts

---

[44]"When religion Steps on Science's Turf," *Free Inquiry Magazine* 18:2, pp. 18–19.

of properties. On the one hand there will be *electro-chemical* or *neurophysiological* properties (NP properties, for short). Among these would be such properties as that of involving n neurons and n^* connections between neurons, properties that specify which neurons are connected with which others, what the rates of fire in the various parts of the event are, how these rates of fire change in response to changes in input, and so on. But if the event in question is really a *belief*, then in addition to those NP properties it will have another property as well: it will have to have a *content*.[45] It will have to be the belief that p, for some proposition p. If it's the belief that Proust is a more subtle writer than Louis L'Amour, then its content is the proposition *Proust is more subtle than Louis L'Amour*. If it is instead the belief that Cleveland is a beautiful city, then its content is the proposition *Cleveland is a beautiful city*. My belief that naturalism is all the rage these days has as content the proposition *Naturalism is all the rage these days*. (That same proposition is the content of the German speaker's belief that naturalism is all the rage these days, even though he expresses this belief by uttering the German sentence 'Der Naturalismus ist diese Tage ganz gross in Mode'; beliefs, unlike sentences, do not come in different languages.) It is in virtue of having a content, of course, that a belief is true or false: it is true if the proposition which is its content is true, and false otherwise. My belief that all men are mortal is true because the proposition which constitutes its content is true, but Hitler's belief that the Third Reich would last a thousand years was false, because the proposition that constitutes its content is (was) false.

Given materialism, therefore, beliefs would be long-standing neural events. As such, they would have content, but also NP properties. Now how is it that we human beings have come to have beliefs, and how is it that we have come to have beliefs with the content those beliefs do in fact have? Naturalists (and of course not only naturalists) ordinarily believe that human beings have come to be by way of evolution; they have evolved according to the mechanisms specified in contemporary evolutionary theory. (The prime candidates are natural selection operating on some source of genetic variability such as random genetic mutation.) We have something of an idea as to the history of those NP properties: structures with these properties have come to exist by small increments, each increment such that it has proved to be useful in the struggle for survival.[46] But what about the *content* of belief? If a belief is a neuronal event, where does its content come from? How does it get to be associated in that way with a given proposition?

---

[45] It is of course extremely difficult to see how a material structure or event could have content in the way a belief does; below (p. 54). I'll argue that in fact such a structure *can't* have content, so that materialism cannot accommodate belief.

[46] Here we can ignore pliotropy and spandrels.

Materialists offer two (or possibly three) main theories here. According to the first, content *supervenes upon* NP properties; according to the second, content *is reducible to* NP properties.

Note that if content properties are reducible to NP properties in the sense of 'reducible' suggested below, then they also supervene upon them. Note also that for present purposes I ignore so-called 'wide content.' If we were to take wide content into account, we'd say that content supervenes, not just on NP properties, but on NP properties together with certain properties of the environment. The same would go, *mutatis mutandis*, for the suggestion that content is reducible to or identical with NP properties. In the interest of simplicity, I ignore wide content; nothing in my argument below hinges on this omission.

Suppose we think about the second theory first. Consider the property of having as content the proposition *Naturalism is all the rage these days*, and call this property C. On the present suggestion, C *just is* a certain combination of NP properties. It might be a disjunction of such properties: where P_1 to P_n are NP properties, C, the property of having the content in question, might be something like (where 'v' represents 'or')

$$P_1 \, \text{v} \, P_3 \, \text{v} \, P_8 \, \text{v} \cdots P_n$$

More likely, it would be something more complicated: perhaps a disjunction of conjunctions, something like (where '&' represents 'and')

$$(P_1 \, \& \, P_7 \, \& \, P_{28} \cdots) \, \text{v} \, (P_3 \, \& \, P_{34} \, \& \, P_{17} \, \& \cdots) \, \text{v} \, (P_8 \, \& \, P_{83} \, \& \, P_{107} \, \& \cdots) \, \text{v} \cdots$$

We could put this by saying that any content property is a Boolean combination of NP properties, that is, a combination constructed from NP properties by disjunction, conjunction, and negation. And to say that content properties are reducible to NP properties is just to say that every content property is some Boolean combination of NP properties. In fact, if we think that any Boolean combination of NP properties is itself an NP property, we could say that content properties just are NP properties—a special sort of NP property, to be sure, but still NP properties. So, on this theory, content properties—e.g., the property of having *Naturalism is all the rage these days* as content—are, or are reducible to, NP properties.

That's one of the two materialistic proposals; the other is that a content property isn't an NP property, or a Boolean combination of NP properties, but rather *supervenes on* NP properties. What does that mean; what is this 'supervenience'? The basic idea is that a set of properties S supervenes on a set of properties S^* just if any pair of objects which agree on the S^* properties must also agree on the S properties. For example, beauty (of a picture, a face) supervenes on molecular constitution; any two pictures (or faces) with the same molecular constitution will be beautiful to the same degree. Content properties supervene on NP properties, then, if and only if any two objects or structures with the same NP properties must have the same content properties. You couldn't have a pair of structures—neuronal events, say—that had the same NP properties but different contents.[47] Content is a *function* of NP properties.

We can put this officially as follows:

> (S) Necessarily, any structures that have the same NP properties have the same content.

This is a *weak* form of supervenience; a stronger one could be put as

> (S[+]) For any possible worlds W and W^* and any structures S and S^*, if S has the same NP properties in W as S^* has in W^*, then S has the same content in W as S^* has in W^*.

If we think of supervenience as involving nomic rather than broadly logical necessity, then in (S[+]) we'll quantify just over nomically possible worlds, not possible worlds *simpliciter*. Those who think that content properties supervene on NP properties for the most part think, I believe, that the former supervene on the latter in the stronger sense (S[+]) (and hence also, of course, in the weaker sense (S)). For present purposes, however, it doesn't matter which sense we employ.

But what about that "necessarily"? Here this supervention suggestion divides into two branches. On the first branch, the necessity in question is broadly logical necessity, the sort of necessity enjoyed by the truths of logic and mathematics, but by many other propositions as well. (For example, such propositions as *No prime minister is a prime number*, *No people are numbers*, *Bachelors are unmarried*, *Dogs are animals*, and *There aren't any things that do not exist*.) Necessary propositions are true in every possible world. If a proposition p is necessary, then every way things could have been is such that if things had been that way, p would have been true. And now the current suggestion is that the proposition *Any structures that have the same NP properties also have the same content* is necessary in that same sense.

According to the other branch of the supervenience theory, the necessity in question isn't broadly logical necessity, but something more obscure—something we could call 'causal' or 'natural' or 'nomic' necessity. The idea is that some propositions aren't necessary in that broadly logical sense, but still enjoy a certain sort of necessity. Consider Newton's Law of Gravitation, for example, according to which any two physical objects attract each other with a force proportional to the sum of their masses and inversely proportional to the square

---

[47] So the second possibility is really a special case of the first: if content properties are reducible to NP properties, then clearly structures with the same NP properties will have the same content properties.

of the distance between them. This proposition doesn't seem to be necessary in the broadly logical sense. It could have been false; there are possible worlds in which it is false.[48] Still, the proposition seems to be necessary in some way; it is certainly not just a coincidence that objects behave in this way. It seems that a pair of objects *must* behave in this way; it isn't that they just *happen* to. So there seem to be two kinds of necessity; hence we can speak of two kinds of supervenience, weak and strong. According to strong supervenience, it is necessary in the broadly logical sense that any two structures that have the same NP properties also have the same content; according to weak supervenience, that proposition has the kind of necessity had by the laws of nature.

Return now to the question that led us into reduction and supervenience: how does it happen that those neural structures, the ones that constitute belief, have *content*? Where does it come from and how do they get it? The basic idea is something like this. As we go up the evolutionary scale, we find neural structures with greater and greater complexity. Near one end of the scale, for example, we find *C. elegans*, a small but charismatic worm with a nervous system composed of only a few neurons. (The nervous system of *C. elegans* has been completely mapped.) At the other end of the scale there are human beings, whose brains contain many billions of neurons connected in complex and multifarious ways, so that the number of different possible brain states is absolutely enormous. And now the idea is that as you rise in the evolutionary scale, as you go through more and more complex neural structures, at a certain point content shows up. At a certain level of complexity, these neural structures start to display content. Perhaps this starts gradually and early on (possibly *C. elegans* displays just the merest glimmer of consciousness and the merest glimmer of content), or perhaps later and more abruptly; that doesn't matter. What does matter is that at a certain level of complexity of neural structures, content appears. This is true whether content properties are reducible to NP properties or supervene on them.

So (given materialism) some neural structures at a given level of complexity acquire content; they thus become beliefs. And the question I want to ask is this: what is the likelihood, *given naturalism*, that the content that thus arises is in fact *true*? In particular, what is the likelihood, given N, that the content associated with *our* neural structures is true? More generally, what is the likelihood, given naturalism, that our cognitive faculties are reliable, thereby producing mostly true beliefs?

We all commonsensically assume that our cognitive faculties are for the most part reliable, at least over a large area of their functioning. I remember where

---

[48] Indeed, according to contemporary physics it is false in the actual world, although it is a good approximation to the truth.

I was last night, that I've just had cold cereal for breakfast, that my elder son's name is not Archibald, that a year ago I lived in the same house I live in now, and much else besides. I can see that the light is on in my study, that the flower garden is overgrown with weeds, and that my neighbor put on weight over the winter. I know a few truths of mathematics and logic, mostly pretty simple, no doubt, but still . . ... The natural thing to assume, and what we all do assume (at least before we are corrupted by philosophy (or neuroscience)), is that when our cognitive faculties aren't subject to malfunction, then, for the most part and over a wide area of everyday life, the beliefs they produce in us are true. We assume that our cognitive faculties are reliable. But what I want to argue is that the naturalist has a powerful reason against this initial presumption and should give it up.

By way of entering this argument, suppose we conduct a thought experiment. Consider a hypothetical species that is cognitively a lot like us: members of this species hold beliefs, make inferences, change beliefs, and the like. And let us suppose naturalism holds for them; they exist in a world in which there is no such person as God or anything like God. Our question, then, is this: what is the probability that their cognitive faculties are reliable? Consider any particular belief on the part of one of these hypothetical creatures. That belief, of course, is a neural structure of a given sort, and one sufficiently complex to generate content. We may add, if we like, that this structure occurs or takes place in response to something in the environment; perhaps it is a certain pattern of firing of neurons in the optical portion of the brain, and perhaps this pattern arises in response to the appearance of a predator in the middle distance. And a certain proposition has somehow come to be associated with this structure, so that the structure acquires belief content and is a belief.

Now what is the probability (given naturalism) that this proposition is true? Well, what we know about the belief in question is that it is a neurological structure that has certain NP properties, properties the possession of which is logically or causally sufficient for the possession of that particular content. We are assuming also that this structure arises in response to the presence of that predator, and we can also assume, if we like, that this structure is a reliable indicator of that kind of predator. This structure, we may suppose, arises when and only when there is a predator in the mid-distance. Even so, the content generated by this structure, on this occasion, need have nothing to do with that predator, or with anything else in the environment. Indication is one thing; belief content is something else altogether, and we know of no reason why the one should be related to the other. Content simply arises upon the appearance of neural structures of sufficient complexity; there is no reason why that content need be related to what the structures indicate, if anything. The proposition constituting that content need not be so much as *about* that predator.

So what, then, is the likelihood that this proposition, this content, is true? Given this much, shouldn't we suppose that the proposition in question is as likely to be false as true? Shouldn't we suppose that the proposition in question has a probability of roughly one/half of being true? Shouldn't we estimate its probability, on the condition in question, as in the neighborhood of .5? That would be the sensible course. Neither seems more probable than the other; hence we estimate the probability of its being true as .5.

The probability we are thinking of here is objective,[49] not the personalist's subjective probability, and also not epistemic probability. (Of course there will be a connection between objective and epistemic probability, perhaps a connection in the neighborhood of Miller's Principle; presumably epistemic probability will in some way follow known objective probability.)[50] But then, in suggesting the first attitude above, am I not relying upon the notorious Principle of Indifference? We are trying to estimate the probability that the content in question is true, given that it is generated by adaptive neural structures; I say that given this condition, for all we can see, it is as likely to be false as to be true; so we should judge that probability to be .5. Isn't that to endorse some version of the Principle of Indifference? And hasn't that principle been discredited?[51] Not really. The Bertrand paradoxes show that certain incautious statements of PI come to grief—ust as Goodman's grue/bleen paradoxes show that incautious statements of a principle governing the projection of predicates or properties comes to grief. But, of course, the fact is we project properties all the time, and do so perfectly sensibly. In the same way, I think, we often employ a principle of indifference in ordinary reasoning, and do so quite properly. We also use it in science—for example, in statistical mechanics.[52] Of course, problems arise where there are equally natural or plausible ways of analyzing a situation into the relevant possibilities.

But suppose, for some reason, we take a somewhat different attitude to this probability: how could we possibly know, we ask, what this probability is? For all we can tell, it is very high; but also, for all we can tell, it is very low. We really can't form any opinion at all as to what it is; this probability is inscrutable for us.

---

[49] See WPF, ch. 9. It's worth noting that the argument can also be conducted in terms of epistemic probability, although I don't have space here to show how.

[50] See WPF p. 163.

[51] See, e.g., Bas van Fraassen's *Laws and Symmetry* (Oxford: Clarendon Press, 1989), pp. 293ff.

[52] ". . . an astonishing number of extremely complex problems in probability theory have been solved, and usefully so, by calculation based entirely on the assumption of equiprobable alternatives." Roy Weatherford, *Philosophical Foundations of Probability Theory* (Routledge and Kegan Paul, 1983), p. 35. See also Robin Collins' "A Defense of the Probabilistic Principle of Indifference" (lecture to History and Philosophy of Science Colloquium, Univ. of Notre Dame, Oct. 8, 1998, presently unpublished).

This, too, seems a sensible option. My argument, fortunately, will work just as well given the premise that the relevant probability is inscrutable.

But aren't we forgetting something important? These hypothetical creatures have arisen, presumably, by way of evolution. They have come to be by way of something like natural selection working on some process of genetic variation—perhaps random genetic mutation. Presumably, then, it has proven adaptively useful for creatures of that sort to display that neural structure in the circumstances in which this creature finds itself. This structure's arising in those circumstances has (or had) survival value; it contributes to the reproductive fitness of the creature in question, presumably by helping cause the right sort of behavior (fleeing, or wary watchfulness, maybe). Whatever exactly the appropriate action is, the neuronal event in question is useful because it is a cause (part-cause) of that behavior. And doesn't that mean that it's likely that the content associated with this structure is in fact a true proposition?

It is crucially important to see that the answer to this question is NO. This neuronal event or structure has NP properties such as sending electrical signals to other parts of the nervous system as well as to muscles and/ or glands. By virtue of these NP properties, it causes adaptive behavior such as fleeing. This neuronal structure also displays NP properties that are sufficient, causally or logically, for the presence of content. As a result of having that neuronal event with that particular constellation of NP properties, the creature in which this event is to be found also believes a certain proposition. But what reason is there to think that proposition *true*? Granted, the structure in question helps cause adaptive behavior. But that doesn't so much as slyly suggest that the content that gets associated with the structure is true. As far as its causing the right kind of behavior is concerned, it simply doesn't matter whether the content, that associated proposition, is true or false. At this point, as far as the truth or falsehood of the content that arises, natural selection just has to take potluck. (Not that it minds—it's interested, so to speak, just in adaptive behavior, not in true belief.) Natural selection selects for structures that have adaptive NP properties; as it happens, these structures are of sufficient complexity to generate content; but there isn't even the faintest reason to think that content true. Given naturalism, it would be sheer coincidence, an enormous cosmic serendipity, if the content that is associated with adaptively useful NP properties should also turn out to be all or mostly true content. Naturalists who think content supervenes on NP properties (and that would be most naturalists) tend to assume automatically (at least when it comes to us human beings) that the content in question *would be* true; but why think that? This assumption is at best a piece of charming but ingenuous piety. Given naturalism, the belief in question is as likely to be false as to be true.

So, with respect to the relevant facts about the origin and provenance of this particular belief on the part of this hypothetical creature, the probability of its being true—i.e., the probability that the content of the neural structure in question should be a true proposition—would have to be estimated as about .5. The associated content in question could, of course, be true; but it could also, and with equal likelihood, be false.

What, then, is the probability that the cognitive faculties of these creatures will be *reliable*? A reliable belief-producing faculty will produce a considerable preponderance of true belief over false belief. We ordinarily think our cognitive faculties are more reliable in some circumstances than in others: we are good at such things as remembering what we had for breakfast or perceiving whether there are any trees in the backyard; we are less good at determining (without artificial aids) whether a mountain goat we see at 500 yards has horns. We are also less reliable when working at the limits of our faculties, as in trying to determine what happened in the first 10^{-33} seconds after the Big Bang. (Given all the disagreements, perhaps we are also less reliable when it comes to philosophy.) But any reasonable degree of reliability, as we ordinarily think of it, requires producing a substantial preponderance of true beliefs. A thermometer that didn't produce more true than false readings (within the appropriate limits of error) would not be reliable.

As we saw above, it's not enough that it produces more true than false readings, or even that it produces only true readings. A reliable thermometer must produce a preponderance of true readings not just in fact, but also in the appropriately close possible worlds. Just how much of a preponderance? Well, of course it won't be possible to come up with a precise figure here; but surely a thermometer that doesn't produce true readings in more than, say, ¾ of the appropriate circumstances can't be accounted reliable.

And the same sort of thing goes for the reliability of cognitive faculties; they, too, are reliable, and reliable in a certain area, only if they produce a preponderance of true beliefs over false. Going back to those hypothetical creatures, what we've seen is that the probability, on the relevant condition, that any given belief of theirs should be true is in the neighborhood of 1/2. This means that the probability that their faculties produce the preponderance of true beliefs over false required by reliability is very small indeed. If I have 1000 independent[53] beliefs, for example, the probability (under these conditions) that three quarters or more of these beliefs are true (certainly a modest enough

---

[53] 'Independent': it could be that a pair of neural structures with content were such that if either occurred, so would the other; then the beliefs in question would not be independent. Similarly when the content of one neural structure entails the content of another: there, too, the beliefs in question won't be independent.

requirement for reliability) will be less than 10^{-58}.[54] And even if I am running a modest epistemic establishment of only 100 beliefs, the probability that ¾ of them are true, given that the probability of any one's being true is 1/2, is very low, something like .000001. So the chances that this creature's true beliefs substantially outnumber its false beliefs (even in a particular area) are small. The conclusion to be drawn is that it is very unlikely that the cognitive faculties of those creatures are reliable.

So far what we've seen is that, given naturalism and the supervenience of content upon NP properties, it is unlikely that the cognitive faculties of these creatures are reliable; this is true even if we add that the content of their beliefs is generated by structures with NP properties that are fitness-enhancing, adaptively useful.

That's how things stand if content *supervenes* upon NP properties. But what about the other option, reductionism? What if content properties (for example, the property of having as content the proposition *Naturalism is all the rage these days*) just *are* NP properties, or complex clusters of NP properties? In this case we get the very same results. To see why, consider, again, a given belief on the part of a given member of that hypothetical group of creatures. That belief, of course, is a neuronal event, a congeries of neurons connected in complex ways and firing away in the fashion neurons are wont to do. This neuronal event displays a lot of NP properties. Again, we may suppose that it is adaptively useful for a creature of the kind in question to harbor neuronal structures of the sort in question in the circumstances in question. The event's having the NP properties it does have is fitness-enhancing in that by virtue of having these properties, the organism is caused to perform adaptively useful action— fleeing, for example. But some subset of these NP properties together constitute its having a certain content, constitute its being associated, in that way, with some proposition. What is the probability that this content is true? What is the probability that the associated proposition is a true proposition? The answer is the same as in the case we've already considered. The content doesn't have to be true, of course, for the neuronal structure to cause the appropriate kind of behavior. It just happens that this particular arrangement of adaptive NP properties also constitutes having content. But again: it would be a piece of enormous serendipity if this content, this proposition, were *true*; it could just as well be false. So the probability that this content is true would have to be rated at about 1/2, just as in the case of supervenience. If this is true for each of the independent beliefs of the organism in question, the probability (on naturalism) that the cognitive faculties of these creatures are reliable would have to be rated as low. The conclusion to be drawn so far, then, is that given naturalism, it is unlikely that these creatures have reliable cognitive faculties.

---

[54] My thanks to Paul Zwier, who performed the calculation.

Now the next step in the argument is to note that of course what goes for these hypothetical creatures also goes for us. Suppose naturalism (construed as including materialism) is in fact true with respect to us human beings: there is no such person as God or anything like God. Then the probability that our cognitive faculties are reliable is low, just as in the case of those hypothetical creatures. For us, too, the main possibilities would have to be supervenience (logical or causal) and reduction or identity. In our case, too, if we focus on any particular belief—say, the belief that naturalism is all the rage these days—on the part of a particular believer, we see that this belief (given materialism) will have to be a neuronal event of some kind. This event will be of sufficient complexity to generate content (by supervenience or reduction); somehow a proposition gets associated with it as its content. We may suppose, if we wish, that it is adaptively useful for creatures like us to harbor structures of that kind in the circumstances in which the believer finds herself. It would be the merest coincidence, however, if the content generated by the structure in question should be *true* content, if the proposition which is the content of the belief in question should turn out to be a *true* proposition. That means that the probability of this belief's being true would have to be judged to be in the neighborhood of 1/2, not much more likely to be true than to be false. But then it will be exceedingly improbable that the whole set of this believer's beliefs should display the preponderance of true belief over false required by the reliability of her cognitive faculties. So our case is like that of those hypothetical creatures; in our case, too, the probability that our cognitive faculties are reliable, given naturalism, is low. Let '$P(.../\_\_\_)$' stand for 'the probability of ... on $\_\_\_$,' let 'R' stand for the proposition that our cognitive faculties are reliable, and 'N' stand for naturalism (construed as including materialism). We can then put this point briefly as '$P(R/N)$ is low.' (If we like, we can include in 'N' the proposition that our cognitive faculties have come to be by way of the processes proposed in current evolutionary theory.)

But now let's take one more step: a person who accepts naturalism and recognizes that $P(R/N)$ is low, thereby acquires a *defeater* for R. A defeater[55] for a belief B I hold—at any rate this kind of defeater—is another belief B

---

[55] Of course there are several kinds of defeaters; here it isn't necessary to canvass these kinds. The kind of defeater presently relevant would be a *rationality* defeater, and an *undercutting* rationality defeater. In addition to rationality defeaters, there are also *warrant* defeaters; these, too, come in several kinds. For more on defeaters, see Michael Bergmann, "Deontology and Defeat," *Philosophy and Phenomenological Research* 60 (2000): 87–102, and "Internalism, Externalism and the No-Defeater Condition," *Synthese* 110 (1997): 399–417, and see my "Reply to Beilby's Cohorts," in *Naturalism Defeated? Essays on Plantinga's Evolutionary Argument Against Naturalism*, ed. J. Beilby (Ithaca, NY: Cornell University Press, 2002), pp. 205–11.

I come to hold which is such that given that I hold B^*, I can no longer rationally hold B. For example, I look into a field and see what I take to be a sheep. You come along, identify yourself as the owner of the field, and tell me that there aren't any sheep in that field and that what I see is really a dog that's indistinguishable from a sheep at this distance. Then I give up the belief that what I see is a sheep. Another example: on the basis of what the guidebook says I form the belief that the University of Aberdeen was established in 1695. You, the university's public relations director, tell me the embarrassing truth: this guidebook is notorious for giving the wrong date for the foundation of the University. (Actually it was established in 1595.) My new belief that the University was established in 1595 is a defeater for my old belief. In the same way, if I accept naturalism and see that $P(R/N)$ is low, then I have a defeater for R; I can no longer rationally believe that my cognitive faculties are reliable.

The problem isn't that I don't have enough *evidence* for R, to believe it rationally. The fact is I don't *need* evidence for R. That's a good thing, because it doesn't seem possible to acquire evidence for it, at least if I have any doubts about it. For suppose I think up some argument for R, and on the basis of this argument come to believe that R is indeed true. Clearly this is not a sensible procedure; to become convinced of R on the basis of that argument, I must, of course, believe the premises of the argument, and also believe that if those premises are true, then so is the conclusion. But if I do that, I am already assuming R to be true, at least for the faculties or belief-producing processes that produce in me belief in the premises of the argument and belief that if the premises are true, so is the conclusion. As the great Scottish philosopher Thomas Reid says,

> If a man's honesty were called into question, it would be ridiculous to refer to the man's own word, whether he be honest or not. The same absurdity there is in attempting to prove, by any kind of reasoning, probable or demonstrative, that our reason is not fallacious, since the very point in question is, whether reasoning may be trusted.[56]

My accepting any argument for R, or any evidence for it, would clearly presuppose my believing R; any such procedure would therefore be viciously circular.

More important, however, is the following. We all naturally assume R, and assume it from our earliest days as cognitive agents. Now rationality is best explained in terms of proper function: a belief is rational, in a given set of circumstances, just if a rational person, one whose cognitive faculties are functioning

---

[56] *Essays on the Intellectual Powers of Man* in *Thomas Reid's Inquiry and Essays*, ed. Ronald Beanblossom and Keith Lehrer (Indianapolis: Hackett Publishing Co., 1983), p. 276.

properly, could hold that belief in those circumstances.[57] But then clearly it is perfectly rational to assume, without evidence, that your cognitive faculties are functioning reliably. We rational agents do this all the time, and do not thereby display cognitive malfunction. You might wind up in a care facility for believing that you are Napoleon, but not for believing that your cognitive faculties are functioning reliably. It is therefore perfectly rational to believe R, and to believe it in the basic way, i.e., not on the basis of propositional evidence.

But that doesn't mean that it is not possible to acquire a defeater for R; even if a belief is properly basic it is still possible to acquire a defeater for it. In the above example about the sheep in the field, my original belief, we may suppose, was basic, and properly so; I still acquired a defeater for it. Here is another famous example to show the same thing. You and I are driving through southern Wisconsin; I see what looks like a fine barn and form the belief *Now that's a fine barn!* Furthermore, I hold that belief in the basic way; I don't accept it on the basis of evidence from other propositions I believe. You then tell me that the whole area is full of barn façades (indistinguishable, from the highway, from real barns) erected by the local inhabitants in an effort to make themselves look more prosperous than they really are. If I believe you, I then have a defeater for my belief that what I saw was a fine barn, even though I was rational in holding the defeated belief in the basic way. It is therefore perfectly possible to acquire a defeater for a belief B even when it is rational to hold B in the basic way. This is what happens when I believe naturalism, and come to see that $P(R/N)$ is low: I acquire a defeater for R. I can then no longer rationally accept R; I must be agnostic about it, or believe its denial.

Perhaps we can see more clearly here by considering an analogy. Imagine a drug—call it XX—that destroys your cognitive reliability. Ninety-five percent of those who ingest XX become cognitively unreliable within two hours of ingesting it; they then believe mostly false propositions. Suppose further that I now believe both that I've ingested XX a couple of hours ago and that $P(R/$ I've ingested XX a couple of hours ago$)$ is low; taken together, these two beliefs give me a defeater for my initial belief that my cognitive faculties are reliable. Furthermore, I can't appeal to any of my other beliefs to show or argue that my cognitive faculties are still reliable. For example, I can't appeal to my belief that my cognitive faculties have always been reliable in the past or seem to me to be reliable now; any such other belief is also now suspect or compromised, just as R is. Any such other belief B is a product of my cognitive faculties; but then in recognizing this and having a defeater for R, I also have a defeater for B.

Of course not just any belief with respect to which R is unlikely is a defeater for R. It is not the case that for just any belief A I have and belief B I acquire,

---

[57] See my WCD, pp. 133–7.

if $P(A/B)$ is low, then B is a defeater, for me, for A. I'm looking (from up close) at a sheep in the field and form the belief that (A) there is a sheep in the field; you come along and tell me that (B) at least 85% of the time there are no sheep there. I take your word for B, and $P(A/B)$ is low; still, B isn't a defeater, for me, for A. I learn that 2483 is prime. Given just that information it is unlikely that there are exactly three books on my desk; I don't thereby acquire a defeater for my belief that there are exactly three books on my desk. Can we state more general conditions under which a belief B will be a defeater, for S, for a belief A? Following and adapting a suggestion of Michael Rea's,[58] we might try:

> (D) B is a defeater for A, for S, if (but not only if) (1) S sees that $P(A/B)$ is low, and (2) there is no experience E S has or proposition P (distinct from A) S believes such that the epistemic probability of A on $B\&E$ or $B\&P$ is high.

The application of (D) to the above cases of defeat is obvious.

But what about the case in question, where the beliefs are:

$P(R/N)$ is low & N,

on the one hand, and R, on the other? Does the former constitute a defeater for the latter, according to (D)? Are there beliefs or experiences X such that the epistemic probability of R on

$P(R/N)$ is low & $N\&X$

is high? Say that a belief X of S is a *defeater-deflector* for R and *$P(R/N)$ is low* & N if the epistemic probability of R on *$P(R/N)$ is low* & $N\&X$ is high. Are there defeater-deflectors for R and *$P(R/N)$ is low* & N? Well it certainly looks as if there are. What about R itself? That's presumably something the naturalist believes. The epistemic probability of R on

$P(R/N)$ is low & $N\&R$

is certainly high. But of course R itself isn't a proper candidate for being a defeater-deflector here. If a belief A could *itself* be a defeater-deflector for a putative defeater of A, no belief could ever be defeated.[59] Which beliefs are such that

---

[58] See his *World without Design: the Ontological Consequences of Naturalism*, p. 205. Rea puts his principle in terms of epistemic probability, not objective probability, and adds to the antecedent a third clause: "(3) A is believed by S not on the basis of evidence."

[59] See *Naturalism Defeated?*, p. 224.

they can properly function as defeater-deflectors? This is the *Conditionalization Problem.*[60] It isn't easy to give a complete answer, but we can say at least the following:[61] first, neither *R* itself nor any proposition equivalent to it (e.g., *(R v (2 + 1 = 4)) & -(2 + 1 = 4))* is a defeater-deflector here. Second, conjunctions of *R* with other propositions *P* the naturalist believes—*(2 + 1 = 3) & R*—will not be defeater-deflectors, unless *P* itself is; more generally, propositions *P* that entail *R* will not be defeater-deflectors, unless a result of deleting *R* from *P*[62] is a defeater-deflector. Finally, no proposition *P* that is evidentially dependent upon *R* for *S*—such that *S* believes *P* on the evidential basis of *R*—is a defeater-deflector for *R*. Thus *either R or naturalism is true* is evidentially dependent, for me, upon *R*, as is *either R or Friesland is larger than the US*, and *there is some true proposition P such that P(R/N&P) is high.* Given this account of defeater-deflection, principle (D) seems at the least plausible.

Two final matters. First, perhaps you believe the thing to think about $P(R/N)$ is not that it is low, but that it is *inscrutable.* How, you ask, can we possibly tell what that probability would be? Return to page 38 and the question of the probability that a belief is true, conditional on its supervening on or being reducible to adaptive NP properties. There I said that this probability should be thought of as in the neighborhood of ½ (in which case it would be unlikely *in excelsis* that the creature's true beliefs should exceed its false with a preponderance sufficient for its cognitive faculties' being reliable). But maybe the right answer is that we just can't tell what that probability is: it's inscrutable.

There may be something to this objection. But all the argument as stated really requires is that the probability in question not be very high; that it isn't very high seems clear enough. Suppose, however, that this probability really is completely inscrutable: we haven't the faintest idea what it is. As far as we can tell, it could be as high as 1; it could also be zero; and it could be anything in between. We still get the same result. If this probability is inscrutable, then so will be $P(R/N)$; but *N&P(R/N) is inscrutable* is a defeater for *R*, just as is *N&P(R/N) is low.* Consider an analogy. You learn that your cousin Sam, whose cognitive faculties you have always assumed to be reliable, has ingested *XX* (above, p. 45). You know that *some* proportion of those who ingest *XX* become wholly unreliable; but you don't know what that proportion is; as far as you are concerned, *P*(Sam's faculties are reliable/Sam has ingested *XX*) is inscrutable. It could be as low as zero; it could be as high as 1; and it could be anything in between. Under these conditions you have a defeater for your assumption that

---

[60] See *Naturalism Defeated?*, pp. 220–5.
[61] and here I follow *Naturalism Defeated?* pp. 224–5.
[62] Where *P* entails *R*, a result of deleting *R* from *P* will be any proposition *Q* such that *Q* is logically independent of *R* And such that *P* is logically equivalent to the conjunction of *R* with *Q*.

Sam's cognitive faculties are reliable. You would also have a defeater for R if you believed you had ingested XX and that $P(R/\text{I've ingested } XX)$ is inscrutable. So what the argument really requires is only that $P(R/N)$ be low or inscrutable.[63]

Finally, there is one more wrinkle, or perhaps fly in the ointment.[64] Consider someone who is cognitively normal, and who comes to believe that she has ingested XX, that reliability-destroying drug mentioned above. This person may very well continue to assume that her cognitive faculties are functioning properly. She may very well carry on her cognitive life in the usual way, even if she becomes convinced she's contracted mad cow disease, a disease, as she believes, that renders its victims cognitively unreliable. And of course the same goes (in spades) if she believes N and sees that $P(R/N)$ is low. But (and this is the crucial point), in so doing, might she not be functioning perfectly properly, without so much as a hint of dysfunction or malfunction? The answer certainly seems to be Yes. If so, however, then given my account of defeat (in terms of proper function), she doesn't have a defeater for R in the belief that she has ingested XX or has contracted mad cow disease, and my argument fails.

Here I can only gesture at the response.[65] The first thing to see is that one who really rejects R is in a state of cognitive disaster. And some modules of our cognitive design plan are aimed not at the production of true beliefs, but at the production of other worthwhile conditions, including avoidance of disaster. For example, if you fall victim to a usually fatal disease, you may somehow think your chances are much better than is indicated by the statistics you know; this is the so-called 'optimistic overrider.' Your faculties may be functioning perfectly properly in producing this belief; this particular bit of the cognitive design plan is aimed, not at producing true beliefs about the possible course of your disease, but beliefs that will maximize your chances of recovery. Still, in some sense those statistics really do give you a defeater for your belief that in all likelihood you will recover. What they give you is a *Humean Defeater*. You have a Humean defeater for a belief B in a given situation if (1) the production of B is governed by a bit of the design plan that is aimed not at the production of true belief, but at some other state of affairs (such as recovery from disease or the avoidance of cognitive disaster), and (2) if only truth aimed processes were at work in this situation, you would have an ordinary rationality defeater for B. One who believes she's taken XX has a Humean defeater for R, as does someone who thinks she has mad cow disease. My claim is that the naturalist who sees that $P(R/N)$ is low has a Humean defeater for R.

---

[63] The first clause of (D) (above p. 46) should thus be amended to '(1) S sees that $P(A/B)$ is low or inscrutable.'

[64] As William Talbott pointed out to me.

[65] For a full version of the response, see *Naturalism Defeated?*, pp. 205–11.

I therefore have a defeater for *R*. But if I consider *R* and do not believe it, then I have a defeater for any belief I take to be a product of my cognitive faculties. Naturally enough, that would be *all* of my beliefs; all of my beliefs are products of my cognitive faculties. The result so far, then, is that if I believe *N* (construed as including materialism) and I also see that the probability of *R* with respect to *N* is low, then I have a defeater for each of my beliefs. Since *N* itself is one of my beliefs, I also have a defeater for it; *N*, therefore, is self-defeating.

Further, if you believe *N* and see that *P(R/N)* is low, you will be enmeshed in that particularly virulent sort of skepticism mentioned above (p. 30). It may be that you can't really reject *R* in the heat and press of day-to-day activities: for example, when you are playing poker with your friends, or building a house, or climbing a cliff. You can't think Humean thoughts about, say, induction when clinging unroped (you're free-soloing) to a rock face 500 feet up the East Buttress of El Capitan. (You won't find yourself saying, "Well, of course I can't help believing that if my foot slips I'll hurtle down to the ground and smash into those rocks, but [fleeting, sardonic, self-deprecatory smile] I also know that I have a defeater for this belief and hence shouldn't take it seriously.") But in the calm and reflective atmosphere of your study, you see that this is in fact the case. Of course you also see that the very reflections that lead you to this position are also no more acceptable than their denials; you have a universal defeater for whatever it is you find yourself believing. This is that really crushing skepticism, and it is this skepticism to which the naturalist is committed.

2. Dualistic naturalism

Now the vast majority of naturalists, I think, are materialists about human beings, and I've been conducting my argument (that naturalism implies skepticism) under the assumption that to be a naturalist is to be a materialist. However, there have been and are at least a few naturalists who are not materialists; at any rate there have been at least a few non-materialists who are in the near vicinity of naturalism.[66] Perhaps these philosophers are moved by the powerful arguments against materialism—for example, the apparent impossibility, as I'll argue below, that a congeries of neurons or any other material processes could be *about* something, or that human beings should be conscious or hold beliefs, if they were in fact material objects. Alternatively, the naturalist might be moved by the thought that it seems possible (in the broadly logical sense) for him to exist, even if neither his body nor any part of his body[67] existed. By virtue of these or other considerations, a naturalist (or near naturalist) might reject materialism about human beings; he might suppose that a human being

---

[66] Among them would be Bertrand Russell, C. D. Broad, possibly G. E. Moore.

[67] Nor any material object coincident with his body, if there are any such things.

is really an immaterial self possessing a body: he might be a dualist. So even though most naturalists are materialists, naturalism doesn't obviously entail or imply materialism. In what follows I want to consider, briefly, whether the naturalist can evade the above argument (that naturalism implies debilitating skepticism and is self-defeating) by rejecting materialism about human beings in favor of dualism.

The dualistic naturalist will add, of course, that an immaterial self of the kind he endorses will stand in close relation to a material body, the body of the person in question. This relation can be as tight as you please: perhaps a self can't exist without being embodied; perhaps, even, an immaterial self supervenes on the body whose self it is. The idea would be that at a certain level of neuro-physiological complication, an immaterial self simply arises. It is a (metaphysically or broadly logically) necessary truth that when that degree of complexity arises—when that particular configuration of properties is instantiated on the part of the brain or nervous system of a material organism—an immaterial self simply emerges. This immaterial self S is so related to the underlying biological body B that B can properly be said to *belong to S*, to be S's body. That is, S sees through B's eyes, feels pleasure and pain in B, can directly cause B to move in various ways, and the like. Furthermore, perhaps S's mental life supervenes on B's neurophysiological properties. If so, every mental act, every act of the self, would require a material substrate, a biological basis in the brain; and if a pair of such bodies exemplify the same NP properties, they will also exemplify the same mental states. But the self itself, so to speak, is not material; and thinking, believing, imagining, loving, hating, desiring—all of the mental activities in which we engage—are really activities on the part of this immaterial self.

Now: does this way of thinking enable the naturalist to avoid the virulent skepticism the materialistic naturalist is committed to? I can't see how. First, note that if the mental life of the self *supervenes* on the NP properties of the body, then the situation here is just as it was with respect to materialism. A certain group of NP properties—presumably a group that is adaptively useful—will give rise to a given belief; but what reason is there, given naturalism, for thinking that belief *true*? It isn't as if, as in theism, the person in question has been created in the image of a God one of whose outstanding characteristics is knowledge and understanding. Given naturalism, it seems that the belief in question would be as likely to be false as true. If so, the probability that this belief is true will have to be rated in the neighborhood of .5. The same goes for the other beliefs of the person in question. But then it is monumentally unlikely that the person's beliefs will display the preponderance of true belief required by her faculties' being reliable, and $P(R/N)$ will be low.

On the other hand, perhaps this person's mental life does not supervene, either logically or causally, upon the properties of her body. Perhaps her beliefs are not determined by the state of her body; they float free of her NP properties.

Then what is the probability, given naturalism, that such a free-floating belief should be true? Given theism, we'd expect that God would have created the self in question in such a way that her beliefs, at least in many areas, would be for the most part true. But given naturalism, there isn't, of course, any God who designs us so as to resemble him in holding true beliefs. It looks as if the probability of the belief in question's being true, given naturalism, would presumably be in the neighborhood of .5. If so, once again the probability that her cognitive faculties are reliable will be very low. If she sees this, she has a defeater for R, and hence for her other beliefs, thus falling into that skepticism. Dualistic naturalism does no better than materialistic naturalism in eluding this objection.

C. *Naturalism vs. belief*

My final criticism of naturalism: if you are a naturalist, then (so I say) you should reject the idea that anyone ever believes anything. This is no trivial matter; one of the most obvious things about us (of course) is that we believe many things. I believe that all men are mortal, that $7 + 5 = 12$, that I live in Indiana, that some of my children live in Brazil, that Paul Q. Zwier isn't much of a tennis player, and much else besides. I believe many things, and as far as I know am not idiosyncratic in so doing; the same goes for you and all other (normal, adult) human beings. What I propose to argue is that if naturalism is true, none of us believes any of these things or anything else. But I do have to offer a caveat. What I really propose to argue is that *materialism* (with respect to human beings) has no place for belief. Most naturalists, of course, are materialists; but it isn't obvious that naturalism implies materialism. I must concede that the present objection to naturalism can be avoided by any naturalist willing to embrace substance dualism. This isn't much of a concession, however. Most naturalists appear to be less than wildly enthusiastic about substance dualism; showing that a view leads to substance dualism, they typically think, is a *reductio ad absurdum* of it.

So most naturalists are materialists. But from the perspective of materialism, there is a real problem with such mental properties as *being conscious* and *being in pain*, and such mental acts as beliefs, desires, hopes, and the like. I'll concentrate on the latter, although the former is every bit as vexing, for a materialist. Beliefs, desires, hopes, fears, and the like, are said to be *propositional attitudes*, attitudes or stances one takes towards propositions. Thus I can hope that there is a dog in my house, fear that there is a dog there, believe that there is, and desire that there be one there. In each case I adopt a certain attitude towards the proposition *there is a dog in my house*. I can believe that proposition, or hope that it is true, or fear that it is, or desire that it be. And I say there is a real problem with beliefs (and these other intentional attitudes) from the perspective of materialism. The problem is that there is no sensible way to think about belief from that perspective; if materialism were true, then (so I'll argue) there wouldn't *be* any beliefs. A materialist should really be an *eliminativist* with respect to beliefs, i.e., someone who thinks there actually aren't any such things as beliefs.[68] According to eliminativists, the thought that there are beliefs is part of what they call 'folk psychology,' a primitive theory (so they think) developed by early and unscientific human beings, and a theory that ought to be replaced by something more scientific and up to date. Materialists, I say, should agree with eliminativists in thinking there aren't any beliefs.

Some might think to finesse this problem by denying that there are any such things as beliefs, in the same spirit that 'adverbialists' with respect to sense data deny that there are sense data. On this way of thinking, there are people, and people believe propositions—e.g., that all men are mortal. It is not the case, however, that there are any such objects or entities as *beliefs*. When, as we say, I believe that all men are mortal, that is not to be thought of as involving *two* things—me and a belief—but only one thing: a person, who is behaving in a certain way or displaying a certain property (the property of believing that all men are mortal). The argument I give below can easily be recast so as to take account of this possibility.

The difficulty I have in mind is not a recent invention. You can find it in Plato, but Leibniz offers a famous and particularly forceful statement of it:

> 17. It must be confessed, moreover, that *perception*, and that which depends on it, *are inexplicable by mechanical causes*, that is by figures and motions. And supposing there were a machine so constructed as to think, feel and have perception, we could conceive of it as enlarged and yet preserving the same proportions, so that we might enter it as into a mill. And this granted, we should only find on visiting it, pieces which push one against another, but never anything by which to explain a perception. This must be sought for, therefore, in the simple substance and not in the composite or in the machine.[69]

Now Liebniz uses the word 'perception' here; he's really thinking of mental life generally. His point, in this passage, is that thinking, mental life generally, cannot arise by way of the mechanical interaction of parts. Consider a bicycle (or, as Leibniz says, a mill): it does what it does by virtue of the mechanical interaction of its parts. Pushing down on the pedals causes the sprocket to

---

[68] For an example of eliminativism, see, e.g., Paul Churchland, "Eliminative Materialism and the Propositional Attitudes," in *Contemporary Materialism*, ed. Paul K. Moser and J.D. Trout (London: Routledge, 1995), p. 151.
[69] *Monadology* 17. There are many translations of the *Monadology*.

which they are attached to turn, which causes the chain to move, which causes the sprocket attached to the back wheel to turn, which causes the back wheel to rotate. By virtue of these mechanical interactions, the bicycle does what it does, i.e., moves from one place to another upon someone's pedaling it. And of course machines generally—jet aircraft, refrigerators, computers, centrifuges—do their things and accomplish their functions in the same way. So Leibniz's claim, here, is that thinking can't arise in this way. A thing can't think by virtue of the mechanical interaction of its parts.

Leibniz is thinking of mechanical interactions as interactions involving pushes and pulls, gears and pulleys, chains and sprockets. But I think he would say the same of other interactions studied in physics, those involving, for example, gravity, electricity , magnetism, the forces holding the nucleus of an atom together, and the like. Call these physical interactions. Leibniz's claim is that thinking can't arise by virtue of physical interaction among objects or parts of objects. According to current science, electrons and quarks are simple, without parts.[70] Presumably neither can think—neither can believe, doubt, want, fear, or feel pain. But then a proton composed of quarks won't be able to think either, at least by way of physical relations between its component quarks, and the same will go for an atom composed of protons and electrons, a molecule composed of atoms, a cell composed of molecules, and an organ (e.g., a brain) composed of cells. If electrons and quarks can't think, we won't find anything composed of them that *can* think by way of the physical interaction of its parts.

Leibniz is talking about thinking generally; suppose we narrow our focus to *belief*. Recall (above, p. 33) that from the viewpoint of materialism, a belief would be a neurophysiological event or structure of some kind, a structure or event involving many neurons connected to each other in various ways, with inputs and outputs from other parts of the nervous system. Furthermore, as we also saw, a belief will have at least two kinds of properties: on the one hand, there will be NP properties; on the other, there will be a property of a different kind: the property of having a certain content. Every belief is the belief that p for some proposition p: that proposition p is then the content of the belief. Thus the content of the belief that Proust is more subtle than L'Amour is the proposition *Proust is more subtle than L'Amour*; the content of the belief that $7 + 5 = 12$ is the proposition $7 + 5 = 12$.

And now the difficulty for materialism is this: how does it happen, how can it be, that an assemblage of neurons, a group of material objects firing away *has a content*? How can that happen? More poignantly, *what is it* for such an event to have a content? What is it for this structured group of neurons, or the

---

[70] Although there are speculative suggestions that quarks may in fact be composed of strings.

event of which they are a part, to be related to the proposition *Cleveland is a beautiful city* in such a way that the latter is its content? A single neuron (or quark, electron, atom, or whatever) presumably isn't a belief; but how can belief, content, arise from physical interaction among such material entities as neurons? How can such physical interaction bring it about that a group of neurons has content? We can examine this neuronal event as carefully as we please; we can measure the number of neurons it contains, their connections, their rates of fire, the strength of the electrical impulses involved, and the potential across the synapses, with as much precision as you could possibly desire; we can consider its electro-chemical, NP properties in the most exquisite detail; but nowhere, here, will we find so much as a hint of content. Indeed, none of this seems even vaguely *relevant* to its having content. None of this so much as slyly suggests that this bunch of neurons firing away is the belief that Proust is more subtle than Louis L'Amour, as opposed, e.g., to the belief Louis L'Amour is the most widely published author from Jamestown, North Dakota. Indeed, nothing we find here will so much as slyly suggest that it has a content of any sort. Nothing here will so much as slyly suggest that it is *about* something, in the way a belief about horses is about horses.

The fact is, we can't see how it *could* have a content. It's not that we see or know this is perfectly possible, but we just don't know how it's done. When light strikes photo-receptor cells in the retina, there is a complex cascade of electrical activity, resulting in an electrical signal to the brain. I have no idea how all that works; but of course I know it happens all the time. But the case under consideration is different. Here it's not merely that I don't know how physical interaction among neurons brings it about that an assemblage of neurons has content and is a belief. No, in this case, we can't see how such an event *could* have content—that is, it seems upon reflection that it could *not* have content. It's a little like trying to understand what it would be for the number seven, e.g., to weigh five pounds (or for an elephant to be a proposition). We can't see how that could happen; more exactly, we can see that it *couldn't* happen. A number just isn't the sort of thing that can have weight; there is no way in which that number or any other number could weigh anything at all. (The same goes for elephants and propositions.) Similarly, we can see, I think, that physical activity among neurons can't generate content. These neurons are clicking away, sending electrical impulses hither and yon. But what has this to do with content? How is content or aboutness supposed to arise from this neuronal activity? How can such a thing be a belief? You might as well say that thought arises from the activity of the wind or the waves. But then no neuronal event can as such have a content, can be *about* something, in the way in which my belief that the number seven is prime is about the number seven, or my belief that the oak tree in my backyard is without leaves is about that oak tree.

Here someone might object as follows. "You say we can't see how a neural event can have content; but in fact we understand this perfectly well, and something similar happens all the time. For there is, after all, the computer analogy. A computer, of course, is a material object, an assemblage of wires, switches, relays, a hard disk, a keyboard, and the like. I can type in a sentence or indeed an entire document; in fact I *am* typing in an entire document. Now take any particular sentence in the document: say the sentence 'Naturalism is all the rage these days'. That sentence is represented and stored on the computer's hard disk. We don't have to know in exactly what *way* it's stored (it's pluses and minuses, or a magnetic configuration, or something else; it doesn't matter). Now the sentence 'Naturalism is all the rage these days' *expresses* the proposition *Naturalism is all the rage these days* (as does the German sentence 'Der Naturalismus ist diese Tage ganz gross in Mode' or any other sentence synonymous with this one). That sentence, therefore, has the proposition *Naturalism is all the rage these days* as its content. But then consider the analogue of that sentence on the computer disk: clearly it, too, expresses the same proposition as the sentence it represents. That bit of the computer disk, therefore, has propositional content. But of course that bit of the computer disk is also a material object (as is any inscription of the sentence in question). Contrary to your claim, therefore, a material object can perfectly well have propositional content; indeed, it happens all the time. But if a computer disk or an inscription of a sentence can have a proposition as content, why can't an assemblage of neurons? Just as a magnetic pattern has as content the proposition *Naturalism is all the rage these days*, so, too, a pattern of neuronal firing can have that proposition as content. Your claim to the contrary is completely bogus." Thus far the objector.

Well, if the sentence or the computer disk really did have content, then I guess the assemblage of neurons could too. But the fact is that neither does—or, rather, neither has the right kind of content: neither has *original* content. For how does it happen that the sentence has content? It's simply by virtue of the fact that we human beings *use* the sentence in a certain way, a way such that if a sentence is used in that way, then it expresses a certain proposition. Upon hearing that sentence, I think of, grasp, apprehend the proposition *Naturalism is all the rage these days* (and of course the same goes for the German sentence and speakers of German). You can get me to grasp, entertain, and perhaps believe that proposition by uttering that sentence. How exactly all this works is complicated and not at all well understood; but the point is that the sentence has content only because of something *we*, we who are already thinkers, do with it. We could put this by saying that the sentence has *secondary* or *derived* content; it has content only because we, we creatures whose thoughts and beliefs already have content, treat it in a certain way. The same goes for the magnetic pattern on the computer disk: it represents or expresses that proposition because we assign that proposition to that configuration. But of course that isn't how it goes (given materialism) with that pattern of neural firing. That pattern doesn't get its content by way of being used in a certain way by some other creatures whose thoughts and beliefs already have content. If that pattern has content at all, then, according to materialism, it must have *original* or *primary* content. And what it is hard or impossible to see is how it could be that an assemblage of neurons (or a sentence, or a computer disk) could have original or primary content. To repeat: it isn't just that we can't see how it's done, in the way in which we can't see how the sleight-of-hand artist gets the pea to wind up under the middle shell. It is rather that we can see, to at least some degree, that it can't be done, just as we can see that an elephant can't be the number 7, and that the number 7 can't weigh seven pounds.

Peter van Inwagen agrees that it is indeed hard to see how physical interaction among material entities can produce thought: "... it seems to me that the notion of a physical thing that thinks is a mysterious notion, and that Leibniz's thought-experiment brings out this mystery very effectively."[71] Now I am taking this fact as a reason to reject materialism, the idea that human beings are physical or material objects with no immaterial parts. I'm taking it as a reason for thinking materialism is false. But if materialism is false, immaterialism must be true; if a material object can't think, then whatever thinks must be an immaterial object. Hence a human being is really an immaterial object (or at least has an immaterial part or element). The simplest view here is substance dualism; this is the view that a human being is an immaterial object, a thing that can think, joined in a special way to a material body. I am an immaterial substance standing in a peculiarly intimate relation to a certain material thing, the thing I call my body. And the fact that it is hard to see how a material object can think (so I say) is a serious difficulty for materialism. It's an argument for substance dualism—but only, of course, if there is no similar difficulty for substance dualism itself.

Van Inwagen thinks there *is* a similar difficulty for dualism:

> For it is thinking itself that is the source of the mystery of a thinking physical thing. The notion of a non-physical thing that thinks is, I would argue, equally mysterious. How any sort of thing could think is a mystery. It is just that it is a bit easier to see that thinking is a mystery when we suppose that the thing that does the thinking is physical, for we can form mental images of the operations of a physical thing and we can see that the physical interactions represented in these images—the only interactions that *can* be represented in these images—have no connection with thought or sensation, or none we are able to imagine, conceive or articulate. The only reason we do not readily find the notion of a non-physical thing that thinks equally mysterious is that we have no clear procedure for form-ing mental images of non-physical things. (p. 176)

So dualism is no better off than materialism; they both have the same problem. What is this problem, according to van Inwagen? The problem for material-ism is that we can't *imagine* a material thing thinking; we can't form a mental

---

[71] *Metaphysics* (Boulder, CO: Westview Press, 2002 (second edition)), p. 176. Hereafter page refer-ences given in the text.

image of a material thing thinking. But the same goes, says van Inwagen, for an immaterial thing: we also can't form a mental image of an immaterial thing thinking. Indeed, we can't form a mental image of any kind of thinking thing: "My point," he says, "is that nothing could possibly count as a mental image of a thinking thing" (p. 177). But then materialism and dualism are so far on a par; there is nothing here to incline us to dualism rather than materialism.

Thus far van Inwagen; but is he right? The thought of a physical thing thinking, he concedes, is mysterious; that is because we can't form a mental image of a physical thing thinking. But this seems to me to mislocate the problem. It is not just that we can't form a mental image of a physical thing thinking that inclines us to reject the idea. There are plenty of things of which we can't form a mental image, where we're not at all inclined to reject them. I can't form a mental image of the proposition *Proust is more subtle than L'Amour* or *Naturalism is all the rage these days*. I can't form a mental image of either of these propositions' being true (or being false). But I'm not in the least inclined on that account to reject the idea that the first, say, is in fact true. As Descartes pointed out, I can't form a mental image of a 1000-sided rectilinear plane figure (or at least an image that distinguishes it from a 100-sided rectilinear plane figure); that doesn't suggest that there can't be any such thing. I can't form a mental image of the number 79's being prime; that doesn't incline me to believe that it isn't prime. I don't believe that a proposition or a set could be red; but it's not because I can't form a mental image of a proposition's (or a set's) being red.

Well, what *is* it, then, that inclines me to think a proposition can't be red, or a horse be an even number? The answer, I think, is that one can just see upon reflection that these things are impossible. I can't form a mental image of a proposition's having members; but that's not why I think no proposition has members, because I also can't form a mental image of a *set's* having members. It's rather that one sees that a set is the sort of thing that has or can have members, and a proposition is not. It is the same with a physical thing's thinking. True, one can't imagine it. The reason for rejecting the idea, however, is not that one can't imagine it. It's rather that one can see that a physical object just can't do that sort of thing. This isn't as clear, perhaps, as that a proposition can't be red; some impossibilities are more clearly impossible than others. But one can see it to at least some degree.[72] And the same *doesn't* go for an immaterial

---

[72] Van Inwagen might be prepared to concede this; he says: ". . . Leibniz's thought experiment shows that when we carefully examine the idea of a material thing having sensuous properties, it seems to be an impossible idea." "Dualism and Materialism: Athens and Jerusalem?," *Faith and Philosophy* 12:4 (Oct. 1995), p. 478. That is (I take it), it seems to be *necessary* that material things don't have such properties. Van Inwagen's examples are such properties as *being in pain* and 'sensing redly'; the same goes, I say, for properties like *being the belief that* p for a proposition *p*.

thing's thinking; we certainly can't see that no immaterial thing can think. (If we could, we'd have an argument against the existence of God: no immaterial thing can think; if there were such a person as God, he would be both immaterial and a thinker; therefore . . . .)

Van Inwagen has a second suggestion as to why it's hard to conceive of a thinking thing:

> In general, to attempt to explain how an underlying reality generates some phenomenon is to construct a representation of the working of that underlying reality, a representation that in some sense "shows how" the underlying reality generates the phenomenon. Essentially the same considerations as those that show that we are unable to form a mental image that displays the generation of thought and sensation by the workings of some underlying reality (whether the underlying reality involves one thing or many, and whether the things it involves are physical or non-physical) show that we are unable to form *any* sort of representation that displays the generation of thought and sensation by the workings of an underlying reality. (pp. 177–8)

The suggestion is that we can't form an image or other representation displaying the generation of thought by way of *the workings of an underlying reality*; hence we can't see how it can be generated by physical interaction among material objects such as neurons. This much seems right. Van Inwagen goes on to say, however, that this doesn't favor dualism over materialism, because we *also* can't see how thought can be generated by the workings of an underlying *non*-physical reality. And perhaps this is also right. But here there is an important dissimilarity between dualism and materialism. The materialist thinks of thought as generated by the physical interaction of such things as neurons; the dualist, however, typically thinks of an immaterial self, a soul, a thing that thinks, as *simple*. An immaterial self doesn't have any parts; hence, of course, thought isn't generated by the interaction of its parts. Say that a property P is *basic* to a thing x if x has P, but x's having P is not generated by the interaction of its parts. Thought is then a basic property of selves, or, better, a basic *activity* of selves. It is also an *immediate* activity of selves, in that a self doesn't think by way of doing something else (in the way, for example, that the referee signals a touchdown by raising his arms). A self doesn't think by way of doing something else. It's not that (for example) there are various immaterial parts of a self whose interaction produces thought; nor is it that a self thinks by doing something else. Of course a self stands in causal relations to its body: retinal stimulation causes a certain sort of brain activity which in turn causes a certain kind of experience in the self. But there isn't any *way* in which the self produces a thought; it does so immediately. To ask 'How does a self produce thought?' is to ask an improper question. There isn't any *how* about it.

An analogy: consider the lowly electron. According to current science, electrons are simple, not composed of other things. An electron has basic properties such as spin and a negative charge. But then the question 'How does an electron manage to have a charge?' is an improper question. There's no *how* to it; it doesn't do something else that results in its having such a charge, and it doesn't have parts by virtue of whose interaction it has such a charge. Its having a negative charge is rather a basic and immediate property of the thing. The same is true of a self and thinking: it's not done by underlying activity or workings; it's a basic and immediate activity of the self. But then the important difference, here, between materialism and immaterialism is that if a material thing managed to think, it would have to be by way of the activity of its parts; and we can't see how that could happen (it seems upon reflection that it can't happen). Not so for an immaterial self. Its activity of thinking is basic and immediate. And it's not the case that we are inclined upon reflection to think this can't happen—there's nothing at all against it, just as there is nothing against an electron's having a negative charge, not by virtue of the interaction of parts, but in that basic and immediate way. The fact of the matter, then, is that we can't see how a material object can think—that is, upon reflection it seems to at least some degree that a material object *can't* think. Not so for an immaterial self.

True, as van Inwagen says, thought can sometimes seem mysterious and wonderful, something at which to marvel. (Although from another point of view thought is more familiar than hands and feet). But there is nothing here to suggest that it can't be done. Part of the mystery of thought is that it is wholly unlike things that are done by material objects; but of course that's not to suggest that it can't be done at all. Propositions are also mysterious and have wonderful properties: they manage to be about things; they are true or false; they can be believed; they stand in logical relations to each other. How do they manage to do those things? Well, certainly not by way of interaction among material parts. Sets manage, somehow, to have members—how do they do a thing like that? And why is it that a given set has just the members it has? How does the unit set of Socrates manage to have just him as a member? Why can't I be a member of it? What mysterious force keeps me out of it? Well, it's just the nature of sets to be like this. These properties can't be explained by way of physical interactions among material parts, but that's nothing at all against sets. Indeed, these properties can't be *explained* at all. Of course if you *began* with the idea that everything has to be a material object, then thought (and propositions and sets) would indeed be mysterious and paradoxical. But why begin with that idea? Thought is seriously mysterious, I think, only when we assume that it would have to be generated in some physical way, by physical interaction among physical objects. *That* is certainly mysterious; indeed it goes far beyond mystery, all the way to apparent impossibility. But that's not a problem for thought; it's a problem for materialism.

Now of course this problem has not been lost on materialists, canny lot that they are. Their attempts to deal with the problem ordinarily take the form of suggestions as to how it might be that a neural object or event could have (original) content after all. Nearly all attempts to do so begin with what we might call *indicators*, or *indication*, or *indicator meaning*.[73] Deer tracks in my backyard indicate that deer have run through it; smoke indicates fire; the height of the mercury column indicates the ambient temperature; buds on the trees indicate the coming of spring. We could speak here of 'natural signs': smoke is a natural sign of fire and the height of the mercury column signifies the ambient temperature. When one thing indicates or is a natural sign of another, there is ordinarily some sort of causal or nomic connection between them by virtue of which the first is reliably correlated with the second. Smoke causes fire, which is why it indicates fire; measles cause red spots on your face, which is why red spots on your face indicate measles; there is a causal connection between the height of the mercury column and the temperature.

The nervous systems of organisms often contain such indicators. A widely discussed example: whenever a frog sees a fly zooming by, there is (so we think) a certain pattern of neural firing in its brain; as a result these neurons, or patterns of firing, are sometimes called 'fly detectors.' Another famous example: some anaerobic marine bacteria have little internal magnets called 'magnetosomes.' These function like compass needles, indicating magnetic north. The direction to magnetic north (in the northern hemisphere) is downward; hence these bacteria, which can't flourish in the oxygen-rich surface water, move towards the more oxygen-free water at the bottom of the ocean. There are also such structures in human bodies. There are structures that respond in a regular way to blood pressure and temperature, to the amount of sugar in the blood, to its sodium content, to light of a certain pattern striking the retina, and the like. Presumably there are structures in the brain that are correlated with features of the environment: it is widely assumed that when you see a tree, there is a distinctive pattern of neural firing (or some other kind of structure) in your brain that is correlated with and caused by it.

The next step is to call these structures, the ones correlated with external or internal conditions of one kind or another, 'representations.' Indeed, the idea that such structures are representations has become so common that it is part of the current background assumptions in cognitive neuroscience. Those patterns of neural firing in the frog's brain are said to be representations of flies, or bugs (or small flying objects); those magnetosomes in anaerobic bacteria are said to represent north, or the direction towards oxygen-free water, or the lines of the earth's magnetic field (there is usually considerable latitude of choice

---

[73] See Fred Dretske's *Explaining Behavior* (Cambridge, MA: MIT Press, 1988), pp. 54ff.

as to what gets represented); the structures in your body that respond to the temperature of your blood are said to represent that temperature.

Now the terms 'represent' and 'representation' are multiply ambiguous. Webster's *Third International* gives a whole host of analogically connected meanings: you can send your representative to a meeting; your state or national representative represents your interests (we hope); an artist can produce a representation of a battle; a musical passage can represent a storm; x's and o's can represent football players and a dotted line can represent where the tight end is supposed to go; a scale model of Mt. Rainier can represent Mt. Rainier. This term is therefore something of a weasel word, and in typical philosophy of mind or cognitive science contexts it is used without definition. As a result, it is often hard to know just what is meant by calling those indicators 'representations'; shall we say that wherever you have causal or nomological correlation, you have representation? Shall we say that smoke represents fire (and fire represents smoke), that the rate at which the wheels of my car turn represent the speedometer reading, and that trees budding represent spring or warmer weather (and vice versa)? Well, I guess we can say these things if we like; it's a free country, and the term 'representation' is flexible enough to allow it.

But here the crucial next step: efforts to understand belief materialistically typically try, somehow, to promote these representations to *beliefs*. In so doing, they don't ordinarily try to solve Leibniz's problem—the fact that it looks as if a material thing can't think, or be a belief; they simply ignore it. But this procedure is also unpromising in its own right: representation of this sort is nowhere near sufficient for belief. The gas gauge on my car may represent the amount of gas (or the weight on the bolts holding the tank to the frame), or the volume of air in the tank, and other things as well; nothing in the neighborhood has beliefs on these scores. The thermostat may represent the temperature; but when the temperature drops and the thermostat starts the furnace, it doesn't believe that it's too cool in here (and neither does the furnace or anything else in the relevant neighborhood). Those magnetosomes perhaps represent the direction to oxygen-free water; neither they nor the bacteria that contain them believe that's the way to oxygen-free water. Certain internal structures indicate and thus represent your blood pressure; these structures don't believe that your blood pressure is thus and so, and neither (most of the time) do you. The thing to see is that no amount of this indication and representation, no matter how gussied up, is sufficient for *belief*. Clearly a material object *can* be a representation in *some* sense: Michelangelo's *David* for example, is a representation of David, and a few weird lines in a cartoon can represent Ted Kennedy. But it doesn't follow that a material structure can be a belief, or that it can have propositional content (original content). And I think we can see that it can't.

There are basically three ways in which materialist thinkers try to promote indicators to belief. First, there is the Millikan/Dennett proposal: an indicator gets to be a belief when evolution confers on it the *function* of causing a certain sort of behavior. Second, there is Jerry Fodor's suggestion. It's natural to think there are certain brain structures that indicate cows; when I see a cow, presumably there will be in my brain a structure that is correlated with cows. But this structure can also be caused by other things—a moose in the twilight, for example, or maybe a very large cat, perhaps after I've had too many martinis. According to Fodor, what confers content on such a structure—the content *cow*—is that there being structures of that sort that are *not* caused by cows is asymmetrically dependent upon there being structures of that sort that *are* caused by cows: "But 'cow' means *cow* and not *cat* or *cow or cat* because *there being cat-caused 'cow' tokens depends on there being cow-caused 'cow' tokens, but not the other way around.*"[74] Third, there is Fred Dretske's work, perhaps the most sophisticated and accomplished attempt to explain belief from a materialist perspective.[75] I don't have the space to look into all of these; a brief examination of Dretske's efforts will have to suffice. But note that all three lines of approach ignore Leibniz's problem. All three simply assume that it is possible for a material thing to think and for a material assemblage of neurons to be a belief.

Dretske begins (as does nearly everyone undertaking this enterprise) with the notion of indication, correlation (perhaps nomic, perhaps causal) between events of one kind and events of another. His attempt to explain belief in terms of indication involves two additional ideas. First is the notion of *function*. All beliefs are representations, and representations essentially involve functions: "The fundamental idea [of representation] is that a system, S, represents a property F, if and only if S has the function of indicating (providing information about) the F of a certain domain of objects."[76] So not all cases of indication are cases of representation: the fuel gauge in my automobile indicates the amount of gasoline in the tank, the weight on the bolts holding the tank to the frame, the amount of air in the tank, the air pressure, the altitude, the temperature, the potential across a certain circuit, and many other things; its *function*, however, is to register the amount of gasoline in the tank. Hence it represents the amount of fuel in the tank and does not represent those other properties and quantities, interesting as they may be. This appeal to function enables Dretske to see representational contexts as like belief contexts in being intentional: it may be that it is the function of something or other to indicate a property *p*, while it isn't its function to indicate a nomically or logically equivalent property *q*.

---

[74] *A Theory of Content and Other Essays* (Cambridge, MA: MIT Press, 1990), p. 91 (original emphasis).

[75] See in particular *Explaining Behavior* and *Naturalizing the Mind* (Cambridge: MIT Press, 1995).

[76] *Naturalizing the Mind*, p. 2.

But just as not every case of indication involves representation, so, according to Dretske, not every case of representation is a case of belief (or proto-belief, as he tends to put it). He cites the case of the noctuid moth, which, upon detecting the bursts of high-frequency sound emitted by the bat's radar, executes evasive maneuvers. Here we have representation; it is the function of those neural structures *N* registering that sound to indicate the presence of bats, to carry the information that bats are present. But these structures, says Dretske, are not beliefs and do not have belief content. Where *C* is a structure representing something or other (and now we come to the second additional idea), belief content is present *only if C causes some motor output or movement M, and the explanation of C's causing M is C's carrying the information that it does.* That is not so in the case of those structures in the noctuid moth: ". . . the explanation of why *this* C is causing *this* M, why the moth is now executing evasive maneuvers—has nothing to do with what *this* C indicates about this moth's surroundings. The explanation lies in the moth's genes".[77] Take a given moth and the neural circuit *C* whose firing causes those maneuvers *M*: the explanation of *C*'s causing *M* is not that *C* indicates the presence of bats, but the way the neural circuitry of this moth is deployed. The fact that in these moths, *C* represents the presence of bats may explain or help explain why moths of this type have survived and flourished; but the fact that in a given moth *C* represents bats does not explain why *C* causes *M*.

If we don't get belief here, where do we get it? Where there is *learning*, says Dretske. Consider a bird that learns to peck at a red spot because it is rewarded when it does. At first the bird pecks aimlessly, now at the red spot, now at the black spot, now at a shadow on the walls of its cage. But then we reward it when it pecks at the red spot. Soon it will peck only or mainly at the red spot; it has learned something. What has happened here? Well, the bird had a red spot detector to start with; by virtue of learning, that structure came to cause the bird to peck at the red spot. And the structure in question causes the motor output in question because that structure indicates a red spot, carries the information that the figure in front of the bird is a red spot. Here, says Dretske, we do have a case of belief content, and the bird can be said to believe (or proto-believe) that there is a red spot in front of it.

As far as I can see, therefore, Dretske's complete account of belief can be put as follows:

(D) *x* is a belief if and only if (1) *x* is a state of an indicating element *E* in a representational system (e.g., the event consisting in the system's being 'on') (2) whose function it is to indicate something *F*, (3) *x* is in the mode or state it is in when it indicates something *F*, (4) *x* causes some movement M, and (5) the explanation of *x*'s causing *M* is that it indicates *F*.

---

[77] *Explaining Behavior*, p. 92.

A comment on (3): it's not necessary that on the occasion in question, x is actually indicating something F perhaps on this occasion x is misrepresenting. We fix red-colored spectacles on the bird: now its red spot indicator causes it to peck at any spot, red or not. But the red spot indicator is still on, as we might say, even when in fact the spot in front of the bird is black.

This is a complex and sophisticated account; some of its complexity can be accounted for in terms of the failure of earlier accounts. For example, someone might say, perhaps with Dennis Stampe, that a belief is any element of an indicator system that is indicating F, or perhaps with Millikan, that x is a belief if x is an element of an indicator system whose function it is to cause some adaptive motion M. These are clearly insufficient, as is shown by such internal indicator systems as those that register blood pressure, blood temperature, and sodium and sugar levels in blood. Here we have elements of indicator systems indicating something F, and having the function of causing some adaptive motion M (adjusting blood temperature, sodium or sugar level, etc.); but nothing in the neighborhood has the relevant beliefs.

Still, sophisticated as it is, Dretske's account, I think, won't anywhere nearly do the job. I've already argued that the notion of proper function can't be accommodated by naturalism and also that a material structure *can't* acquire or have content; for present purposes let's waive these more general objections and consider some that are a bit more specific. First, a couple of semi-technical objections. I believe that $7 + 5 = 12$; nothing, however, carries the information that $7 + 5 = 12$, and indeed *7 + 5's being equal to 12* isn't information. That is because, according to Dretske's (Shannon) conception of information, information is always a matter of reduction of possibilities; but *7 + 5's equaling 12* doesn't reduce the possibilities with respect to anything. The account is therefore too strong; it rules out beliefs that are logically necessary in either the broad or the narrow sense. And just what kind of possibilities are we thinking of here? If causal or nomic possibilities are relevant, then the account also fails to work for nomologically necessary beliefs, such as that (as current physics has it, anyway) nothing travels faster than light (more exactly, nothing accelerates from a velocity less than that of light to a velocity greater than that of light). This doesn't reduce the nomic possibilities. And what about beliefs about the past? Given that past propositions are 'accidentally necessary,' nothing *now* carries the information that Brutus stabbed Caesar (in Dretske's technical Shannon sense—obviously some textbooks carry that information in the ordinary sense).

Further, I believe that Proust is more subtle than L'Amour; is it even remotely plausible to suppose that I must therefore have a Proust-is-more-subtle-than-L'Amour-indicator, a neural structure whose function it is to indicate that Proust is more subtle than L'Amour? Or a structure that fires when one person is a more subtle writer than another? And even if there were such structures, would they have to cause *motion* of one sort or another for me to believe that Proust is more subtle than L'Amour? Maybe I've always believed this, but never said so, or in any other way displayed this belief in my behavior.

Still further, return to that noctuid moth. Perhaps it was designed by God; and perhaps God designed it in such a way that C, the structure causing that evasive motion, causes that motion because C indicates the presence of bats. Then it would be true that C causes M because of what it indicates, and on Dretske's account, the moth would on the appropriate occasions believe that there are bats present. So if the moth came to be by undirected evolution it doesn't have beliefs (or at least doesn't have the belief that bats are present when its bat indicator is activated); if God has designed it, however, then it does have that belief on those occasions. Can that be right? In the same way there are all those internal indicators I mentioned a bit ago: structures whose function it is to indicate blood pressure, temperature, sodium level, sugar level, and the like. These indicators are in fact so constituted that they cause certain kinds of movements. If human beings have been designed by God, then presumably they cause those movements because of what they indicate; that's why God designed the system in such a way that they *do* cause those movements. But then on Dretske's account, these structures, or we who contain them, would hold the associated beliefs about our blood temperature, pressure, sodium level, sugar level, and the like. But we don't; if Dretske's account were right, therefore, this would constitute an argument against the existence of God. Clearly it doesn't.

Insofar as they can't accommodate necessary beliefs and beliefs about the past, Dretske's conditions are too strong: they aren't necessary for belief. But they are also too weak: they aren't sufficient either. If his account were correct, then if we have been designed by God, we hold all those beliefs about blood pressure, temperature, sodium content, and the like; but we don't. You may or may not think we have in fact been designed by God or anyone else; but even if we haven't it is certainly possible that we have; hence it's possible that Dretske's conditions hold when no beliefs are present. And really, why should the fulfillment of Dretske's conditions have anything at all to do with belief? So there is a structure that has the function of indicating something and causes what it does because of what it indicates; does that really so much as slyly suggest that something in the neighborhood of this structure holds the appropriate belief, or any belief at all? Consider again the lowly thermostat. The bimetallic strip indicates the temperature, and has the function of indicating it. Further, when it bends enough to close the circuit, thereby causing furnace ignition, it causes what it causes because of what it indicates; we designed the thermostat in such a way that when that strip indicates 67°F, it causes the furnace to ignite. The explanation of its causing that movement is that it is indicating that the temperature is 67°F. But neither the bimetallic strip nor the thermostat, nor the furnace nor anything else need believe that the temperature is 67°F. Dretske's account, therefore, won't anywhere nearly serve as an explanation of how there could be beliefs if materialism about human beings is true.

That's the third problem for naturalism, construed so as to include materialism: if it were true, there would be no such thing as belief content, no such thing as primary intentionality, and no such thing as belief. There are, of course, various responses to this problem. As I said above, several materialists hold that there simply aren't any such things as beliefs; the fact is no one ever believes a proposition. These ideas—belief, content, intentionality, aboutness, and the like—belong to the infancy of our race. They belong to folk psychology, a way of thinking that is now outmoded, even if we all rely upon it. We may expect, so they tell us, that the categories of folk psychology will be replaced by more adequate ways of thought, categories, and concepts coming from science. Just as we no longer believe that the earth is flat, just as we no longer believe that the stars are slits in a giant canvas stretched over the earth every night to give us a good night's sleep, so (so the claim goes) we will at some point no longer believe in beliefs, desires, aboutness, and the like. But then the fact that naturalism has no room for belief is really nothing against it. This response seems to me the strongest a naturalist can muster. Of course it does have one real problem: it seems utterly crazy to think that people never hold beliefs.

Conclusion

What we've seen, so far, is that naturalism cannot accommodate proper function and the things that go with it: health, illness, flourishing, pathology, and the like. If naturalism is true, neither people nor other living things nor their systems or organs function properly (or improperly). Most naturalists are also materialists about human beings; if both naturalism and materialism are true, so I say, there aren't any such things as beliefs. Finally, we've also seen that naturalism is self-defeating; a reflective naturalist has a rationality defeater for naturalism itself, and is thus irrational in believing naturalism. Indeed, the reflective naturalist has a defeater for anything he believes and is thus thrown into that profound, many-layered, reflexive skepticism both feared and endorsed by David Hume.

So what's a naturalist to do: what options are available to him, once he recognizes these consequences? I see three basic possibilities. The first is a kind of fictionalism. Maybe there really aren't any desires or beliefs or other intentional phenomena (or alternatively the question whether there are has no answer); these things are mere fictions. Still, fiction has its uses. You can adopt the *intentional stance* towards (alleged) other persons and some machines:

you can treat them and think of them as if they really did possess desire and belief.[78] You can make with respect to them the predictions and predications you would make if you thought they really did possess those properties. If you do so, your predictions about their behavior and responses to what you do will be substantially enhanced and will go more easily and smoothly.[79]

There is no doubt that fiction can sometimes enable us to achieve a level of understanding and control not otherwise available. In physics we think about frictionless planes, point particles, true vacuums. Perhaps there aren't any such things; even so, we can learn much by thinking about them. (Thinking about these fictions is also of practical benefit: we use them in the design and construction of space shuttles, linear accelerators, Olympic bobsleds, and so on.) Of course it requires a certain sophistication to see how fiction can help us gain genuine understanding; but the thought that it can goes back at least to Hobbes and Locke, with their fictional notion of an aboriginal contract signed and sealed by our remote ancestors hoping for relief from their miserable lives in the state of nature. The prime modern sources of this notion of useful fictions are perhaps Leibniz and Kant. Speaking of something like useful fiction with respect to some of the very ideas under consideration (purpose, goal, design plan, proper function and their colleagues) Kant has this to say:

> . . . an object, or state of mind, or even an action is called purposive, although its possibility does not necessarily presuppose the representation of a purpose, merely because its possibility can be explained and conceived by us only so far as we assume for its ground a causality according to purposes, i.e. in accordance with a will which has regulated it according to the representation of a certain rule.[80]

Kant's idea is that there are natural phenomena of which we can gain proper understanding only by way of such notions as purpose and function—despite the fact that nature itself can't properly be seen as displaying (or even covertly harboring) purpose or function. And perhaps the naturalist can follow Kant, adopting an intentional stance with respect to belief and also with respect to proper function and its colleagues.

Now these anti-realist stances are refined and highly sophisticated—in fact, a bit contorted. And, as any rock climber knows, unnatural stances become

---

[78] See Daniel Dennett's *Consciousness Explained* p. 76

[79] Another reason for adopting the intentional stance: perhaps for reasons of your own you want to preserve verbal agreement with those with whom you really disagree; you may want to speak with the vulgar but think with the learned.

[80] *Critique of Judgment*, tr. with an Introduction by J. H. Bernard (New York: Hafner Press, 1951), 55/6, pp. 54–5.

awkward and uncomfortable if held for any length of time. If in one way a fiction can help you understand a phenomenon, in another it can harm your understanding of it. You think the fact is there is no such thing as belief (or proper function); you find yourself nonetheless ineluctably compelled, in your non-philosophical life, to adopt a stance presupposing that there *are* such things. Of course no one really *adopts* such a stance, any more than you adopt your parents; we all take it utterly for granted from earliest consciousness that others have desires and beliefs. Similarly, we all take it for granted that there is such a thing as proper function for the heart, or kidney, or lung. More poignantly, there is such a thing as *mal* function for these things. The fictionalist stance is awkward: to adopt it you are to think that George's heart isn't *really* malfunctioning (or that there isn't any truth of the matter as to whether it is), but you are to treat it and think about it, somehow, as if it *were* malfunctioning. Can you really avoid doublethink and false consciousness? Alternatively, can you avoid what from your own perspective is illusion and error? Illusion, as Freud and Marx tell us, has its uses; but helping to achieve straightforward understanding is not among them.

This line of thought, therefore, is not really attractive. We can turn again to contemporary philosophy of mind for a second alternative. This is for the naturalist to follow the eliminativists in philosophy of mind, who say the same about belief, desire, hope, acceptance, and the other mental states recognized by what they call (in a disparaging tone of voice) 'folk psychology.'[81] We ordinary folk organize our entire lives around the idea that people, ourselves included, believe some propositions, withhold others, and disbelieve still others. We all believe that people, ourselves included, desire some outcomes and hope to avoid others. The eliminativist, however, regards these notions—belief, desire, etc.—as part of an outmoded theory. A proper science of mind will have no place for them (or, presumably, for the notion of mind itself). The naturalist can follow suit, display the courage of his naturalistic convictions, and stoutly declare that there are no such things as belief and/or proper function. These declarations are simply the costs exacted by naturalism; if we want to be naturalists, we will have to pay the price.[82]

But here we meet a very natural question: why should we *want* to be naturalists? If it requires giving up all these things, presumably we should weigh

---

[81] See, e.g., Churchland, "Eliminative Materialism and the Propositional Attitudes," p. 151.

[82] What about the Humean skepticism to which I said the naturalist falls prey? The eliminativist naturalist can perhaps reply that my argument is stated in terms of the categories of belief and defeaters; if, as he proposes, there simply aren't any such things as beliefs, my argument is of doubtful relevance. Of course the naturalist, even the eliminativist naturalist, will presumably still need something *like* the categories of belief and defeater; he'll still want to propose or advance or endorse certain propositions and reject others; he'll still hold that there are right and wrong

the cost of accepting naturalism against its proposed benefits. On the one side of the scale are the arguments for naturalism; on the other, our reasons for the ordinary beliefs we must give up if we wish to be naturalists. And it will be sensible to adopt naturalism, clearly enough, only if the arguments for it are stronger than the reasons for those ordinary beliefs. But where *are* the arguments for naturalism? Perhaps it would be sensible to give up all those ordinary ways of thinking if there were powerful arguments for naturalism. But where are those powerful arguments? As far as I can see, there aren't even any *decent* arguments, let alone powerful arguments, for naturalism. So I suggest a third possibility: give up naturalism, and perhaps accept instead some form of theism.[83]

(or useful and fruitless) ways of doing this; and he'll still want to hold that one can come to endorse something such that endorsing it makes it right, or useful, or appropriate to stop endorsing something. His job will be to try to reconstruct something of the categories of folk psychology in terms of the categories he accepts; and perhaps the argument for Humean skepticism can also be reconstructed in terms of those categories.

[83] My thanks to Michaels Rea and Bergmann.

2
Does God Exist?

Michael Tooley

Introduction

Is belief in the existence of God epistemically justified? I shall argue that, unfortunately, it is not, and the reason that I shall offer is that the argument from evil, properly formulated, shows that the existence of God is unlikely—indeed, *very* unlikely—in the light of facts about the evils found in the world. The latter claim is, of course, highly controversial. But, in addition, even if it can be shown that the evils that are found in the world render the existence of God unlikely, it might still be the case that the existence of God is not unlikely *all things considered*. For perhaps the argument from evil can be overcome by appealing either to positive arguments in support of the existence of God, or to the idea that belief in the existence of God is properly basic, or non-inferentially justified.

I think that it can be shown that neither of these things is the case. For reasons of space, however, I shall not address these two responses in my opening statement. I shall, instead, deal with them at appropriate points later in this debate.

My opening statement is divided into four parts. The first deals with various preliminary matters, while the second surveys a number of arguments for atheism. Then, in part 3, I consider how the argument from evil should be formulated. Finally, in part 4, I offer a detailed statement and defense of the argument.

Three preliminary matters will be addressed in part 1. First, there is the question of the relevant concept of God. Secondly, there is the question of the relation between God, so conceived, and the gods of various historical religions—in particular, the Western monotheistic religions of Judaism, Christianity, and Islam. Thirdly, there is the question of whether it is preferable to formulate the issue in terms of whether it is possible to have knowledge of the existence of God, or in terms of whether belief in the existence of God can be epistemically justified, or justified in some other way.

In part 2, I briefly survey a number of arguments for atheism. These I divide into three main groups. First, there are *a priori* arguments against the existence of God. Here we shall see that while most of these arguments are not without force, they apply to conceptions of God that involve one or more metaphysical elements that are not part of the concept of God that is relevant here. This is not true, however, in the case of one of the *a priori* arguments. That argument has, however, a somewhat modest conclusion—namely, that, as regards the choice between theism, atheism, and agnosticism, atheism is the default position.

Next, there are *a posteriori* arguments against the existence of God, and they can be divided into two importantly different sub-groups. The one consists of arguments that do not involve any *moral* claims. The thrust of these arguments is typically that what we now know about the nature of the world either makes it likely that materialism is true, or, more modestly, makes it likely that reality does not contain any immaterial minds.

Finally, there are *a posteriori* arguments that do involve moral claims—namely different versions of the argument from evil, including the special version known as the argument from the hiddenness of God. The most forceful arguments in support of atheism are to be found, I believe, within this third general group.

In the third part, I turn to a consideration of the argument from evil. Setting out that argument properly is, as we shall see, rather more difficult than has generally been appreciated, and so my discussion, in this part, will center upon some important general issues concerning how the argument from evil is best formulated. Among the things on which I shall focus are the following four distinctions: first, abstract versus concrete formulations of the argument from evil; secondly, incompatibility versus evidential formulations; thirdly, subjective versus objective formulations; and, fourthly, axiological versus deontological formulations.

The final part of my discussion is then devoted to setting out a deontological formulation of the evidential argument from evil, and to examining the crucial inductive step involved in that argument. I shall argue that the inductive step in question can be justified, and this, together with the truth of the premises, means that the evidential argument from evil, properly formulated, is an 'inductively sound' argument, and a very forceful one, for the conclusion that God does not exist.

1   Some Preliminary Issues

In this first part, I shall focus upon four preliminary matters. First, what is the relevant concept of God in the present discussion? Secondly, what is the relation between God, so conceived, and the gods of various historical, revealed religions, such as Judaism, Christianity, and Islam? Thirdly, does it make any difference to the argument from evil if one holds that God is identical with the god of some particular, revealed religion? Fourthly, is it preferable to formulate the basic issue here in terms of whether it is possible to have knowledge of the existence of God, or in terms of whether belief in the existence of God can be epistemically justified, or justified in some other way?

1.1   The relevant concept of God

The term 'God' is used in many ways, but these uses tend to fall into two main groups. On the one hand, there are metaphysical interpretations of the term. According to some of these, God is a being that possesses some special property, or that stands in some unique relation to other things. Thus, for example, God may be defined as an unmoved mover, or as a first cause, or as a necessary being that has its necessity of itself, or as a being that is pure act, devoid of all potentiality, or as a being whose essence is identical with its existence, and so on. Alternatively, God may be conceived of in metaphysically more austere terms, and it may be held that God, rather than being one entity among others—however special—is instead to be identified with the ground of being, or with being itself. Or, more radically still, it may be held that God is, instead, an ultimate reality to which no concepts at all apply: God is the ineffable One that lies beyond all distinctions and concepts.

On the other hand, there are interpretations of the term 'God' that, rather than arising out of a metaphysical inquiry, are connected instead, in a direct, straightforward, and positive way, with religious attitudes, such as that of worship, and with very important human desires and concerns, such as the desire that good should ultimately triumph over evil, and that justice will be done, or the desire that the world not be one where death marks the end of an individual's existence, or one where, ultimately, all conscious existence ceases, and one is left with a purely material universe, devoid of all consciousness, thought, and purpose.

What properties must something have if it is to play the roles just mentioned—that is, if it is to be an appropriate object of worship, and if it is to provide grounds for thinking that there is at least a reasonable chance that the fundamental human hopes in question will be fulfilled? A very natural and plausible answer is that God must be a person, and one who, at the very least, is a very powerful, very knowledgeable, and morally very good person, and who, ideally, is omnipotent, omniscient, and morally perfect, since otherwise it will be an open question both whether God's purposes will, without exception, be morally admirable ones, and whether those morally good purposes will ultimately be achieved.

These very properties that suffice to render a being an appropriate object of the attitudes and hopes in question also give rise, however—and in a very natural and straightforward way—to serious grounds for doubting whether such a being does in fact exist, since, given the supposition that there is a very powerful, very knowledgeable, and morally very good person, it seems very puzzling why the world contains various highly undesirable states of affairs. For, in the first place, many of the most undesirable states of affairs that the world contains are such as could be prevented—or, at least, be very quickly eliminated—by a being who was only moderately powerful. Secondly, given that humans have knowledge of such evils, a being certainly does not need to be exceptionally knowledgeable to be aware of the existence of the evils in question. Finally, even a moderately good human being, given the power to do so, would prevent or eliminate those evils. Why, then, do such extremely undesirable states of affairs exist if there is a being who is omnipotent, omniscient, and morally perfect—or even a being who is merely very powerful, very knowledgeable, and very good?

The argument that I shall set out bears upon the existence of God, thus understood. But it is also relevant, of course, if, rather than *defining* God as a being with very great (or unlimited) knowledge, power, and goodness, one begins by defining God in purely metaphysical terms, but then goes on to argue that a metaphysical entity with the relevant properties will also be at least very powerful, very knowledgeable, and morally very good.

By contrast, if God is conceived of in a purely metaphysical way, and if *no* connection is forged between the relevant metaphysical properties and the possession of significant power, knowledge, and goodness, the argument that I shall be developing ceases to be relevant. Could there, then, be some such purely metaphysical entity—such as a first cause, or an unmoved mover, or a necessary being that has its necessity of itself, and that is a cause of all other beings? In some cases, I would hold that there are other arguments that constitute a decisive objection to the existence of such an entity, while, in other cases, I would hold merely that none of the arguments that has been offered in support of the existence of the relevant metaphysical entity is sound, and that there is no good reason to believe in the existence of that entity. But as my concern in the present discussion is simply with the existence of God as defined above, these are not conclusions for which I shall be arguing here.

1.2 *The god of theism versus the gods of historical religions*

A second preliminary issue that calls for comment concerns the relation between God, thus conceived, and the deities believed in by people who embrace various historical religions, and here the basic point is this. On the one hand, Christians usually want to say that the god that they worship is, if he exists, identical with God as defined above. Similarly, Muslims would, I think, identify Allah with God, thus conceived, while Jews would do the same for their deity, Yahweh.

But, on the other hand, these identifications are by no means unproblematic, since it is not clear that the deities associated with these historical religions can be characterized as perfectly good. Suppose, for example, that Allah, as the Koran indicates, favors holy wars against infidels—that is, against people who reject Islam.[1] Is Allah, then, plausibly described as perfectly good? Or suppose that, as the Roman Catholic Church teaches, and as Protestant Fundamentalists believe, Hell exists, and that most of the human race will wind up there, suffering unending torment.[2] Can this god of Catholicism and Protestant Fundamentalism be characterized as morally perfect?

It is important to keep this issue sharply in focus. For, though I am an atheist, I should very much like it to be the case that I am mistaken, and that it turns out that God, as I have defined him, does exist. For while the existence of such a being does not guarantee that we are in the best of all possible worlds, it greatly increases, at the very least, the chances that the world is a very good one. But, on the other hand, the existence of the god of Protestant Fundamentalism, or of Roman Catholicism, or of Islam, is not something that I would welcome, for it would mean that the world, while certainly not the worst imaginable, would be very bad indeed.

1.3   Revealed religions and the argument from evil

Suppose that a believer in Judaism insists, contrary to what I've claimed, that Yahweh, understood as a deity who performed all of the actions attributed to him in the Torah, is morally perfect, and also omnipotent and omniscient. Or that a Christian insists, contrary to what I've claimed, that the deity whose actions are described in both the Old Testament and the New Testament is morally perfect, and also omnipotent and omniscient. Or that a Muslim insists that Allah, understood as a deity whose actions are described in the Koran, is morally perfect, and also omnipotent and omniscient. Will this make any difference as regards the argument from evil?

It would seem that it will. First of all, in standard versions of the argument from evil, the only *action* on the part of a potential deity that one can appeal to is the (admittedly very far-reaching) action of creating the world. Otherwise, one has to appeal, instead, to cases where, if there is an omnipotent and

---

[1] As regards the treatment of infidels, a famous verse at sura 9.5 says: "Slay the idolaters wherever you find them." There are, of course, many passages in the Koran that preach tolerance, but they are all from early suras of the Meccan period, and are abrogated by the above verse, which is from a Medinan, and hence later, sura. (For a discussion of the Islamic doctrine of abrogation, see Warraq, 1995, pp. 114–15.)
[2] Among the passages on which these beliefs are based are Matthew 25:41, 25:46, 7:13–14, and 22:13–14.

omniscient deity, that deity has, by *failing* to act in certain ways, done something that is *prima facie* wrong. By contrast, given a claimed revelation, one may be able to appeal to many cases where actions that the deity is believed to have performed are *prima facie* wrong.

Thus, for example, in the case of Orthodox Judaism, or of Protestant Fundamentalism, one can appeal to such things as the following: (1) Yahweh's decision to drown all men, women, and children in a great flood, with the exception of a single family—as described in the story of Noah's ark (Genesis, Chapters 6–8); (2) Yahweh's action of killing all of the firstborn children (and animals) of all Egyptian families[3]; (3) Yahweh's affirmation, when setting out the Ten Commandments, that he will punish the children of parents who reject him and who worship some other god[4]; (4) Yahweh's command to Saul, to kill all of the Amalekites[5].

Similarly, in the case of forms of Christianity that do not set aside passages in the New Testament that some find troubling, one can appeal, for example, to the decision of the Christian deity to create a place where most of the human race will suffer eternally, and to the action of the Christian deity in holding that, because of Adam's sin, all men are born with original sin, and so deserve damnation—as affirmed by Paul in his letters.

In the second place, in some instances one will have not only a number of highly problematic actions that one can use in formulating the argument from evil, but also information about the deity's *reason* for performing the act in question. So, for example, in the case of the story of Noah and the Flood, we are not forced to speculate as to why Yahweh killed all men, women, and children, with the exception of Noah's family, and all animals, except for those that were on the ark, since Genesis 6:5–7 gives us God's reason for thus acting:

> The Lord saw that the wickedness of man was great in the earth, and that every imagination of the thoughts of his heart was only evil continually. And the Lord was sorry that he had made man on the earth, and it grieved him to his heart.

---

[3] "At midnight the Lord struck down the firstborn in the land of Egypt, from the firstborn of Pharaoh who sat on his throne to the firstborn of the prisoner who was in the dungeon and all the firstborn of the livestock. Pharaoh arose in the night, he and all his officials and all the Egyptians; and there was a loud cry in Egypt, for there was not a house without someone dead." Exodus 12:29–30.

[4] "You shall not make for yourself an idol, whether in the form of anything that is in heaven above, or that is on the earth beneath, or that is in the water under the earth. You shall not bow down to them or worship them; for I the Lord your God am a jealous God, punishing children for the iniquity of parents, to the third and fourth generation of those who reject me, but showing steadfast love to the thousandth generation of those who love me and keep my commandments." Exodus 20:4–6.

[5] "Go now and fall upon the Amalekites and destroy them, and put their property under ban. Spare no one; put them all to death, men and women, children and babes in arms, herds and flocks, camels and asses." 1 Samuel, 15:3.

> So the Lord said, "I will blot out man whom I have created from the face of the
> ground, man and beast and creeping things and birds of the air, for I am sorry
> that I have made them."

Those not committed to holding that Genesis is the revealed Word of God
will probably find the claim that every imagination of the thoughts of almost
every human "was only evil continually" somewhat implausible. The idea here,
however, is simply to take the passage as it stands, and then to ask whether the
reason that Yahweh gives for destroying virtually all life on earth, including not
just the apparently very naughty adults, but almost all children, and almost all
non-human animals, is such as suffices to make that action morally justified.

Similarly, in the case of the story of the devastation that, according to Exodus
6–12, Yahweh inflicts upon the Egyptians, to say that Yahweh must have
had some morally sufficient reason for killing all of the firstborn children
(and animals) of all Egyptian families, but that we have no way of knowing, at
present, what it was, would be to ignore, for example, Exodus 10:1–2, where
Yahweh states his reason:

> Then the Lord said to Moses, "Go in to Pharaoh; for I have hardened his heart
> and the heart of his servants, that I may show these signs among them, and that
> you may tell in the hearing of your son and of your son's son how I have made
> sport of the Egyptians and what signs I have done among them; that you may
> know that I am the Lord."

One can consider, then, whether Yahweh's reasons do in fact serve to make
such actions as the infliction of the plagues upon all Egyptians, and the killing
of all of the firstborn, actions that are morally right, all things considered.

In short, when it is claimed that the god of some revealed religion is an
omnipotent, omniscient, and morally perfect person, one is no longer restricted,
in formulating the argument from evil, to appealing mainly to actions that God
might have performed, but did not, since one can appeal to actions ascribed
to the deity in the relevant revelation, and also, in some cases, to information
about the deity's reasons for performing those actions, and one can ask whether
those actions are morally right.

1.4 Knowledge, warrant, and epistemically justified belief

The term "warrant" is used by Plantinga to refer to whatever it is that must
be added to true belief in order to constitute knowledge. Given that concept,
how should the issue of the choice among theism, agnosticism, and atheism be
formulated? In terms of knowledge? In terms of warrant? Or in terms of epistemically justified belief? The last of these, I suggest, is the appropriate notion,
for the following reasons.

In the first place, whether a belief is epistemically justified, and, if it is, the extent to which it is, is a function of the epistemic probability of the relevant proposition. The latter fixes, non-epistemic factors aside, what degree of assent to the proposition in question is appropriate. Then that degree of assent, in turn, enters into the determination of what actions are rational in the circumstances. As long as the epistemic probability of a given proposition remains fixed, whether one does or does not *know* that the proposition is true makes no difference to what degree of assent is rational, or to what actions are rational. Similarly, as long as the epistemic probability of a proposition remains fixed, whether acceptance of that proposition is *warranted* or not makes no difference with respect to rational belief or rational action.

But what is epistemic probability? One answer is that it is logical probability relative to one's total evidence. But what is one's total evidence? Does it consist of all of one's prior, justified beliefs? That view seems problematic, since the extent to which one is justified in believing different things may vary enormously, and so it would seem that not all beliefs should count equally.

A natural response to this problem is to say that the epistemic probability of a proposition, rather than being equal to its logical probability relative to one's total evidence, is equal instead to its logical probability relative to the propositions that one is non-inferentially justified in accepting. But then questions arise both as to whether all such properly basic beliefs should receive the same degree of assent, and whether that degree of assent should be equal to one. If one is an indirect realist with regard to both perception and memory, one *may* be able to maintain that both of these things are the case. Or, alternatively, an indirect realist may be able to hold that the epistemic probability of a proposition is its logical probability relative to the propositions describing one's 'basis' states—that is, those states in virtue of which various beliefs are non-inferentially justified. But if one is, instead, a direct realist, I think it can be shown that neither of these options is satisfactory, and that an account of epistemic probability will have to involve not just the idea of logical probability, but also some idea of 'foundational' probability—where the probability that a proposition that one is non-inferentially justified in believing is independent of its relations to any other propositions.

The second reason for not formulating the issue in terms of the concept of warrant is that that concept is too narrow, since, while all warranted beliefs are presumably epistemically justified, not all epistemically justified beliefs are warranted, as is shown by Gettier-style cases. Suppose, for example, as in one of Gettier's examples, that Smith has knowledge that constitutes extremely strong evidence for the proposition that Jones owns a Ford. As a result, Smith adopts the belief that Jones owns a Ford—a belief that is surely epistemically justified. Smith then goes on to adopt the disjunctive belief that either Jones owns a Ford, or Brown is in Barcelona, where the proposition that Brown is in

Barcelona is one that Smith has no reason at all for thinking is true. Indeed, let us suppose that Smith has excellent evidence that the latter proposition is false. It will still be the case that the probability for Smith that the disjunctive proposition—that either Jones owns a Ford, or Brown is in Barcelona—is true will be slightly greater than the probability that Jones owns a Ford, and so it will be very high indeed. So surely Smith is justified in accepting that disjunctive belief. Suppose, finally, that it turns out that Jones does not own a Ford, but that, surprisingly, Brown is in Barcelona. Then Smith's disjunctive belief is justified and true, but not, Gettier claims—and surely rightly—a case of knowledge. But if it is not a case of knowledge, then it cannot be a warranted belief, and so there can be epistemically justified beliefs that are not warranted.

Finally, because of Getter's counterexamples to the thesis that knowledge is justified true belief, together with other counterexamples that have also been advanced, the question of the correct account of the concept of knowledge has become a matter of immense controversy, with many competing accounts on offer. When warrant is defined as whatever must be added to true belief to constitute knowledge, all of that controversy, and all of the competing proposals, are exactly carried over into the question of the correct account of what constitutes warrant. It would be nice if, in discussing the relative merits of theism, agnosticism, and atheism, one could avoid getting enmeshed in all of this, and I claim that one can. For if it could be shown, for example, that the epistemic probability of theism was high, one would no longer be justified in remaining an atheist or an agnostic, and this would be so regardless of whether it was true that one could know that God existed, or be warranted in so believing.

I shall frame my discussion, accordingly, in terms of the notion of epistemic probability, and I shall attempt to show, then, that the epistemic probability of there being an omnipotent and omniscient being that, given certain moral standards, is morally perfect, is very low, and, therefore, that the belief that such a being does not exist is, unless there are countervailing considerations, epistemically justified, and highly so.

2   Arguments Against the Existence of God

In this part, I shall briefly survey a number of arguments against theism. These can be divided into three main groups by distinguishing, first of all, between *a priori* arguments and *a posteriori* arguments, and then, secondly, in the case of *a posteriori* arguments, between those that involve moral claims, and those that do not.

With regard to *a priori* arguments against the existence of God, what we shall see is that while some arguments of this sort are not without force, they tend to apply only to conceptions of God that involve some metaphysical element not entailed by the properties of omnipotence, omniscience, and moral perfection. One *a priori* argument, however, does apply to God, so defined; however, that argument supports only a rather modest conclusion—namely, that as regards the choice between theism, atheism, and agnosticism, atheism is the default position.

The second group of arguments consists of *a posteriori*, or empirical, arguments that do not involve any moral claims. The basic thrust of these arguments is usually that our present knowledge of the nature of the world makes it unlikely that God exists, because it makes it unlikely that any immaterial minds at all exist.

Finally, there are *a posteriori* empirical arguments that involve moral claims. These consist of different versions of the argument from evil, including the special form known as the argument from the apparent hiddenness of God. It is, I suggest, within this third general group of arguments that the most powerful arguments in support of atheism are to be found.

2.1 A priori *arguments*

Arguments of this first sort can be divided into three main types. First, there are arguments that attempt to show, not that atheism is true, but, more radically, that statements about the existence of God, though they may possess some sort of meaning, are not cognitively significant—that is, are not such as are either true or false. Secondly, there are arguments that attempt to show that the concept of God involves an implicit contradiction—so that it is logically impossible that God exists. Thirdly, there are arguments that attempt to establish only the much more modest conclusion that the existence of God is *a priori* less likely than the non-existence of God.

2.1.1   Are theistic statements cognitively significant?

Many philosophers have held, and some still hold, that theism is to be rejected, not because it is false, but because sentences about the existence of God are literally devoid of any cognitive sense: they express no propositions; they say nothing that is either true or false. Such a contention is typically supported by an appeal to some version of the verifiability principle of cognitive content, as in the case of the most famous exposition of this view—namely, that found in A. J. Ayer's book *Language, Truth, and Logic* (1936).

The version of the verifiability principle that Ayer appealed to was a particularly vigorous one, as in addition to entailing that theological statements were devoid of cognitive content, it also entailed that while statements about one's own experiences, understood as involving qualitative, phenomenal properties, were cognitively significant, the same was not true of statements about the experiences of other people. But even if one shifts to less radical versions of the verifiability criterion of cognitive content, there are very strong objections both to any version of the verifiability principle, and to any attempt to use such a principle to show that theological statements are neither true nor false—as I argued in "Theological Statements and the Question of an Empiricist Criterion of Cognitive Significance" (1975), and as a number of theists have argued, including Richard Swinburne in his book *The Coherence of Theism* (1977).

2.1.2   Some arguments for the logical impossibility of theism

Let us set aside, then, the claim that theological statements are neither true nor false, and consider what sorts of arguments can be offered for holding that God does not exist. First of all, a number of *a priori* arguments have been offered in support of the claim that the concept of God involves a contradiction. Properly developed, some of these arguments do establish, I believe, that the particular concepts of God against which they are directed are problematic. But they do not, I shall argue, show that there is anything contradictory about the concept of God that is relevant here.

Let me briefly sketch, then, some typical examples of such *a priori* arguments. I shall then go on, in the next subsection, to indicate why they do not show that there is anything problematic about the idea of an omnipotent, omniscient, and morally perfect deity.

(1) Omniscience and immutability. It is sometimes maintained that God is an absolutely immutable being. It can be argued, however, that this is not compatible with God's being omniscient. For suppose that it is now exactly 12:20 p.m. If God is omniscient, then God must know that it is now precisely 12:20 p.m., and so he must believe that it is now exactly that time. Suppose, next, that five minutes have now passed. Then God now knows that it is now exactly 12:25 p.m., and so it cannot be the case that God now believes that it is now precisely 12:20 p.m. Hence God must be in a different state now than he was in five minutes ago, and, therefore, God cannot be changeless.[6]

(2) The problem of a timeless agent. It is sometimes held that God is eternal, not in the sense of existing at every moment of time, but in the sense of being outside of time—perhaps in the way that necessarily existent entities, such as numbers, or Platonic Forms, if such there be, are outside of time. However, God is also a person who created the world, and who acts in human history—or, at

---

[6]This type of argument was advanced and defended by Norman Kretzmann in his article "Omniscience and Immutability" (1966). (He then later rejected it in the article "Eternity" (1981), which he co-authored with Eleonore Stump.)

least, who is capable of so doing. But are these two properties really compatible? If something acts, and brings about the existence either of the world, or of specific events in time, must not such a being itself be within time?

This incompatibility claim seems to me right. It is not, however, a claim that can be taken to be self-evident: an argument is needed. But I think that such an argument can be developed. The most promising way of doing so, I believe, is by arguing that there is a connection between causation and time. One might, for example, attempt to demonstrate that a cause is necessarily earlier than its effect, and one way of doing that would be to argue for a causal theory of temporal priority—as I have done elsewhere (1997, chapter 9). If some such argument can be sustained, then one will have shown that nothing that lies outside of time can enter into causal relations.

(3) Omniscience, moral perfection, and an indeterministic world. Consider, first, the idea of being omniscient in an indeterministic world. Could an omniscient being know, for example, that a certain Uranium-238 atom would decay in the next five seconds? If radioactive decay were a deterministic process, there would be no problem, since such a being would know how things were in the universe as a whole at earlier times, and so would know of some total state of the universe at a certain time that it was either a sufficient cause of the atom's undergoing radioactive decay at some point in the next five seconds, or else a sufficient cause of that not happening. But what if the laws governing radioactive decay were indeterministic—as seems to be the case in our universe? Could an omniscient being still know whether or not an atom would decay?

If backward causation is logically possible, there is no problem. For then the atom's decaying in three seconds' time can cause the relevant belief in the omniscient being via a temporally backwards, causal process. Many philosophers, however, contend that backwards causation is logically impossible. To show that this is so is, admittedly, not an easy matter.[7] But if that claim can be sustained, then this solution is ruled out.

Another possible response is that if there are counterfactuals of freedom concerning what actions would be performed by a particular individual with libertarian free will in a given situation, and if an omniscient being, by knowing which counterfactuals of freedom are true, can know what a free agent will do at any future time, why cannot there also be 'counterfactuals of chance' that enable an omniscient being to know whether a given atom will decay?

---

[7] For a discussion of why many standard attempts to show that backward causation is logically impossible do not succeed, see my *Time, Tense, and Causation* (1997), section 3.2.

A full discussion of this proposal would require considerable space. My view, however, is that, as Robert Adams (1977) and others have argued, so-called "middle knowledge"—that is, knowledge of such counterfactuals—is impossible, and the grounds that I would offer is that any serious correspondence theory of truth rules out the idea of counterfactuals of freedom.

A final response involves the idea that while it is true that if God were located in time, he would not be able to know whether an indeterministic event would occur at a later time, God is outside of time, and this enables him to have knowledge of any event at any point in the temporal series. But if the earlier argument—to the effect that the idea of a timeless agent involves a contradiction—is right, this solution is also ruled out. Consequently, unless there is some other solution that we have not considered, it might seem that we can conclude that an indeterministic universe rules out the existence of an omniscient being.

But even if this were right, how would it show that there is any contradiction in the idea of an omniscient person? Is not the conclusion at most that the existence of such a person is incompatible with the existence of an indeterministic world?

If one assumes only that the person is omniscient, this is right. But suppose that one considers a being that is also omnipotent and morally perfect. If one could somehow argue both that such a being would create at least some other people, and that those individuals would possess libertarian free will, then one would be able to conclude that if there is a being that is omnipotent, omniscient, and morally perfect, then the world must be at least partly indeterministic. So if omniscience is logically incompatible with the existence of an indeterministic world, it would have been shown that the existence of a being who is omnipotent, omniscient, and morally perfect is implicitly self-contradictory.

(4) Paradoxes of omnipotence. It is sometimes argued, as follows, that the concept of omnipotence involves a contradiction. If one is omnipotent, one is able to bring about any logically possible state of affairs. One logically possible state of affairs, however, is that the world should contain a rock that is too large for anyone to lift. An omnipotent being must be able to bring it about, therefore, that there is such a rock. Suppose, then, that an omnipotent being does this. Then there is a rock that no one, including the omnipotent being, can lift. But any rock must be such that it is logically possible to lift it. So there is now a logically possible action—the lifting of a certain rock—that the being that we are considering cannot perform. Therefore, that being is not omnipotent. The assumption that there is an omnipotent being leads, accordingly, to a contradiction.

(5) The impossibility of a logically necessary person. Suppose that one introduces the concept of God by treating that concept as itself a theoretical entity that is implicitly defined by the following, simple theory, T_G:

(a) For any x, the concept of God applies to x only if x is omnipotent, omniscient, and morally perfect.

(b) It is logically necessary that if there is an x such that the concept of God applies to x, then it is logically necessary that there is an x such that the concept of God applies to x.

One can then transform this implicit definition into an explicit one by using, for example, the Ramsey/Lewis method of defining theoretical terms. So replace all occurrences of "the concept of God" in (a) and (b) by the expression "the concept C"—where 'C' is a variable that ranges over concepts. Then one has the following two open sentences:

(a*) For any x, the concept C applies to x only if x is omnipotent, omniscient, and morally perfect.

(b*) It is logically necessary that if there is an x such that the concept C applies to x, then it is logically necessary that there is an x such that the concept C applies to x.

One can then explicitly define the concept of God as follows:

The concept of God is identical with that unique concept C that satisfies the conjunction of (a*) and (b*).

Assume, now, that the concept thus defined is not implicitly contradictory, so that it is logically possible that there is an x to which the concept of God truly applies. One can then show that it follows that there exists an x to which the concept of God truly applies. For let us use the term 'p' to represent the proposition that there is an x to which the concept of God applies, and let us assume that the following are analytic truths:

(LN) A proposition is logically necessary in any given world if and only if it is true in every possible world.

(LP) A proposition is logically possible in any given world if and only if it is true in at least one possible world.

(T) A proposition is true if and only if it is true in the actual world.

The argument can then be set out as follows:

(1) The proposition, that p, is logically possible.   Assumption.

(2) There is a possible world—call it W—in which the proposition, that p, is true.

From (1) and (LP).

(3) The proposition that if p, then it is logically necessary that p, is itself logically necessary.

From the definition of the concept of God.

(4) The proposition, that if p, then it is logically necessary that p, is true in every possible world.

From (3) and (LN).

(5) The proposition, that if p, then it is logically necessary that p, is true in world W.

From (4).

(6) The proposition, that it is logically necessary that p, is true in world W.

From (2) and (5).

(7) The proposition, that p, is true in every world.

From (6) and (LN).

(8) The proposition, that it is logically necessary that p, is true in every world.

From (7) and (LN).

(9) The proposition, that it is logically necessary that p, is true in the actual world.

From (8).

(10) The proposition, that it is logically necessary that p, is true.

From (9) and (T).

One can then discharge the assumption made at (1), thereby generating the following result:

(A) If it is logically possible that God exists, then it is logically necessary that God exists.

The idea is then to establish the following claim:

(B) It is not logically necessary that God exists.

For (A) and (B) then yield:

(C) The existence of God is logically impossible.

Clearly, the crucial step in this argument is establishing that (B) is true. Later, when I consider the ontological argument—of which the argument at (1) through (10) is one version—I shall indicate how one might argue for (B).

2.1.3   The irrelevance of these arguments in the present context

None of these arguments, it seems to me, provides one with any ground for concluding that the general idea of an omnipotent, omniscient, and morally perfect person involves any inconsistency. First, as regards the argument that attempts to show that omniscience and immutability are incompatible, it seems to me that that argument is sound. But the argument does not bear upon the present concept of God. For while it may very well follow, given certain scholastic, and highly metaphysical, conceptions of God, that God is absolutely free of all change, and necessarily so, this is certainly not the case when God is defined as an omnipotent, omniscient, and morally perfect person. Indeed, on the contrary, there is a strong reason—namely, the very argument we are now considering—for concluding that any omniscient being must undergo change.

Some writers have, it is true, attempted to resist this argument. In particular, Eleonore Stump and Norman Kretzmann (1981) have tried to show that an appropriate account of the concept of eternity provides a basis for concluding that omniscience is not incompatible with immutability. Their argument rests, however, upon a failure to recognize that ordinary tensed sentences contain indexicals.[8] The relevance of this is that it can be shown (Perry, 1979) that the knowledge that can be expressed by an indexical thought (or utterance) cannot be expressed by a non-indexical thought, and this entails that if tensed sentences contain indexicals, then no being that does not undergo change can possibly have knowledge of what time it is at any two distinct times.

The gist of the second argument was that something cannot be both timeless and an agent. This argument also seems to me to be sound. But once again, it does not tell against the concept of God being employed here, since there is no reason at all for holding that an omnipotent, omniscient, and morally perfect God will be outside of time. On the contrary, there is least two strong reasons for holding that God, so conceived, will be in time. In the first place, the present argument, which appeals to connections between being an agent and entering into causal relations, and between the relation of causation and that of temporal priority, provides grounds for holding that God must be in time. In the second place, the conclusion of the first argument does the same, for if God is mutable, then he is certainly in time.

---

[8] It is sometimes claimed that ordinary tensed sentences do not contain indexicals. For a refutation of that view, see my *Time, Tense, and Causation* (1997, pp. 217–23), and "Basic Tensed Sentences and their Analysis" (2003, pp. 418–32).

Why, then, have some religious thinkers been inclined to hold that God is outside of time? One line of thought is that God is immutable, and that if God is immutable, then he must be outside of time. But this argument is unsound. First of all, as we have seen, the claim that God is immutable should be rejected. Secondly, the move from the idea that God is immutable to the conclusion that God is outside of time is also highly problematic. For what support can be offered for that inference? The only serious possibility, I believe, involves an appeal to the claim that there is a certain conceptual connection between time and change—to wit, that time presupposes change. But this claim is open to two very strong objections. First, there is the argument against this claim set out and defended by Sydney Shoemaker in his paper "Time without Change" (1969). Secondly, the claim that time presupposes change can be shown to be incompatible with the fact that nothing prevents there being causal connections between qualitatively indistinguishable states of affairs—including total states of the universe at a time.

The third argument focused, in effect, upon the familiar theological problem of whether an omniscient being could have foreknowledge of free human actions, and then attempted to convert an argument for the conclusion that it is impossible to have foreknowledge of the free actions of others into an argument for the conclusion that omniscience is incompatible with omnipotence and moral perfection by appealing to the idea that an omnipotent, omniscient, and morally perfect being would create agents who enjoyed libertarian free will.

Both parts of this argument are, I believe, problematic. In the case of the second part, it appears that a defense of that part will have to appeal to the consequentialist view that one is morally required to perform the action (or one of the actions) that produces the best balance of good states of affairs over bad states of affairs. But consequentialism, it seems to me, is open to serious objections.

As regards the first part, many attempts have been made to show that foreknowledge of the free actions of others is logically possible,[9] but all of the attempts with which I am familiar are, I believe, unsound.[10] Nevertheless, it seems to me that there is a perfectly satisfactory answer to the argument—namely, that if the argument does establish that foreknowledge of the free actions of others is logically impossible, then the absence of such knowledge does not entail that one is not omniscient: just as omnipotence is not the ability to perform any action, including ones that it is logically impossible to perform,

---

[9] For a very useful survey and discussion of the most important approaches, see Zagzebski (1991).

[10] For criticisms of some approaches, see my article "Freedom and Foreknowledge" (2000).

so omniscience is to be characterized, not as a matter of knowing every true proposition, but as a matter of knowing every proposition that it is logically possible to know at the relevant time.

The fourth argument attempted to show that the concept of omnipotence gives rise to contradictions. This argument seems to me clearly unsound, and this can be seen if one simply makes explicit the times at which the being acts, or possesses some property. For suppose A is omnipotent at a specific time t_1. Then A can act at that time to bring it about that there is a rock that no one can lift. But at what time does the latter state of affairs first exist? It cannot be time t_1, since, I would argue, a cause cannot be simultaneous with its effect. So let us suppose that A acts at time t_1 to bring it about that there is, at some later time t_2, a rock that no one can lift. It then follows that A either no longer exists at time t_2, or does exist at time t_2, but is no longer omnipotent. So to bring it about that there is a rock that no one can lift—including himself—an omnipotent being must either commit suicide, or at least bring it about that he is no longer omnipotent at the relevant time. This is not, presumably, something that a sensible person—let alone a morally perfect one—would be likely to do. But there is no contradiction in the proposition that A, who is omnipotent at time t_1, either does not exist at some later time t_2, or else exists at that time, but is not omnipotent. Accordingly, there is no paradox of omnipotence.

The fifth and final argument sketched above claimed that the idea of a being who is omnipotent, omniscient, and morally perfect, and whose existence, in addition, is logically necessary, is self-contradictory, and this is a claim that I shall be defending later on, since if this claim is not correct, then the argument set out in the preceding section—at steps (1) through (10)—is a sound proof of the necessary existence of an omnipotent, omniscient, and morally perfect person. But the incoherence, as I shall be claiming, of that concept of God arises precisely because of the postulate that if such a God exists, then its existence is logically necessary, and so the conclusion of the present argument provides no grounds for thinking that the concept of a being who is omnipotent, omniscient, and morally perfect, but not logically necessary, is in any way problematic.

The upshot is that while three of the above five *a priori* arguments for the non-existence of God—namely, the first, the second, and the fifth—do appear to constitute strong objections to certain metaphysical conceptions of God, they do not tell against the concept that is relevant here.

2.1.4   The argument from logical probability: atheism as the
        default position

Let us now turn to a very different sort of *a priori* argument, namely, an argument that, rather than being directed to showing that the concept of God is implicitly self-contradictory, and thus that the existence of God is logically impossible, aims at establishing the much more modest conclusion that atheism is the default position—that is, that in the absence of any positive ground for, or evidence in support of, belief in the existence of God, it is reasonable to hold that God does not exist, and unreasonable either to believe in God, or to suspend belief on this matter.

How might one try to support this contention? One way would be to consider what one does with respect to beliefs concerning the existence of other types of things in cases where there is no positive evidence in support of their existence. Consider, for example, fairies and leprechauns. The vast majority of people surely think that it is *very unlikely* that there are such things. But is this because we have positive evidence against the existence of fairies and leprechauns? Or is it, rather, simply because we have no positive evidence in support of their existence? As it is not easy to see what the positive evidence in question could be, the natural answer is that we take the fact that there is no evidence in support of the existence of such things as itself grounds for concluding that it is very unlikely that fairies and leprechauns exist. If so, and if we are justified in taking this view in the case of fairies and leprechauns, then must it not equally be the case that, in the absence of positive evidence in support of the existence of God, the correct view to take is that it is very unlikely that God exists?

One way of attempting to rebut this argument would be by arguing that the case of God differs from that of fairies and leprechauns in that we are non-inferentially justified in believing in God, but not in believing in fairies and leprechauns. On the face of it, this is not an immensely plausible claim. Closer consideration of it, however, is certainly called for. But rather than tackling this issue in my opening statement, I shall turn to it when I am responding to Plantinga's defense of the view that theistic belief is properly basic.

A more compelling response, it seems to me, is as follows. Compare the following two propositions:

(1) Living things now exist on a planet circling Alpha Centauri.

(2) Living things now exist on some planet in the universe, besides the Earth.

Ignoring what may now be the case, it seems true at least that, before Darwin and the Theory of Evolution, people had no positive evidence in support of either (1) or (2). But is it true that it would have been reasonable to hold that both (1) and (2) are unlikely to be true? One thing that is clear is that (2) is much less unlikely than (1), and given that that is so, one might well think that it is an open question just how likely or unlikely (2) is. But if this is an open question, might it not turn out that (2), rather than being unlikely, is actually at least more likely than not?

In short, the existence of some things for which we have no positive evidence may be much more likely than the existence of other things for which we also have no positive evidence. Moreover, it seems possible that the existence of some things for which we have no positive evidence may very well be more likely than not. If so, then any argument that appeals to the general claim that, if one has no positive evidence in support of the existence of some thing, then one is justified in holding that the existence of that thing is unlikely, cannot be sound.

The conclusion, in short, is that each case needs to be considered on its merits. Let us do that, then, in the case of the existence of God. The question, then, is how one can form an estimate of the likelihood of God's existing, in the absence of supporting evidence. Ideally, one would like to appeal to a complete system of logical probability that would entail a precise answer to the question of the logical probability that the proposition that God exists is true, given only tautological evidence. But even if, as I maintain, there is such a system, what form it takes is a controversial matter.

Fortunately, there is a way of finessing this problem, and which, though it will not yield an exact value for the probability in question, does enable one to generate various upper bounds. The idea is this. First, incorporate whatever attributes you want into the definition of God—such as that of being absolutely perfect—as long as something cannot be God unless it is omnipotent, omniscient, and morally perfect. It then follows that the logical probability that God exists cannot be greater than the logical probability that there is an omnipotent, omniscient, and morally perfect person. Secondly, given this, the basic strategy involves finding possible entities whose existence is logically incompatible with the existence of an omnipotent, omniscient, and morally perfect person, and whose *a priori* probability of existing can plausibly be equated with the *a priori* probability of an omnipotent, omniscient, and morally perfect person. It will then follow that the *a priori* probability that such a being exists cannot be less than the *a priori* probability that God exists.

One such candidate, for example, is a being who is omnipotent, omniscient, and perfectly evil. For, in the first place, it seems clear that it is logically impossible for there to be two omnipotent beings at one and the same time, since if one willed that some contingent future state of affairs obtain, while the other willed that it not obtain, they could not both succeed. Secondly, the fact that an omnipotent, omniscient, and perfectly evil being differs from an omnipotent, omniscient, and morally perfect one only in being perfectly evil, rather than perfectly good, strongly suggests that it is *a priori* just as likely that there is an omnipotent, omniscient, and perfectly evil being as that there is an omnipotent, omniscient, and perfectly good being.

A possible objection here emerged once in a conversation with Peter Geach, who, when the possibility of an omnipotent, omniscient, and perfectly evil person was raised, replied that Spinoza had shown that such a person was logi-cally impossible. When asked how the argument went, Geach replied that the basic idea was that while the virtues are all logically compatible, the vices are not—a claim that he illustrated by appealing to the idea that boundless pride was incompatible with completely unbridled lasciviousness.

It was tempting, at this point, to mention one or two philosophers as possi-ble counterexamples. The essential point here, however, is simply that when one speaks of a perfectly evil person, one does not normally have in mind someone who, among other things, suffers from complete cowardliness, perfect slothfulness, and total weakness of the will. What one generally has in mind, rather, is a person who is perfectly malevolent, and, on the face of it, that concept does not seem any more problematic than the concept of a person who is perfectly benevolent.

In the absence of a stronger objection, then, it appears reasonable to hold that the existence of an omnipotent, omniscient, and perfectly evil being is *a priori* just as likely as that of an omnipotent, omniscient, and perfectly good being. Are there other, equally likely candidates? Another that might plausibly be suggested, I think, is an omnipotent and omniscient being who falls pre-cisely between the perfectly good and perfectly evil deities—that is, a being who, rather than either wanting to see others flourish, or wanting to see them suffer, is indifferent as to whether others fare well or badly.

The suggestion, then, is that it is reasonable to view the following three pos-sible beings as *a priori* equally probable:

(a) an omnipotent, omniscient, and perfectly good being;

(b) an omnipotent, omniscient, and perfectly evil being;

(c) an omnipotent, omniscient, and morally indifferent being.

But if that is right, then the *a priori* probability that God exists cannot be greater than one-third, and so the *a priori* probability that God does not exist must be at least two-thirds. Consequently, in the absence of a positive reason in support of the existence of God, it is reasonable to believe that God does not exist. Atheism is the default position.

There is, however, a line of thought that, if correct, refutes the above argu-ment. It involves the famous Socratic thesis that it is impossible to do some-thing that one knows is morally wrong. For if this meta-ethical claim were true, then any omniscient being would necessarily be morally perfect, and so the probability of there being an omnipotent and omniscient being who was either perfectly evil or morally indifferent would be equal to zero. Socrates' thesis, however, seems very implausible—unless one is prepared to argue that humans do not possess any moral knowledge—since, on the face of it, it would seem that many people do in fact do things that they know to be morally wrong.

But even if one sets aside the strong, Socratic thesis, there are related, but more moderate, meta-ethical theses that might seem to undercut, at least in part, the present argument. In particular, consider the claim that there is at least some necessary connection between knowledge that an action is morally wrong and a disposition not to perform the action, other things being equal. If that is the case, then an omnipotent and omniscient being will, in the absence of countervailing motivation, be more likely, on any given occasion, to perform an action that is morally right, rather than one that is morally wrong. From this, it might then seem to follow that the *a priori* probability of there being an omnipotent, omniscient, and perfectly good being should be at least somewhat greater than that of an omnipotent, omniscient, and perfectly evil being.

Is it true that moral knowledge is, at least to some extent, intrinsically and necessarily motivating? This is a very difficult, and much disputed, issue in meta-ethics, but there is an argument in support of an affirmative answer that seems to me to have force. The argument starts from the question of what it means to say that an action is wrong, all things considered. Suppose that one replies that an action is morally wrong all things considered if and only if the wrongmaking properties of the action outweigh its rightmaking properties. This immediately leads to the question of what is meant by rightmaking and wrongmaking properties. Suppose that, in response, one says that the properties of being a rightmaking property and of being a wrongmaking property are second-order properties of properties, of which one is directly aware. Does one now have a satisfactory answer to our original question? I do not think that one does, for even if one accepts the claim that that one is directly aware of those two second-order properties, one still faces the question, in effect, of which is which. What is it that makes one of those second-order properties the property of being a rightmaking property, and the other the property of being a wrongmaking property?

One answer, offered by J. L. Mackie (1977), is that a second-order property is the property of being a rightmaking property if and only if the knowledge that any action has a property with that second-order property necessarily motivates one, to some extent, to perform the action, and, similarly, that a second-order property is the property of being a wrongmaking property if and only if the knowledge that any action has a property with that second-order property necessarily motivates one, to some extent, not to perform the action. On this view, moral knowledge is necessarily connected with motivation.

To avoid this conclusion, the moral realist needs to show that there is some other plausible way in which to analyze the relevant concepts. I think that it is doubtful that there is. But rather than pursue that issue, let us simply consider whether the thesis that moral knowledge is intrinsically motivating undermines the above argument.

It seems to me clear that it does not. If moral knowledge is necessarily motivating, then an omniscient being will always have some inclination to do what is right, and this means that it will be more likely to do that on any given occasion. But that does not mean that such a being is likely always to do what is right. Moreover, even if the inclination to do what is right always brought it about, as a matter of fact, that an omniscient being always did what was right, that would not mean that the being in question was perfectly good, since always doing the right thing does not suffice to make one perfectly good: to be perfectly good one must possess a trait of character that *ensures* that one will never do what is wrong, regardless of whatever circumstances may arise.

The answer to the objection, in short, is that the difference between an omnipotent, omniscient, and perfectly good being and an omnipotent, omniscient, and perfectly evil being lies in the possession of different enduring dispositions, and neither dispositional trait is more likely than the other.

If this is right, the earlier conclusion stands: the *a priori* probability that God exists cannot be greater than one-third. But then it also seems likely that one can argue for a much lower upper bound on the *a priori* probability that God exists, since there are many possibilities other than (a), (b), and (c): an omnipotent and omniscient being might possess any degree of goodness intermediate between moral indifference and perfect goodness, and any degree of evilness between being morally indifferent and being perfectly evil. So consider, for example, the property of having a moral character that falls halfway between moral indifference and moral perfection, or the property of having a moral character that is halfway between that of a morally indifferent person and that of a perfectly evil person. Is there any reason that can be given for assigning to the existence of an omnipotent and omniscient person who exhibits one of these properties a lower *a priori* probability than possibilities (a), (b), and (c)? If not, then we must conclude that the *a priori* probability that God exists cannot be greater than one-fifth.

A serious downward spiral is now on the horizon, since it might be argued that there are an infinite number of possibilities between the extreme of being perfectly good and that of being perfectly evil. If all of those possibilities are on a par with the three originally cited, then the probability of there being an omnipotent and omniscient being that realizes any particular possibility will be infinitesimal, and so the *a priori* probability that God exists will be infinitesimal.

It may be possible to block this by arguing that the possibilities we are now considering are more complex than those of a perfectly good being, a perfectly evil being, and a perfectly indifferent being, and so must have lower *a priori* probabilities. But even if this view can be defended, it does not affect the present argument, since the first three possibilities, which do seem to be on a par, are sufficient to establish that atheism is the default position. In addition, even if the other possibilities are more complex, and so have a lower probability, there does not seem to be any reason for holding, for example, that it is *a priori* more likely that there is a perfectly evil being than that there is a being whose moral character falls *somewhere* between that of a perfectly indifferent person and that of a perfectly evil person. So it seems plausible that the additional possibilities beyond the first three will certainly enable one to ratchet down, considerably further, the upper bound on the *a priori* probability that God exists.

But even if this is so, the conclusion in question is still much more modest than the extremely strong conclusion that would be established by the earlier *a priori* arguments if they were sound, and applicable to the concept of God that is relevant here—namely, that the existence of God is logically impossible—and a theist could perfectly well accept the present argument, but then go on to argue either that there is satisfactory positive evidence in support of the existence of God, or else that belief in the existence of God not only could be, but is, non-inferentially justified.

Nevertheless, in the absence of a satisfactory defense of either of these possibilities, the conclusion of the present argument will stand, and atheism will be the epistemically rational position. As a consequence, a person who embraces theism by a Kierkegaardian or Jamesian leap of faith will not, as is often thought, simply be choosing to believe in the existence of God when that belief is as likely to be false as it is to be true: he or she will, instead, be choosing to believe something that is much more likely to be false than it is to be true.

2.2   An empirical argument: immaterial minds and physical reality

This concludes my survey of some *a priori* arguments for atheism. Let us now turn to the second main type of argument for atheism—namely, *a posteriori*, or empirical, arguments that do not involve any moral claims. Here I shall focus upon the claim that our present knowledge of the nature of the world makes it unlikely that God exists by making it unlikely that there are any immaterial minds at all.

Consider the following. First, if one suffers a substantial—but not too serious—blow to the head, one may be temporarily immobile, and so unable to exhibit any of the behavior typically associated with a conscious person. But, in addition, we speak of such a person as being unconscious—thereby indicating that we believe that the person is not, at the time in question, enjoying any experiences, or any thoughts, or other mental states. Moreover, we surely have good reason for this belief, for if such persons were merely immobile through a stretch of time, then we would expect them, when they recovered, to be able to tell us what they had been thinking about during the period of immobility. But they do not do this: they remember nothing, and they make no claims to have been conscious during that time.

Secondly, more serious blows to the head may damage the brain in ways that render the person in question permanently unable to exhibit the behavior typically displayed by a conscious person. In such cases, we cannot appeal to what the individuals tell us when they recover as evidence for the conclusion that they enjoyed no thoughts, or feelings, or experiences during the period of inactivity. Nevertheless, it is surely reasonable to hold that such people are unconscious, since if the reason that a person cannot exhibit the behavior associated with consciousness, in the case of minor and temporary injuries to the brain, is that the person is unconscious, it would seem reasonable to believe that the explanation of the absence of behavior associated with consciousness, in the case of more serious and permanent injuries to the brain, is the same—namely, that the injury has made it impossible for any conscious states to be present.

Many people have believed, and many still do, that the human mind is an immaterial substance, and that all of one's psychological abilities—including the capacity for consciousness, the capacities for thought and feeling, the ability to remember, and so on—reside in an immaterial mind. But how can this belief be plausible in the light of the facts just mentioned? An injury to the brain might well impair the ability of an immaterial mind to receive new information from the external world, or the ability of such a mind to initiate bodily movement, and thus to communicate with others. But how could such injury prevent the mind itself from functioning? If the capacity for thought resides in an immaterial mind, then there is no reason why one should not be able to continue to think after one's brain has been damaged, be it slightly or very severely. The natural conclusion to draw, therefore, from the fact that brain damage can result in unconsciousness is that the capacities for thought, feeling, and experience, rather than being capacities that reside in an immaterial mind, are instead capacities whose categorical bases lie instead in complex neural circuitry.

Thirdly, consider brain damage that does not destroy the capacity for consciousness, but affects mental functioning in other ways. Such damage might be due to external trauma, or to a cerebral hemorrhage, or to aging, or to a disease such as Alzheimer's. In such cases, precisely what mental impairment occurs depends upon what regions of the brain are affected.

Once again, if the human mind were an immaterial substance, it would be very puzzling why damage to the brain should have any effect upon mental functioning. In addition, it would be even more puzzling why there is a correlation between which psychological capacities are affected and the specific regions of the brain that have been damaged. By contrast, if psychological capacities are based upon different neural circuits in different regions of the brain, then the observed facts are just what one would expect.

Fourthly, there are excellent reasons for attributing at least rudimentary states of consciousness—including pleasure and pain—to at least many non-human animals. Then, however, unless one holds that such animals also possess immaterial minds, one is embracing a theory according to which the capacity for consciousness is, in the case of humans, a capacity of an immaterial mind, but, in the case of other species, a capacity of the organism's brain.

In addition, many animals also have many other psychological capacities, including the ability to remember, to solve problems of various sorts, and—in the case of at least some species, such as chimpanzees and gorillas—the ability to use language, and, arguably, to enjoy rudimentary thoughts. So again, unless one is prepared to attribute immaterial minds to such animals, one who believes that humans have immaterial minds will have to hold that there are a number of psychological capacities that, in the case of humans, are capacities of immaterial minds, but that, in the case of non-human animals, are capacities that reside in something purely physical—the brain—and this seems like an extraordinarily disparate picture of the capacities in question.

Fifthly, when one compares the psychological capacities of adult human beings with the psychological capacities of adult members of non-human species, it turns out that the similarities and differences are very strongly connected with the presence or absence of certain structures within the brains of the animals in question—structures that are present within the human brain. Moreover, the mental capacities possessed by animals belonging to different species become increasingly complex, and impressive, as the brain becomes more complex. If humans had immaterial minds, the existence of such correlations would be a remarkable fact for which there would be no explanation, whereas if human psychological capacities are based on structures in the brain, everything falls into place.

Finally, in the case of individuals belonging to a single species, the developing organism appears to start out with no mental life at all, and then gradually acquires various psychological capacities as it matures. Moreover, the capacities that an organism has at any given time are correlated with the degree of development of neuronal circuitry in relevant regions in the brain. If psychological capacities depend on the presence of certain brain structures, this is, once again, precisely what one would expect, whereas if psychological capacities, at least in the case of humans, were capacities of an immaterial mind, the existence of these correlations would be without explanation.

In short, there are excellent reasons for believing that human psychological capacities, rather than residing in an immaterial mind, have their basis instead in complex neurological structures. From this, many present-day philosophers and psychologists have gone on to contend that a further conclusion can be drawn—namely, that human mental states and psychological processes are identical with brain processes, and involve no properties beyond ones that are completely reducible to the entities, properties, and relations that are postulated by physics.

Not all philosophers and scientists, however, accept this further conclusion. One of the main reasons for not doing so is that experiences seem to involve phenomenal, or qualitative, properties—including colors, sounds, tastes, smells, tactile properties, and so on—that, arguably, cannot be reduced to the properties and relations postulated by physics. If this latter view is right, the human mind may, in a certain sense, be identical with the brain, but, if so, the brain involves capacities—such as capacities for giving rise to experiences with phenomenal properties, and to thoughts and feelings—that cannot be reduced to the stuff of physics.

The question which of these views is correct is a matter of continuing debate within present-day philosophy. Fortunately, the answer to this question is not crucial for the present argument. What matters is simply that there is very good reason to accept the following conclusion:

> All of the mental states and psychological processes—both human and non-human—of which we have knowledge, rather than being states of an immaterial mind that could exist in the complete absence of anything physical, are either identical with brain processes, or else causally dependent upon purely physical, neurological structures and processes.

The conclusion, in short, is that complex neurological states of affairs appear to be *causally necessary* conditions for the existence of both rudimentary states of consciousness and higher mental processes, such as thought—and, indeed, for the existence of absolutely all mental states. But if there is strong evidence for such causal laws, the question becomes why one is not justified in concluding that such laws probably hold throughout the universe, and thus that it is likely that *any* thoughts or beliefs or preferences or states of consciousness that exist anywhere are either identical with complex physical processes, or else causally dependent upon such processes. But if this projection of the conditions that we find to be causally necessary in the case of all the minds with which we are acquainted is justified, then we have arrived at the following conclusion: it is unlikely that there are any immaterial minds.

The term 'God' is often interpreted in such a way that it is necessarily true that God is immaterial, either because the definition of the term 'God' involves the idea of being immaterial, or because it involves some other property that entails that God is immaterial—such as the property of being the creator of everything physical. When this is the case, it is an immediate corollary of the above conclusion that it is unlikely that God exists.

But what if one defines God simply as an omnipotent, omniscient, and morally perfect person? Does this entail that God must be an immaterial mind? Contrary, I suspect, to what many philosophers would hold, I do not think that it does. However, I think that a related proposition is plausible—namely, that in our universe, a mind that was either identical with, or dependent upon, in the way indicated above, complex neural structures could not be either omniscient or omnipotent, since, assuming that at least some of the basic causal laws of our world are probabilistic, any physical structure is capable of not functioning properly, and so any capacities based on a physical structure could always fail.

The idea, in short, is that in a world such as ours, no mind that was either identical with, or based upon, certain physical structures could be omnipotent or omniscient. If so, then it follows from the conclusion that it is unlikely that our world contains any immaterial minds that it is also unlikely that God—defined as an omnipotent, omniscient, and morally perfect person—exists.

2.3   The argument from evil and the argument from the apparent hiddenness of God

The third and final type of argument for atheism appeals both to empirical facts about the world and to moral principles, and the basic idea involved is as follows. First, our world appears to contain states of affairs that are highly undesirable—involving, for example, intense suffering endured by animals, by young children, and by adults who seem to have lived morally admirable lives. Suppose, however, that there was an omnipotent and omniscient person. Being omniscient, he would know of such suffering. Being omnipotent, he would be able to prevent it. So if such a being exists, he has refrained from preventing intense and apparently undeserved suffering in an enormous number of cases.

Secondly, given that this is so, are we not justified in concluding that if there is such a being, he is very far from being perfectly good? For, in everyday life, we often draw conclusions about the moral character of another person from information about what that person has either done, or intentionally refrained from doing. Moreover, we are often very confident about such conclusions, and we believe that our confidence is justified. But if such inferences are justified in the case of finite human persons, why should they not also be justified when we are dealing with a possible person who is much more powerful and knowledge-able—or even infinitely so?

Formulations of the argument from evil typically focus upon undeserved suffering and death. But there is a special version of the argument that does not do so, and that deserves mention, both because of its intrinsic interest, and because it has recently been the focus of substantial discussion. This is the argument from the apparent hiddenness of God, and it focuses instead upon the purported, epistemic fact that the existence of God is either not evident, or not as evident as it could be—something that it is claimed is undesirable, and, indeed, seriously so.

It is, I believe, versions of the argument from evil that give rise to the strong-est objections to belief in the existence of God, and, in the next two parts,

I shall defend the view that the argument from evil, properly formulated, shows that it is extremely unlikely that God exists.

3   The Argument from Evil and the Existence of God

The idea that at least some of the evil that is present in the world constitutes an objection to belief in the existence of God is both an ancient idea—going back at least to Job, and presumably beyond—and a very natural one. How best to develop that basic thought, however, and to convert it into an explicitly formulated argument in support of the non-existence of God, has remained rather unclear. For, in the first place, there are at least four important choices that arise concerning the form of the argument. First, there is the choice between purely deductive formulations of the argument from evil, and inductive ones. According to the former, the proposition that God exists is logically incompatible with the existence of evil, or with certain types, or with certain instances, of evil; according to the latter, certain facts about evil in the world, though logically compatible with the existence of God, render it more or less unlikely that God exists. Secondly, there is the choice between very abstract formulations of the argument from evil, and much more concrete ones. Formulations of the former sort incorporate at best a minimum amount of information about the evils to be found in the world, whereas formulations of the latter sort refer either to types of evils that are characterized in a very detailed way, or else to actual, specific, instances of evils. Thirdly, there is also an important choice between axiological formulations of the argument, which focus simply upon undesirable states of affairs, and deontological formulations, which refer instead to rightmaking and wrongmaking properties of actions. Finally, there is the choice between formulations that presuppose the existence of objective values, and formulations that are subjective, and which focus instead upon the question of whether belief in the existence of God can be epistemically justified if certain other beliefs are epistemically justified, and if one also accepts certain values.

In the second place, if one opts for an evidential, or inductive, formulation of the argument from evil, the question then arises as to what the precise form of the inductive step in the argument is, and whether that step can be justified. For while, initially, one might not expect to encounter any serious difficulties here, it turns out that finding a satisfactory account of the inductive inference is considerably more problematic than one might have expected.

My discussion is divided into two main parts. In this, the first part, I shall discuss the four choices mentioned above, with an eye to determining how the argument from evil is best formulated, and I shall argue that the most promising type of formulation will be concrete, inductive, and deontological.

The argument from evil that I shall set out will also be formulated in terms of claims about objective moral values. But, as I shall also argue in this first part, that is not a crucial feature, since if one is skeptical about the existence of objective moral values, one can easily recast the argument in subjective terms.

Having determined the general form that the argument from evil should take, I shall then turn, in the next part, to the task of offering a detailed formulation of the argument, and of showing that the argument, thus formulated, is sound.

3.1 Deductive/incompatibility formulations versus inductive/ probabilistic/evidential formulations

The argument from evil focuses upon the fact that the world appears to contain states of affairs that are bad, or undesirable, or that should have been prevented by any being that could have done so, and it asks how the existence of such states of affairs is to be squared with the existence of God. But the argument can be formulated in two very different ways. First, it can be formulated as a purely deductive argument that attempts to show that there are certain facts about the evil in the world that are logically incompatible with the existence of God, and one especially ambitious form of this first sort of argument attempts to establish the very strong claim that it is logically impossible for it to be the case both that there is *any* evil at all, and that God exists.

An argument of this sort might be put as follows:

(1) Any omniscient being knows about every possible way in which any evil can come into existence.

(2) Any omnipotent being who knows of every possible way in which any evil can come into existence has the power to prevent all evils.

(3) Any morally perfect being wants to prevent all evils.

Therefore:

(4) Any omniscient, omnipotent, and morally perfect being both has the power to prevent all evils, and wants to prevent all evils.

(5) If there is a being who both has the power to prevent all evils, and wants to prevent all evils, then no evils exist.

Therefore:

(6) If there is an omniscient, omnipotent, and morally perfect being, no evils exist.

(7) Evils exist.

Therefore:

(8) There is no omniscient, omnipotent, and morally perfect being.

(9) If God exists, he is omnipotent, omniscient, and morally perfect.

Therefore:

(10) God does not exist.

This form of the argument initially has a striking and perhaps impressive quality. Moreover, the reasoning is certainly valid. It seems very doubtful, however, that the argument is sound. The reason is that the claim that a morally perfect being would want to prevent all evils is not unproblematic. For one of the things that this claim can be seen to rest upon, when scrutinized, is the assumption that no evil is ever logically necessary for some good state of affairs that outweighs it. Is this claim true? Some people have argued that it is not. For example, some people have argued that the world is a better place if people develop desirable traits of character—such as patience, and courage—by struggling against obstacles, including suffering. But if this is right, then the prevention of *all* suffering might well make the world a worse place by depriving people of the chance of developing desirable traits of character through responding appropriately to suffering that they undergo.

The examples that are usually advanced of cases where some evil is logically necessary for a greater good that outweighs the evil do not seem to me convincing. But, on the other hand, I do not think that one can establish, without appealing to some substantive, and probably controversial, moral theory, that there cannot be cases where some evil is logically necessary for a greater good that outweighs it.

What if one shifts from the claim that the existence of God is logically incompatible with the existence of absolutely any evil to the claim, for example, that the existence of God is logically incompatible with the existence of a large number of horrendous evils? Does that change the situation? It is hard to see how it can, since if it is logically possible that a single, unimpressive evil might be logically necessary for some greater good, must this not also be possible in the case of a horrendous evil? But, then, if this is possible in the case of a single, horrendous evil, how could it not be so in the case of a multitude of horrendous evils?

As a consequence, it seems to me that the argument from evil needs to be formulated in a different way—namely, not as a deductive argument for a very strong claim, such as that it is logically impossible for both God and evil to exist, or for both God and a certain quantity of evil, or certain types of evil, to exist, but as an inductive (or evidential or probabilistic) argument for the more modest claim that there are evils that actually exist in the world that make it unlikely—indeed, very unlikely—that God exists.

3.2   *Abstract formulations versus concrete formulations*

Any version of the argument from evil claims that there is some fact concerning the evil in the world such that the existence of God—understood as an omnipotent, omniscient, and morally perfect person—is either logically precluded, or rendered unlikely, by that fact. But versions of the argument often differ quite significantly with respect to what the relevant fact is. Sometimes the appeal is to the mere existence of any evil whatever, while sometimes it is to the existence of a certain amount of evil. Sometimes the appeal is to the existence of evils of a very general sort—such as natural evil—while sometimes the appeal is to the existence of evils of a much more specific sort. Finally, sometimes the appeal, rather than being to some type of evils, is instead to particular cases of evil that have occurred.

To formulate the argument from evil in terms of the mere existence of any evil at all is to abstract in the most extreme way possible from detailed information about the evils that are found in the world, and so one is assuming, in effect, that such information has no crucial bearing upon the argument. Is such an assumption plausible? It is very hard to see how it can be. For, in the first place, while one might well feel that the world would be better off without the vast majority of evils, it is not at all clear that this is so for absolutely all evils. Some would argue, for example, that the frustration that one experiences in trying to solve a difficult problem is far outweighed by the satisfaction of arriving at a solution, and therefore that the world would not be a better place if it did not contain such evils.

Another reason for rejecting this assumption is connected with the idea of libertarian free will. Thus, many people would claim that the world is a better place if it contains individuals who possess libertarian free will, rather than individuals who are free only in a compatibilist sense. If this claim can be made plausible, one can then argue, first, that God would have a good reason for creating a world containing individuals who possess libertarian free will, and then, secondly, that if God did choose to create such a world, even he could not ensure that no one would ever choose to do something morally wrong. The good of libertarian free will requires, in short, the possibility of moral evil.

Neither of these lines of argument is unproblematic. The basic point here, however, is that the idea that either the actuality of certain undesirable states of affairs, or at least their possibility, may be logically necessary for goods that outweigh them is not without some initial plausibility, and if some such claim can be sustained, it will follow immediately that the mere existence of evil cannot be *incompatible* with the existence of an omnipotent, omniscient, and morally perfect being. But, in addition, if there can be such evils, it would seem that the mere existence of evil cannot really provide *very* much in the way of *evidence* against the existence of God.

What if one shifts to slightly less abstract formulations of the argument from evil, based upon the premise that the world contains a certain amount of evil, or upon the premise that the world contains at least some natural evil? Then one is including marginally more information. But one is still assuming, in effect, that most of the detailed information about the evils found in the world is irrelevant to the argument from evil.

A little reflection brings out how implausible this assumption is. Consider a world that contains a billion units of natural evil. Initially, this may seem like a very good starting point for the argument from evil. Upon reflection, however, it can be seen, I suggest, that whether this fact is an impressive reason for questioning the existence of God depends on further details about the world. If those billion units are uniformly distributed over trillions of people whose lives are otherwise extremely satisfying and ecstatically happy, it is not clear that there is a serious problem of evil. But if, on the other hand, the billion units of natural evil fell upon a single, innocent person, and produced a life that was throughout one of extraordinarily intense pain, then it would indeed seem that there was a very serious problem posed by evil.

Details concerning such things as how suffering and other evils are distributed over individuals, and the nature of those who undergo those evils, would certainly seem to be, then, of crucial importance. Thus it seems relevant, for example, that many innocent children suffer agonizing deaths. It also seems relevant that animals suffer, and that they did so before there were any persons to observe their suffering, and to feel sympathy for them. It seems relevant, too, that, on the one hand, the suffering that a person undergoes apparently bears no relation to the moral quality of his or her life, and, on the other hand, that it bears a very clear relation to the wealth and medical knowledge of the societies in which he or she lives.

The prospects for a successful abstract version of the argument from evil would seem, therefore, rather problematic. It is conceivable, of course, that it does follow from correct moral principles that there cannot be any evils whose actuality, or possibility, makes for a better world. But to attempt to set out a version of the argument from evil that requires a defense of that thesis is certainly to swim upstream. A much more promising approach, surely, is simply to focus upon those evils that are thought, by the vast majority of people, to pose at least a *prima facie* problem for the rationality of belief in an omnipotent, omniscient, and morally perfect person.

For much of the second half of the twentieth century—although there were certainly exceptions, as is illustrated by John Hick's book *Evil and the God of*

Love (1966 and 1978)—the focus of discussion tended to be upon highly abstract formulations of the argument from evil, and this was especially so in the case of Alvin Plantinga's much-discussed work during this period on the argument from evil. Thus, in *God and Other Minds* (1967), in *The Nature of Necessity* (1974b), and in *God, Freedom, and Evil* (1974a), for example, Plantinga focuses mainly on the question of whether the existence of God is compatible with the existence of any evil at all, although there are also short discussions of whether the existence of God is compatible with the existence of a given quantity of evil, and of whether the existence of a certain amount of evil renders the existence of God unlikely. (The latter topic is then the total focus of attention in Plantinga's long, 1979 article, "The Probabilistic Argument from Evil.")

In 1979, however, William Rowe published "The Problem of Evil and Some Varieties of Atheism," where he offered a concrete formulation of the argument from evil in which he focused upon the agonizing death of an animal in a forest fire. The result of this article was a gradual shift away from abstract formulations of the argument from evil to a consideration of much more concrete formulations.

Let us briefly consider, then, a concrete version of the argument from evil, based upon a single, horrific evil. Here I shall use a case mentioned by Rowe in a later article "Evil and Theodicy" (1988), in which a young girl, whom he refers to as "Sue", was brutally raped and then murdered by her mother's boyfriend. Using that case, the argument might be put as follows:

(1) The brutal rape and murder of Sue is a state of affairs that (a) is intrinsically bad, or undesirable, and (b) is such that any omnipotent and omniscient person would have the power to prevent that event without thereby either allowing an equal or greater evil, or preventing an equal or greater good.

(2) Any omnipotent, omniscient, and morally perfect person would prevent the existence of any state of affairs that is both (a) intrinsically bad, or undesirable, and (b) such that he could prevent its existence without either allowing an equal or greater evil, or preventing an equal or greater good.

Therefore:

(3) Any omnipotent, omniscient, and morally perfect person would prevent the brutal rape and murder of Sue.

Therefore:

(4) If there were an omniscient, omnipotent, and morally perfect person, then the brutal rape and murder of Sue would not have taken place.

(5) But that event did take place.

Therefore:

(6) There is no omniscient, omnipotent, and morally perfect person.

(7) If God exists, then he is an omniscient, omnipotent, and morally perfect person.

Therefore:

(8) God does not exist.

This formulation of the argument from evil is by no means unproblematic, since serious objections can be directed against the premises introduced at steps (1) and (2). Thus, as regards the former, one can ask, for example, how one can know that the brutal rape and murder of Sue is intrinsically bad, all things considered, for while it certainly seems so relative to the goodmaking and badmaking properties that we are aware of, perhaps there are goodmaking properties of which we have no knowledge, and in virtue of which the event in question is not intrinsically bad, all things considered.

I shall offer quite a different concrete version of the argument from evil in part 4—one that is designed to avoid central objections to which the above argument is exposed. My goal at this point, however, is simply to make vivid the contrast between abstract versions of the argument from evil, and concrete ones, and to bring out the intuitive difference.

Thus, if the mere existence of *any* evil posed an objection to the existence of God—be it via a deductive argument or an inductive one—then a minor quarrel between a husband and wife would either rule out the existence of God, or at least render it unlikely, and that does not seem at all plausible: the world might well have been a better place without the quarrel, but would it also have been better if God had intervened to prevent the quarrel? Or would it be morally wrong for God not to intervene? By contrast, confronted with the brutal rape and murder of Sue—where one certainly thinks that any human who could have prevented that event should have done so—the question of how God could have allowed such an event may well be deeply troubling.

In the light of this, the idea of formulating the argument from evil on the basis of particular cases of terrible evils, rather than in an abstract fashion, seems both natural and much more promising. Nonetheless, some philosophers seem to feel that concrete versions of the argument from evil do not really represent an advance on abstract formulations. In particular, Plantinga seems to believe that if it can be shown that the existence of God is neither incompatible with, nor rendered improbable by, either (a) the mere existence of evil, or (b) the existence of a specified amount of evil, then no *philosophical* problem remains. People may find, of course, that they are still troubled by the existence of *specific* evils, but this, Plantinga seems to believe, is a *religious* problem, and what is called for, he suggests, is not philosophical argument, but "pastoral care" (1974a, pp. 63–4).[11]

In what follows, I shall attempt to show that this view is mistaken.

3.3 Axiological versus deontological formulations of the argument from evil

The two versions of the argument from evil that were set out in the previous two subsections have a feature in common that seems to me very important, but that is not often commented upon. This feature, which they also share with most contemporary formulations of the argument from evil, consists of the fact that they are formulated in terms of *axiological* concepts—specifically, in terms of the goodness or badness, the desirability or undesirability, of states of affairs. As a result, such arguments are exposed to a certain type of objection, as emerges if one considers statement (2) in the version of the argument offered in the previous subsection:

> (2) Any omnipotent, omniscient and morally perfect person would prevent the existence of any state of affairs that is both (a) intrinsically bad, or undesirable, and (b) such that he could prevent its existence without either allowing an equal or greater evil, or preventing an equal or greater good.

How is this premise to be justified? One response would be that a certain common consequentialist claim is true—namely, the claim that an action is morally wrong if it fails to maximize the balance of good states of affairs over bad states of affairs. But the difficulty then is that such a claim is, within ethical theory, deeply controversial, and likely to be rejected by many theists, and others.

The problem, in short, is that axiological formulations of the argument from evil are typically incomplete in a crucial respect, since they generally fail to make explicit *how* a failure to bring about good states of affairs, or a failure to prevent bad states of affairs, entails that one is acting in a morally wrong way. Moreover, the natural way of removing this incompleteness is by appealing to what are in fact controversial ethical claims. The result, in turn, is that discussions of the argument from evil can easily become sidetracked on issues that are, in fact, not really crucial—such as, for example, the question of whether God would be morally blameworthy if he failed to create the best world that he could create.

---

[11] For additional critical discussion of this, see Conway (1988, p. 35), and Adams (1985, pp. 225 and 240).

The alternative to an axiological formulation is a deontological formulation. Here the idea is that rather than employing concepts that focus upon the value or disvalue of states of affairs, one instead uses concepts that focus upon the rightness and wrongness of actions, and upon the—rightmaking or wrongmaking—properties that determine whether an action is one that ought to be performed, or ought not to be performed, other things being equal. When the argument is thus formulated, as I shall do below, there is no problematic bridge that needs to be introduced connecting the goodness and badness of states of affairs with the rightness and wrongness of actions.

3.4   *Subjective versus objective formulations*

A fourth important issue centers upon the distinction between what might be called subjective and objective formulations of the argument from evil. Consider, for example, the following remarks by Richard Swinburne:

> It will be important for me to distinguish among the inquirer's doubts between moral doubts and doubts about contingent non-moral facts, and for this purpose I need to establish a position on the status of moral judgments. I hold that they have truth-values; some are true and some are false. I do not need to argue for that aspect of my position in this context, since anyone who thinks that evil raises for theism the 'problem' which I have described must think this. There could only arise an issue as to whether certain evils were *compatible* with the existence of a good God if goodness and evil were properties which belonged to persons, actions, and states of affairs, and judgments which affirmed or denied their existence had a truth value. (Swinburne, 1988, p. 290)

Embedded in what is otherwise a very thoughtful discussion, these claims by Swinburne—that the problem of evil arises only if moral judgments are either true or false, and only if goodness and evil are real properties of persons, actions, and states of affairs—are rather jarring, as they are not at all plausible. To see why, let us suppose that John Mackie's error theory of value is correct, and that, although we are indeed ascribing non-natural properties to actions when we characterize them as right or wrong, and to states of affairs when we describe them as good or bad, the world in fact contains no instances of such properties (1977, pp. 15–49). All of our 'positive' ethical beliefs would be false in that case, but that would not be a barrier to some of John's ethical beliefs being logically inconsistent with some of Mary's, or to some of John's ethical beliefs being mutually inconsistent, or to their giving rise to inconsistencies when combined with some of his non-moral beliefs about the world.

What about Swinburne's other claim—namely, that the problem of evil does not arise unless moral judgments have truth-values? Swinburne does not spell out his grounds for this claim, but it appears to rest upon the idea that the only sentences that can stand in logical relations with one another are *statements*. But that, surely, is not so. The reason is, first, that any number of psychological states can stand in logical relations to one another. Just as it is logically impossible for both the belief that Peano's postulates are true and the belief that there is a largest prime number to be true, so it is logically impossible for both the desire that Peano's postulates be true and the desire that there be a largest prime number to be satisfied, and similarly for the corresponding hopes, fears, etc. Then, secondly, because various psychological states can exhibit this sort of inconsistency, sentences that 'express' those psychological states can also exhibit inconsistency. So, for example, the two optative sentences, "Would that all the windows were closed" and "Would that at least one window were open," uttered by the same person at the same time and place, are mutually incompatible.

This general point is central to R. M. Hare's account (1952) of the meaning of ethical language. Hare maintains that any adequate account of the meaning of ethical language must be able to explain the logic of moral argument, and his response to this requirement involves arguing, first, that there is a logic of imperatives, and that arguments involving imperatives can be valid or invalid in precisely the same sense that arguments involving statements can be, and, secondly, that the idea that moral language is related to what he refers to as "universalized" imperatives provides a good initial model for understanding the logic of moral discourse.

Suppose, then, that ethical judgments, rather than being either true or false, are really universalized imperatives. That will not affect the logical relations between ethical judgments, or the logical relations within sets of sentences, some of which are ethical, and some of which describe non-moral states of affairs. So whether or not the characterization of some states of affairs as evil is compatible with the characterization of some being as not only omnipotent and omniscient, but also as perfectly good, cannot depend upon whether a cognitivist meta-ethics is correct.

But if the logical relations in question are unaffected by whether ethical judgments have truth-values, then it would seem that it must be possible to formulate versions of the argument from evil that, rather than involving implicit reference to correct moral principles, refer instead to the moral principles that happen to be accepted by a given individual, or group of individuals. And surely this is so. For suppose that Jack is a philosopher who is a theist and a hedonistic utilitarian, while Mary is an atheist who accepts a slightly different ethical outlook. Does Mary have to convert Jack to her moral outlook before she can employ the argument from evil? Clearly not, since she can point out that if there were a being that was omnipotent and omniscient and morally perfect as judged by Jack's own moral standards, then one would expect the world to be a hedonistic paradise. But that doesn't seem to be the case, and so Mary can attempt to show that it is unlikely that there is any being that is omnipotent, omniscient, and morally perfect as judged by the principles of hedonistic utilitarianism. If she succeeds, she will have shown that there is something irrational about the system of beliefs and values that Jack accepts.

The general idea may be put as follows. Consider any objective formulation of the argument from evil. It can be changed into a subjective formulation by the following two steps. First, replace all of the moral terms by expressions that involve explicit reference to the set, *C*, of correct moral principles, so that, rather than referring to intrinsically undesirable states of affairs, one refers to states of affairs that are intrinsically undesirable as judged by *C*, and rather than referring to a morally perfect person, one refers to a person who is morally perfect as judged by *C*. Next, replace all references to *C* by references to any other set, *S*, of moral principles—where *S* is the set of moral principles accepted by the person in question. The first change will not affect the content. The second change will, but it will not affect the logical relations between statements. The result will be a subjective formulation that refers to the moral principles that are, as a matter of fact, accepted by a specific person, but the logical relations within the argument, thus formulated, will be precisely the same as those within the original, objective formulation of the argument.

The possibility of subjective formulations of the argument from evil is, I believe, an important one, given that disagreements concerning fundamental values are not always easily resolved, since the availability of subjective formulations means that it may be possible to show that a given person's belief in the existence of God is irrational without having to question the moral values that he or she accepts.

4   The Evidential Argument from Evil

4.1   Formulating the evidential argument from evil: an overview

I have argued that the most promising formulations of the argument from evil will be concrete, inductive, and deontological. The version I shall offer also involves claims about objective moral values. As we have just seen, however, that is not a crucial feature, since if one is skeptical about the existence of objective moral values, one can easily recast the argument in subjective terms by simply replacing all references to objective moral values by corresponding references to values accepted by the relevant person or persons.

Let me now turn, then, to the task of setting out a sound version of the evidential argument from evil. In the present section, I shall do two things. First, having argued earlier, in section 3.2, for the considerable implausibility of the idea that a satisfactory version of the argument from evil can abstract from most details concerning the evils that one actually finds in the world, I shall begin by briefly listing some of the types of undesirable states of affairs to which one might very well appeal in formulating a concrete version of the argument from evil. Then, secondly, I shall outline a deontological and evidential version of the argument from evil that can be formulated in terms of wrongmaking properties of actions connected with one or more of those undesirable states of affairs.

At that point, we shall still be left with the question of whether there is any acceptable inductive justification of the crucial probabilistic claim that the argument involves, and that issue will therefore be the focus of the discussion in subsequent sections.

4.2   A brief catalogue of some notable evils

What, then, are some of the undesirable states that might enter into a concrete formulation of the argument from evil? The answer is that there are quite a number of different types, including at least the following. First, there are *extreme moral evils*, including the suffering and the deaths brought about by heinously evil individuals—such as Hitler and Stalin—by acts of attempted genocide, by great wars—including religious wars—by the Inquisition, by the persecution of 'witches,' and so on.

Secondly, there is *the suffering endured by innocent children*, including the suffering caused by lack of food in many parts of the world, by diseases such as muscular dystrophy, leukemia, cerebral palsy, and so on, and by abuse inflicted upon children by adults—including horrific cases, such as that of Sue. Such suffering, endured by children, is frequently appealed to in formulations of the argument from evil, since the implausibility of the claim that young children are morally blameworthy for things they have done more or less precludes the idea that they are being justly punished for wrongs they have committed.

Thirdly, there is *the suffering that adults endure as a result of terrible diseases*—such as cancer, mental illness, Alzheimer's disease, and so on. Here, of course, there is at least some room for the idea that adults deserve to suffer because they have acted wrongly. But this is open to the response that one can often form very plausible judgments concerning the moral quality of a person's life, and that what one finds is that many fundamentally good people often suffer to an extent that is totally out of proportion to the wrongs they have committed.

Fourthly, there is *the suffering of animals*. This will include such things as suffering at the hands of other animals, and suffering due to natural disasters. (Here Rowe (1988) cites a Bambi-type case, where a deer endures an agonizing death due to a forest fire.) The case of animal suffering is especially important because, unless the idea of reincarnation is true, such suffering cannot be viewed either as punishment for wrongdoing or as an opportunity for moral growth.

All of the types of evils just mentioned could be prevented by a very powerful and knowledgeable person. But the God of theism, if he exists, is not just a being who *now* has the power to intervene: he is also a being who created everything else that exists. Consequently, one can also raise the question of how satisfactory the world is. When one does this, it appears, for example, that there are a number of '*design faults*' in human beings that contribute greatly to human suffering and unhappiness, and where either no benefits at all are apparent, or else no benefits sufficient to counterbalance the negative effects. Included in this fifth class of evils we have, for example, the following:

(1) The sinuses are misdesigned: the lower sinuses open upward, and thus they do not drain properly, with the result that they may become infected and cause, in some cases, severe headaches.

Evolution, of course, provides an explanation of both good 'design' and bad 'design.' Thus, for example, our sinuses would be fine if we were four-legged animals, rather than two-legged ones. But this explanation is not available to the creationist, and if the theist who is not a creationist attempts to appeal to this idea, he or she needs to say why an omnipotent, omniscient, and morally perfect being would employ evolution as a way of designing different species. Why leave things at the mercy of a morally unguided process that has had, as one would have expected, a number of bad results?

(2) As in the case of the sinuses, so with the human spine: while its design is not too bad in the case of four-legged animals, it is a very unsatisfactory piece of engineering in the case of two-legged animals. This bad design, in turn, means that many humans suffer from back problems, some of which are very debilitating and painful indeed.

(3) Another example of what would seem to be an easily correctable 'design fault' is the presence of wisdom teeth. Most people today in affluent societies, of course, have their wisdom teeth extracted. That operation can itself lead to complications, in the form of sinus infections, and damage to nerve pathways leading to the lower lip and the tongue. But one needs only to go back to the nineteenth century to find a situation when the presence of wisdom teeth had much worse consequences, since impacted wisdom teeth, by becoming infected, could then lead not only to considerable pain, but to septicemia, and to death.

(4) A fourth illustration is provided by childbirth. The size of the human head relative to the size of the birth canal has three unfortunate consequences. First, humans are born in a much more underdeveloped, and therefore more vulnerable, state than newborns of other species. Secondly, childbirth is often a very painful experience. Thirdly, childbirth is potentially a very dangerous event for the woman. Today, of course, a much smaller proportion of women die in childbirth, especially in more affluent countries, because of the use, for example, of birth via Cesarean section, and also because women tend to have far fewer children than previously—though various religious groups, such as Orthodox Jews, still have many children. In the past, however, many women died in childbirth and many continue to do so in less affluent countries.

(5) Men and women differ in various ways. One interesting way, recently discovered, involves a gene called gastrin-releasing peptide receptor— or GRPR for short—which is linked to abnormal growth of lung cells. It had been noted by earlier medical researchers that women were more likely to develop lung cancer than men, without smoking more, and it turns out that the explanation is that while the GRPR gene in not active in men unless they smoke, it is active in 55% of non-smoking women. (The reason for this is connected with the fact that the gene is on the X chromosome, of which women have two, and men only one.) So greater susceptibility to lung cancer is programmed into women.

(6) Another striking source of considerable suffering is declining hormone levels as one grows older. This affects men as well as women, but the effects are especially dramatic in the case of women, where the fall in the level of estrogen, which has been programmed in either by a creator or by evolution, has a number of negative effects. Of these, the most familiar is the greater likelihood of osteoporosis, which often leads to significant suffering and loss of mobility because of bones that break easily, and which, in turn, may lead—especially in the case of hip fractures—to earlier death.

More recent research has also shown, however, that estrogen has a number of important effects upon the brain: (a) it increases blood flow to the brain, and hence the supply of oxygen and glucose that the brain needs to function; (b) it increases the amounts of several brain chemicals—including acetylcholine, which plays a crucial role in memory, and serotonin, which helps to maintain a good mood; (c) it increases the number of synapses between nerve cells in the hippocampus, where memory resides; (d) it helps neurons to grow and regenerate; and (e) it decreases the occurrence of inflammation, thereby inhibiting a process that appears to hasten aging. Because of these effects of estrogen upon the brain, a decline in the level of estrogen increases the probability of impaired mental functioning in general, and, in particular, the probability that a woman will develop Alzheimer's disease.

(7) The body is equipped with sensors that detect injury, and announce the presence of bodily damage via painful sensations. These injury-detectors are badly designed, in at least four ways. First, they are not sensitive to the presence of many life-threatening bodily changes. In particular, the presence of cancer is often detected only after it is too late to do anything about it. Secondly, these injury-detectors often produce high levels of pain when there is no condition that poses a serious health risk to the individual. Consider, for example, migraine headaches. These can make a person very miserable indeed, but the condition that causes such headaches is not a health-threatening condition. (Compare Hume's remark in his *Dialogues Concerning Natural Religion*: "what racking pains, on the other hand, arise from gouts, gravels, megrims, toothaches, rheumatisms; where the injury to the animal-machinery is either

small or incurable?" (199)) Thirdly, there is no way of shutting down these injury-detectors in situations where, rather than providing the individual with a useful warning of bodily damage, they only contribute to the person's misery by producing ongoing pain sensations. Fourthly, the injury-detection system produces levels of pain that are often unbearably intense and that are in no way needed to serve the purpose of alerting one to bodily damage. So the injury-detectors, which failed to warn a person of the early presence of cancer, swing into action when it is too late, at which point they fill the dying person's last weeks with excruciating pain. (Compare, again, Hume's remarks: "But pain often, Good God, how often! rises to torture and agony; and the longer it continues, it becomes still more genuine agony and torture." (*Dialogues*, 200))

(8) A more radical point about the body's injury-detection mechanisms was also made by Hume—namely, that the use of pain to alert one to bodily damage is itself a design fault. Hume's own proposal was that one could be motivated instead by a reduction in pleasure. This suggestion reflects, I think, the unsound idea that every desire or preference must be either a desire for pleasure or a desire to be free of pain. But an alternative, and more satisfactory, proposal is readily at hand. When some part of the body is being damaged, the injury-detectors, rather than giving rise to pain associated with that part of the body, could, where possible, immediately generate an automatic withdrawal response, and, where this is not possible, they could instead give rise to a belief that a certain part of the body was being injured, along with a strong desire to take action that would prevent further damage.

(9) When people become overweight, there is no reduction in appetite, nor is the mechanism that enables one to make use of stored fat an effective and well-designed one. Nor does the body cease extracting and storing calorie-rich compounds, such as fats, from the food that it is processing. The result, once again, is enormous suffering because people are overweight—with much overeating resulting from the fact that food can provide comfort when one is under stress.

(10) The body contains a variety of defense mechanisms to deal with threats posed by bacteria, viruses, toxins, and so on. But viruses are often capable of countermeasures—sometimes of quite a sophisticated sort—that enable them to foil the body's defense mechanisms. A better designed defense system would not be thwarted by such countermeasures.

(11) A disease that has caused many deaths is malaria. There is a gene, however, that provides an effective defense against malaria, and that works by destroying any red blood corpuscles that have been occupied by any of the types of parasitic protozoans that cause malaria. So far, so good. But if one has inherited the relevant gene from both of one's parents, the result is sickle cell anemia, in which sickle cells crystallize within red blood corpuscles, distorting them, and thereby clogging blood vessels, which then gives rise to intense suffering.

(12) Humans are sexually mature some time before they exhibit significant emotional maturity, with the upshot that quite young girls can bear children

long before they have developed the emotional responsibility and commitment needed to care for children satisfactorily.

(13) The association of intense pleasure with sexual activity also appears to be a design fault. For while sexual pleasure can certainly contribute to human happiness, it appears that when everything is taken into account, the world might well be better off if people reproduced simply because they wanted to have children, and if people were not seduced by the very great pleasure associated with sexual activity into actions that have far-reaching and often quite disastrous consequences.

(14) Conscience seems to be quite a fragile thing, and many people seem to have a very weak sense of right and wrong. One's awareness of right and wrong could be much clearer, and more vigorous, so that people were more strongly motivated to do what was right, and not what was wrong—especially things that are heinously wrong, like torture and murder. Would not such a stronger and clearer sense of right and wrong make the world a better place?

(15) Humans are subject to aging, a decline in physical functioning that, in addition to being unwelcome in itself, is often accompanied by suffering resulting from such conditions as arthritis, and by the deterioration of one's mental capacities, sometimes including the complete destruction of those capacities that make one a person.

(16) The mind can be damaged not only by processes connected with aging, but by strokes and other injuries to the brain. Such possibilities of severe damage to a person's mind seem highly undesirable, and if mental faculties, rather than being dependent upon the brain, were instead faculties of an immaterial soul, such unwelcome occurrences would be totally absent from the world.

(17) More radically, embodied persons could be constructed of tougher stuff, so that all bodily injury was ruled out: they could be supermen and superwomen, in a world without kryptonite.

(18) Finally, there is the brief span of human life, and the inevitability of bodily death. This feature of human life seems very unsatisfactory from a moral point of view, as it both places a severe limit upon the possibilities for personal growth and intellectual development, and ends relationships between people that are often deep and enduring. In a well-designed world, surely, the lives of people, and the relationships between them, would be completely open-ended, free to develop indefinitely, with no terminus imposed from without.[12]

'Design faults' are not limited, however, to human beings, and so a sixth class of evils involves features of the world outside of human beings that contribute greatly to suffering, either by humans or by other sentient beings. Thus, in

---

[12] I am indebted to a number of people for entries on this list of 'design faults': (2) was suggested by Ed Curley; (3) and (11) by Graham Oddie; (4) and (7) by Darryl Mehring.

the first place, the earth is misdesigned in many ways that give rise to natural disasters resulting in enormous suffering and loss of life, for both humans and animals. This includes earthquakes, volcanic eruptions, cyclones, hurricanes, tornadoes, floods, tidal waves, and epidemics. Thus, for example, in 1970, a tidal wave from the Bay of Bengal, driven by a cyclone, killed at least 200,000 people, while the Indian Ocean tsunami in 2004 killed more than 225,000 people. Since 1556, there have been 16 earthquakes where more than 50,000 people were killed, and 3 volcanic eruptions where more than 25,000 people died. In four of those earthquakes, more than 200,000 people were killed—the worst of them in China, in 1556, when over 800,000 people were killed.

Secondly, the world contains bacteria and viruses that cause very great suffering and death, sometimes in the form of great epidemics, such as the great plagues of the Middle Ages, and the outbreak of Spanish influenza in the United States in 1918, which killed over 500,000 people, while, more recently, an enormous number of people, including children, have died because of the HIV virus.

Thirdly, there is the enormous suffering that results from the existence of carnivorous animals. When one considers the extremely long period of time during which carnivores have roamed the earth, the amount of suffering that has resulted from this 'design feature' is extraordinarily horrendous indeed. (Not surprisingly, then, people who believe in a 'Young Earth'—with an age of the order of 6,000–12,000 years—sometimes appeal to the enormous suffering that would be involved in a much older earth as the basis of an argument, given the assumption that God exists, in support of the view that the earth is only a few thousand years old.)

Fourthly, the world is one where the resources that exist are too limited to provide for populations of humans, and other animals, that are expanding at natural rates. The world could instead have been an infinite plane, or have had inhabitable planets that were easily accessible.[13]

One final comment on 'design faults.' Most of those listed above can be classified as a matter of faulty engineering, in the sense that, given the laws of nature as they are, a change in the design of the world, or of human beings, or of animals, could have prevented the evils in question. But, as Quentin Smith has pointed out in his article "An Atheological Argument from Evil Natural Laws" (1991), at least some 'design faults' rest on more than bad enginering, involving, as they do, laws of nature. So consider, for example, the possibility of intense suffering. That possibility surely presupposes a relevant psychophysical law. Precisely what form that law takes depends on what the correct account of pain is. If it turns out that painfulness itself is an intrinsic property of sensations of a certain type, then the relevant law will be one linking the

---

[13] This 'design fault' was also suggested by Graham Oddie.

non-pain-quality of a sensation to the pain-quality. If, on the other hand, and as I am rather inclined to think, pain is not itself an intrinsic property of sensations of a certain type, but a matter of the negative preference that is evoked by such sensations, then the relevant law will instead be one linking the non-pain-quality of a sensation to the relevant negative preference. But in either case, the basic point is the same: namely, that an omnipotent creator could have chosen different laws—laws that would not give rise, be it directly or indirectly, to the extraordinarily intense levels of pain that humans and other sentient beings can experience in the world as it presently is.

4.3 The argument from evil: appealing to a single case

Given a list of evils such as that just set out, how should an inductive version of the argument from evil be formulated? In section 3.3, I distinguished between axiological formulations of the argument and deontological ones, and indicated why the former seem problematic. In this section, accordingly, I shall offer a deontological formulation of the argument.

Central to a deontological formulation of the argument are the concepts of rightmaking and wrongmaking properties, and these can be defined as follows. First, one can set out a theory, such as the following, that 'implicitly defines' the relevant concepts:

> There are two second-order properties—namely, the property of being a rightmaking property and the property of being a wrongmaking property—such that if an action possesses at least one property that is a wrongmaking property, and no property that is a rightmaking property, then the action is morally wrong, while if an action possesses at least one property that is a rightmaking property, and no property that is a wrongmaking property, then the action is morally obligatory, or at least morally permissible.

Then, if one wishes, one can use some standard method for defining theoretical terms—such as a Ramsey/Lewis approach (Lewis, 1970)—to convert that implicit definition into explicit definitions of 'rightmaking property' and 'wrongmaking property.'

A complete moral ontology must involve more, however, than qualitative rightmaking and wrongmaking properties, since such properties cannot by themselves determine the status of actions that have both rightmaking and wrongmaking properties, or of actions where the objective probabilities of various rightmaking and wrongmaking properties being present have values other than zero and one. If such actions are to have a determinate moral status, there must be quantitative rightmaking and wrongmaking properties, so that there are numbers associated with rightmaking and wrongmaking properties that represent the moral weight, or seriousness, of the properties in question.

The idea of quantitative rightmaking and wrongmaking properties can be explicated by whatever method seems most satisfactory for quantitative properties in general. Then, given the idea of quantitative rightmaking and wrongmaking properties, we can say that when an action possesses both rightmaking and wrongmaking properties, its moral status depends upon the moral weights of the various properties. Thus, for example, if the weight of the wrongmaking properties, taken together, is greater than that of the rightmaking properties, taken together, then the action is morally wrong, all things considered, while if the weight of the rightmaking properties, taken together, is greater than that of the wrongmaking properties, taken together, then the action is either morally permissible, all things considered, or else morally obligatory.

Given these concepts, one can also introduce the idea of an action's being *prima facie* wrong, in the following way. Relative to (possibly incomplete) information about an action's rightmaking and wrongmaking properties, an action is *prima facie* wrong if the weight of its known wrongmaking properties, taken together, is greater than the weight of its known rightmaking properties, taken together.

The basic idea involved in a deontological formulation of the argument from evil is then as follows. First, it is claimed that the world contains certain states of affairs such that any action of allowing any of those states of affairs to obtain would involve one or more known wrongmaking characteristics that would outweigh the sum total of any known rightmaking characteristics that the action would have. If this is right, then any such action is *prima facie* wrong, relative to the total information that one presently has concerning the action's rightmaking and wrongmaking characteristics. Secondly, the crucial question is then whether there is any sound inductive argument that will take one from the conclusion that such an action is *prima facie* wrong to the further conclusion that the action is probably wrong all things considered. If there is, one will then have an 'inductively sound' version of the evidential argument from evil.

Let me now turn to the task of setting out such an argument. My exposition involves three main steps. First, in the present section, I shall outline an evidential version of the argument from evil that focuses upon a single concrete evil—namely, the earthquake that destroyed Lisbon in 1755, which was felt as far away as southern France and North Africa, and which killed approximately 60,000 men, women, and children. The conclusion of this initial part of the argument will be a somewhat modest, though not insignificant, one—namely, that it is more likely than not that God did not exist at the time in question.

That argument, as we shall see, turns upon a certain crucial, probabilistic claim, and so the second stage in my discussion involves asking how that claim is to be justified. There I shall argue, first, that one very natural way of attempting to justify it—put forward in a formulation of the argument from evil advanced by William Rowe—does not work; but, secondly, that there is an alternative justification that is sound.

Throughout these first two stages in the exposition of the argument, everything will be formulated in terms of a single, concrete case of evil. The third step of my exposition then involves considering how the argument can be modified to appeal to as many cases of evil as one cares to cite. Such an extension is important, because it takes one from an argument for the conclusion that the existence of God is unlikely to an argument for the much stronger conclusion that the existence of God is *extremely* unlikely.

A point that will emerge in that final stage is that precisely how the argument is to be formulated depends upon whether God, is defined as simply an omnipotent, omniscient, and morally perfect person—as I have done—or whether, instead, it is also part of the concept of God, either that God is the creator of the physical universe, or that God exists at all times. What we shall see is that if either of the latter properties is made part of the concept of God—as is the case with theism as normally understood—this final stage of the argument is quite straightforward, whereas if both properties are omitted, a more complicated argument is needed.

Both the first part of the argument, which I am setting out in this section, and the extension of it, to be set out later, have the following overall structure. First, one establishes that one or more entailments of the following form obtain: "Its being the case that a state of affairs S exists at time t, such that it is morally wrong, all things considered, to allow S to exist, *logically entails* that God does not exist at time t." The idea is then to combine that proposition (or those propositions) with a relevant probabilistic claim—which will be established later via an appeal to inductive logic—to generate the ultimate conclusion.

Let us now turn to the details. The argument begins with the following general claim:

(1) It is logically necessary that, for any possible state of affairs S, if the action of choosing not to prevent S is morally wrong, all things considered, then an omnipotent, omniscient, and morally perfect person would never perform that action.

I now want to apply this general claim to the case of the Lisbon earthquake. A natural way of proceeding would be to replace 'S' by 'the Lisbon earthquake.' But such a substitution within a modal context appears problematic. One can, however, proceed differently, through the use of a conditional proof. Let us begin, then, by introducing the following assumption to serve as the basis of the conditional proof:

(2)* The Lisbon earthquake occurred, and the action of choosing not to prevent the Lisbon earthquake is morally wrong, all things considered.[14]

Next, the modal statement at (1) entails the following non-modal statement:

(3) For any possible state of affairs S, if the action of choosing not to prevent S is morally wrong, all things considered, then an omnipotent, omniscient, and morally perfect person would never perform that action.

Then, from assumption (2)* together with (3) we have:

(4)* An omnipotent, omniscient, and morally perfect person would never perform the action of choosing not to prevent the Lisbon earthquake.

Next, a premise is needed that connects up the property of being omnipotent and omniscient at the relevant time with the action of choosing not to prevent the Lisbon earthquake:

(5) It is logically necessary that if the Lisbon earthquake occurred, and if an omnipotent and omniscient person existed at the very start of the Lisbon earthquake, then that omnipotent and omniscient person must have chosen not to prevent that earthquake.

But then (4)* together with (5) entails:

(6)* If an omnipotent and omniscient person existed at the very start of the Lisbon earthquake, then that omnipotent and omniscient person was not morally perfect.

The final necessary truth that is needed in the conditional proof follows from the definition of 'God' that I am employing:

(7) It is logically necessary that, for any person P, if P is God at time t, then P is omnipotent, omniscient, and morally perfect at time t.

From (6)* and (7) we then have:

(8)* God did not exist at the very start of the Lisbon earthquake.

---

[14] As with this step, subsequent steps that depend upon this assumption will be indicated by an asterisk following the number.

At this point we can complete the conditional-proof part of the argument by discharging the assumption that was introduced at (2)*:

(9) If the Lisbon earthquake occurred, and the action of choosing not to prevent the Lisbon earthquake is morally wrong, all things considered, then God did not exist at the very start of the Lisbon earthquake.

Notice, finally, that all of the premises used in the conditional proof either were, or followed from, logically necessary truths. Because of this, (9) must also have the status of a necessary truth. So we have:

(10) It is logically necessary that if the Lisbon earthquake occurred, and the action of choosing not to prevent the Lisbon earthquake is morally wrong, all things considered, then God did not exist at the very start of the Lisbon earthquake.

This in turn immediately entails:

(11) Its being the case that the Lisbon earthquake exists, and that any action of choosing not to prevent the Lisbon earthquake is morally wrong, all things considered *logically entails* that God did not exist at the very start of the Lisbon earthquake.

We can now move on to the second stage of the argument, where a crucial probabilistic claim is introduced. This part is as follows:

(12) The property of choosing not to prevent an event that will cause the death of more than 50,000 ordinary people is a wrongmaking property of actions, and a very serious one.

(13) The Lisbon earthquake killed approximately 60,000 ordinary people.

Therefore, from (12) and (13):

(14) Any action of choosing not to prevent the Lisbon earthquake has a very serious wrongmaking property.

A claim about the Lisbon earthquake, and our moral knowledge concerning it, is now introduced:

(15) No rightmaking properties that we know of are such that we are justified in believing both that an action of choosing not to prevent the Lisbon earthquake would have had those rightmaking properties, and

that those properties are sufficiently serious to counterbalance the relevant wrongmaking property.

At this point, it will be helpful to introduce an abbreviation that will make for less wordy formulations. In particular, let

There are no rightmaking properties that are known to be counterbalancing

stand for

There are no rightmaking properties that we know of such that we are justified in believing both that the action in question has those rightmaking properties, and that those properties are sufficiently serious to counterbalance any relevant, known, wrongmaking property (or properties).

When then is done, (15) can be formulated more compactly as:

(15) Any action of choosing not to prevent the Lisbon earthquake has a known wrongmaking property such that there are no rightmaking properties that are known to be counterbalancing.

The next step involves the introduction of a probabilistic premise that is very controversial, but which lies at the heart of the present formulation of the argument from evil:

(16) For any action whatever, the logical probability that the total wrongmaking properties of the action outweigh the total rightmaking properties—including ones of which we have no knowledge—given that the action has a wrongmaking property that we know of, and that there are no rightmaking properties that are known to be counterbalancing, is greater than one half.

Next, a premise is introduced that connects up the idea of rightmaking and wrongmaking characteristics with the idea of an action's being morally wrong, all things considered:

(17) It is a logically necessary truth that, for any action C, if the total wrongmaking properties of the action outweigh the total rightmaking properties—including ones of which we have no knowledge—then action C is morally wrong, all things considered.

The next step involves drawing a conclusion about the overall moral status of an action of choosing not to prevent the Lisbon earthquake. The route to the desired conclusion requires the following proposition from the theory of logical probability:

(18) If the logical probability of q, given p, is greater than one half, and if q logically entails r, then the logical probability of r, given p, is also greater than one half.

It then follows, from (16), (17), and (18):

(19) For any action whatever, the logical probability that the action is morally wrong, all thing considered, given that the action has a wrongmaking property that we know of, and that there are no rightmaking properties that are known to be counterbalancing, is greater than one half.

This conclusion, together with (15), then entails:

(20) The logical probability that an action of choosing not to prevent the Lisbon earthquake is morally wrong, all things considered, given that choosing not to prevent the Lisbon earthquake has a wrongmaking property that we know of, and that there are no rightmaking properties known to be counterbalancing, is greater than one half.

It then follows from the conclusion of the first part of the argument—namely, (11)—together with (18) and (20) that

(21) The logical probability that God did not exist at the time of the Lisbon earthquake, given that choosing not to prevent the Lisbon earthquake has a wrongmaking property that we know of, and that there are no rightmaking properties known to be counterbalancing, is greater than one half.

Let us consider, now, both the logic of the argument, and the premises. As regards the former, the situation seems unproblematic, since all of the steps are deductive, and I have tried to set the argument out in sufficient detail that the validity of the argument is clear. In any case, the validity of the argument could easily be established by translating it into an appropriate formal language.

The argument stands or falls, accordingly, with the acceptability of the premises. As can be seen from the above statement of the argument, it involves nine premises—set out at steps (1), (5), (7), (12), (13), (15), (16), (17), and (18). So let us consider each of these in turn.

Statement (1) advances a slightly less general version of the claim that an omnipotent, omniscient, and morally perfect person would never perform a morally wrong action. If one wanted, one could argue for this premise by appealing to necessary truths concerning omnipotence, omniscience, and moral perfection; however, this first premise is surely very plausible as it stands.

Statement (5) could be supported by arguing that an omnipotent and omniscient being both would have the power to prevent earthquakes, and would know when an earthquake was starting. Such a being could therefore prevent any particular earthquake, so if he does not do so, it must be because he chooses not to.

Next, the premise introduced at (7) is trivially analytic, being true in virtue of the concept of God that I am employing here.

Statement (12) makes a moral claim, but one that does not seem at all problematic, while statement (13) makes a historical claim for which there is, I believe, very good evidence. But if (13) turned out to be false, statements (12) and (13) could easily be replaced by slightly different statements, involving smaller numbers.

Statement (15) makes a claim that would be challenged by philosophers who respond to the evidential argument from evil by offering a theodicy. Nevertheless, the claim seems very reasonable, given the relevant facts about the world, together with the moral knowledge that we possess. For what right-making properties can one point to that one has good reason to believe would be present in the case of an action of allowing the Lisbon earthquake, and that would be sufficiently serious to counterbalance the wrongmaking property of allowing more than 50,000 ordinary people to be killed?

Statement (16) introduces a premise that both lies at the very center of the present formulation of the argument from evil, and is very controversial. It requires, then, very careful consideration.

Finally, the premise introduced by statement (17) obtains by virtue of the concepts of rightmaking and wrongmaking characteristics, together with the concept of an action's being wrong, all things considered, while the premise introduced by statement (18) follows from the theory of logical probability. Both premises are, then, unproblematic.

The upshot is that the argument is deductively valid, and it seems that the only premise that could be seriously challenged is the one introduced at step (16). It would appear, then, that the argument stands or falls with the crucial probabilistic claim advanced at that step. Let us consider, then, whether that claim can be justified.

4.4   Justifying the probabilistic claim: a natural attempt

Let us begin by considering one rather natural way of attempting to justify the crucial, probabilistic premise set out at step (16). The basic idea is that that premise can be justified by an appeal to the standard inductive procedure of projecting a regularity that has been found to hold in all observed cases to cases not yet observed.

This type of approach was defended by William Rowe in his article "Ruminations about Evil" (1991), and initially it certainly seems both very natural and very plausible. We shall see, however, that it does not, in the end, appear to be sound.

4.4.1 An appeal to simple, instantial generalization?

Rather than considering statement (16) itself, let us consider a related statement that refers specifically to an action of allowing the Lisbon earthquake, namely:

(*) The logical probability that the total wrongmaking properties of the action of intentionally allowing the Lisbon earthquake to occur outweigh the total rightmaking properties of doing so—including ones of which we have no knowledge—given that allowing the Lisbon earthquake to occur has a wrongmaking property that we know of, and that there are no rightmaking properties known to be counterbalancing, is greater than one half.

This statement, however, is a bit wordy, and it will make things more perspicuous if we introduce the following abbreviations :

p: The action of intentionally allowing the Lisbon earthquake to occur has a wrongmaking property that we know of, and there are no rightmaking properties known to be counterbalancing.

q: The total wrongmaking properties of the action of intentionally allowing the Lisbon earthquake to occur outweigh the total rightmaking properties of that action—including rightmaking properties of which we have no knowledge.

Then the above statement can be formulated much more compactly as follows:

(*) The logical probability of *q* given *p* is greater than one half.

So how can (*) be justified? A very natural idea is to introduce the following statement:

r: The action of intentionally allowing the Lisbon earthquake to occur has a wrongmaking property that we know of, and there are *no* rightmaking properties—including rightmaking properties of which we have no knowledge—that counterbalance the wrongmaking property in question.

The thought is then that one will be able to establish the following claim:

(**) The logical probability of *r* given *p* is greater than one half.

But if one can do this, then (*) will follow, since *r* entails *q*, and that fact together with (**) will then entail (*).

So how is (**) to be established? A natural approach involves two ideas. First, an inference from p to r can be shown to have the following logical form:

(1) All known Ps are Qs.

Therefore, it is likely that:

(2) All Ps are Qs.

Secondly, this is precisely the form exhibited by certain standard, everyday, inductive inferences (cf. Rowe, 1991, pp. 72–4).

For if, in statements (1) and (2) one replaces 'P' by 'rightmaking property,' and 'Q' by 'rightmaking property that is not sufficient to counterbalance a certain wrongmaking property possessed by the Lisbon earthquake,' then one has the following two statements that would seem to be logically equivalent, respectively, to statements 'p' and 'r':

(1*) All known rightmaking properties are rightmaking properties that are not sufficient to counterbalance a certain wrongmaking property possessed by the Lisbon earthquake.

(2*) All rightmaking properties are rightmaking properties that are not sufficient to counterbalance a certain wrongmaking property possessed by the Lisbon earthquake.

So are we not justified in concluding, on pain of being forced to reject a certain type of standard, everyday, inductive inference, that p makes r probable, and thus that (**) is justified? But then p must also make q probable, since r entails q. Accordingly, do we not have a justification for statement (*)—and, by a simple generalization of this reasoning, a justification for the corresponding, general, probabilistic claim expressed by statement (16)?

4.4.2   The problem with this account

To see why this account does not work, notice, first of all, that it is important to distinguish between the following two inductive inferences:

All known Ps are Qs	All known Ps are Qs
Therefore, it is likely that	Therefore, it is likely that
The next P is a Q.	*All Ps are Qs.*

The first of these is an inductive inference to the next instance, and it says that if one has observed a (sufficient) number of Ps, and all of them have been Qs, then it is likely that the next *P* observed will also be a *Q*. But this may be so without it being the case that it is likely that all *P*s are *Q*s. For suppose that one has observed a number of *P*s, all of which have been *Q*s, with the result that the probability that the next, randomly selected *P* is a *Q* is 0.99. Then the probability, for example, that, if one goes on to select 75 *P*s at random, *all of them* will be *Q*s, will not only not be 0.99, it will be less than one half, and so the probability that *all P*s are *Q*s certainly need not be greater than one half. Consequently, the second of the above patterns of inductive inference involves a significantly stronger claim, and one that is, therefore, harder to justify.

It is crucial to ask, then, which type of inductive inference is needed in the above attempt to justify the probabilistic claim advanced at step (16), and the answer is that it is the second: one has to show that it is unlikely that there is *any* rightmaking property that is both present and sufficiently weighty, and not merely that it is unlikely, given any randomly selected rightmaking property, that *that particular property* is both present and sufficiently weighty.

The question, accordingly, is under what circumstances the second type of inference is justified. Moreover, given that a conclusion about all further instances is a much stronger conclusion than one that is merely about a single, additional instance, one might well wonder whether, in the present case, an inference of the first sort is justified, while one of the second sort is not.

I want to suggest that this is, in fact, the case, and one way of supporting that claim is by arguing—as I have done elsewhere (1977, p. 693, and 1987, pp. 129–37)—that when one is dealing with an *'accidental'* or *non-nomological generalization* of the form "All *P*s are *Q*s," then, provided that the logical width of the predicate '*Q*' is not infinitesimally close to one,[15] the probability that the regularity in question will obtain gets closer and closer to zero, without limit, as the number of potential instances gets larger and larger, and that this is so regardless of how large one's evidence base is.

But how is it ever possible, then, to justify universal generalizations? The answer is that if laws are more than mere regularities—and, in particular, if they are second-order relations between universals—then the obtaining of a law, and thus of the regularity entailed by it, may have a very high probability upon even quite a small body of evidence. So universal generalizations can be justified *if* they obtain in virtue of underlying laws.

The question then becomes whether *r* expresses a law—or a consequence of a law. If, as seems to me plausible, it does not, then, although it may be true that one is justified in holding, of any given, not yet observed morally relevant

---

[15] The logical width of a predicate is equal to the *a priori* logical probability that the predicate will be true of any given individual. Some predicates do have a logical width that is infinitesimally close to one. For example, the *a priori* probability that something will not have a mass of *exactly* 3.2 kg is presumably infinitesimally close to one.

property, that it is likely to have property Q, it may very well be the case that it is not probable that *all* rightmaking properties have property Q. It may, on the contrary, be probable that there is *some* rightmaking property that does not have property Q.

This objection could be overcome if one could argue that it is unlikely that there are many unknown rightmaking properties. For if the number is small, then the probability of r may still be high even if r does not express a law, or a consequence of a law. Moreover, I am inclined to think that it may well be possible to argue that it is unlikely that there are many unknown, morally relevant properties, since the idea that there are a large number of morally significant properties of which we have, at present, no knowledge seems most unwelcome. But I also think that it is very likely that any attempt to establish this conclusion would involve one or more controversial meta-ethical claims. As a consequence, given the present state of meta-ethics, I shall not pursue such a line of argument here.

4.5   Inductive logic and the crucial step

We have seen that one very natural account of the justification of the crucial probabilistic claim introduced at step (16) in the above formulation of the evidential argument from evil appears to be unsatisfactory. Could it be, then, that there is no acceptable defense of that premise, and that the evidential argument from evil, at least as formulated above, is simply unsound? Given the desirability of the existence of God, that would certainly be a happy conclusion. Unfortunately, that does not seem to be the case, since, as I shall now argue, there is an alternative route to (16) that does appear to be sound.

4.5.1   An alternative defense of the crucial probabilistic claim

My defense of the crucial probabilistic claim focuses upon what beliefs are reasonable, given only fundamental principles of inductive logic, together with information about the *existence* of rightmaking and wrongmaking *properties*, considered in themselves—as contrasted with detailed information about *instances* of such properties.

In setting out the argument, it will be helpful to use the sort of diagram shown in Figure 2.1. In this diagram, the region to the right of the vertical axis represents actions that one ought to perform, all things considered, and the farther to the right an action is located, the stronger the obligation to perform it is. Similarly, the region to the left of the vertical axis represents actions that are morally wrong, all things considered, and the farther to the left an action is located, the more wrong it is.

We need to represent rightmaking and wrongmaking properties, both known and unknown. Rightmaking properties will be represented by arrows

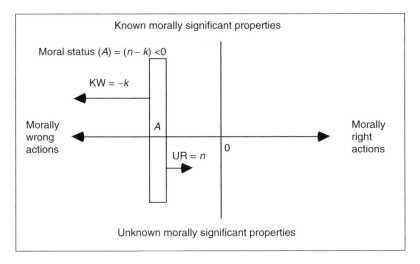

Figure 2.1

pointing to the right, and wrongmaking properties by arrows pointing to the left, with the lengths of the arrows representing the seriousness of the properties involved.

Finally, to distinguish between known and unknown morally significant properties, the former will be represented by arrows above the horizontal axis, and the latter by arrows below the horizontal axis.

Thus, in the Figure 2.1, there is a known wrongmaking property—KW—of magnitude $-k$, and an unknown rightmaking property—UR—of magnitude n. Since the absolute value of $-k$ is greater than that of n, action A is, accordingly, morally wrong all things considered, and its moral value is equal to $(n - k)$.

The argument may now be put as follows. Consider some action A that, as regards rightmaking and wrongmaking properties that one is aware of, has one very serious wrongmaking property, and no rightmaking properties, and which is therefore an action that is, *prima facie*, morally very wrong. If action A does not have any unknown and relevant rightmaking or wrongmaking properties, the situation can be represented by Figure 2.2.

But what about the possibility that action A has some morally significant properties of which one has no knowledge, and that are relevant to the moral status of action A, given the knowledge and power of the agent? Here I want to begin by advancing the following three claims:

(1) Judged from a purely *a priori* point of view, the mere existence of wrongmaking properties is *no less likely* than the existence of rightmaking properties.

(2) Judged from a purely *a priori* point of view, the *likelihood* that there exists a rightmaking property with a moral weight whose absolute value is

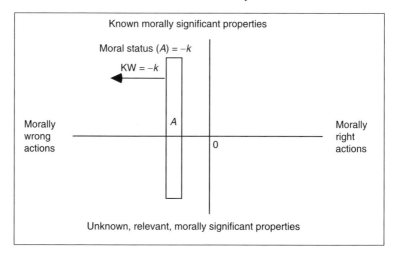

Figure 2.2

equal to M is no greater than the likelihood that there exists a wrongmaking property whose absolute value is equal to M.

(3) Judged from a purely *a priori* point of view, the *likelihood* that there is a rightmaking property with a moral weight whose absolute value is equal to M that is *relevant* to the moral status of the action in question, given the knowledge and power of the agent, is no greater than the likelihood that there is a wrongmaking property whose absolute value is equal to M that is relevant to the moral status of the action.

Is the situation different if one takes into account the knowledge that we have about (a) the existence of rightmaking and wrongmaking properties—whether properties that are instantiated or properties that are not—(b) their moral weights, and (c) the connections between rightmaking and wrongmaking properties, given the power and knowledge of the agent? Do we know, for example, that there are more rightmaking *properties* (not: instances of rightmaking properties) than wrongmaking properties? Or do we know that rightmaking properties are typically more weighty than wrongmaking properties? Or do we know that wrongmaking properties are more likely to be connected to rightmaking properties than to other wrongmaking properties? I do not believe that the moral knowledge that we have supports affirmative answers to any of these three questions. So I suggest that, judged from an *a posteriori* point of view, first, the existence of wrongmaking properties is no less likely than the existence of rightmaking properties; secondly, wrongmaking properties are not likely to have less moral weight than rightmaking properties; and, thirdly, wrongmaking properties are no more likely to be connected to rightmaking properties of a given moral weight than to other wrongmaking properties of that same moral weight.

In short, the following claim seems plausible:

The Symmetry Principle with Respect to Unknown, Rightmaking, and Wrongmaking Properties

Given what we know about rightmaking and wrongmaking properties in themselves, for any two numbers, M and N, the probability of there being an unknown rightmaking property with a moral weight between M and N is equal to the probability of there being an unknown wrongmaking property with a (negative) moral weight whose absolute value is between M and N.

Consider, then, some action A such that, judged only by our current knowledge of rightmaking and wrongmaking properties, together with our non-moral knowledge, it is reasonable to believe that action A is *prima facie* morally very wrong. It is certainly possible, however, that there are rightmaking properties that *we* are not aware of, that are connected, given the power and knowledge of the agent, to the known wrongmaking property involved in A, and that make it the case that the agent's performing action A would not be morally wrong, all things considered, if the agent had knowledge of those properties.

It is possible, then, both that action A has some unknown, relevant, rightmaking property, and that, as depicted in Figure 2.3, that unknown and relevant rightmaking property—UR—is weightier than the known wrongmaking property—KW—with the result that the overall moral status of action A is positive, so that, in the absence of superior alternatives, it is morally permissible for a person with the relevant knowledge to perform action A.

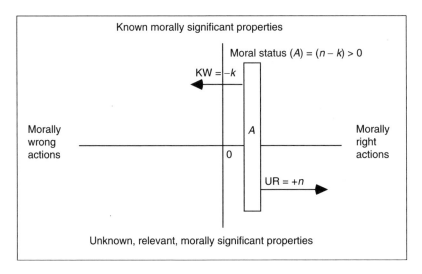

Figure 2.3

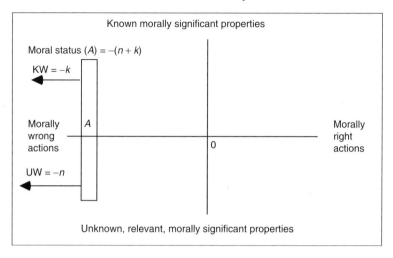

Figure 2.4

If the claim advanced in the Symmetry Principle is correct, then it is *just as likely* that any unknown and relevant rightmaking and wrongmaking properties that exist make it the case, instead, that performing action A is *morally much worse* than it already is relative to known rightmaking and wrongmaking properties, as that they make it the case that performing action A is something that is morally permissible, all things considered.

In particular, it is no less likely that the situation, rather than being as in the diagram just set out, is instead as shown in Figure 2.4.

What, then, is the *probability* that it is not morally wrong, all things considered, to perform action A? A precise answer to this question would require very substantial theorems of inductive logic. But, simply on the basis of the preceding, one can say that it is more likely than not that performing action A is morally wrong, all things considered. For, first of all, a shift of a given amount in the direction of greater moral wrongness is, in view of the Symmetry Principle, just as likely as a shift of an equal amount in the direction of less moral wrongness, and we are starting with an action, A, such that, judged by known rightmaking and wrongmaking properties, and relevant non-moral knowledge, performing that action is *prima facie* very seriously wrong. Secondly, it is possible that there is no shift at all, either because there are no unknown, relevant, rightmaking or wrongmaking properties, or because, although there are, they exactly cancel one another. We have, therefore, the following conclusion:

(C_1) If A is an action that, judged by known rightmaking and wrongmaking properties, is *prima facie* very seriously wrong, then the probability that action A is morally wrong, all relevant rightmaking and wrongmaking properties considered, both known and unknown, is greater than one half.

But the same is also true with respect to the probability, all relevant things considered, that action *A* is morally *very* seriously wrong, and the reasons are the same as in the case of (C_1). So we also have this second conclusion:

(C_2) If *A* is an action that, judged by known rightmaking and wrongmaking properties, and relevant non-moral knowledge, is such that performing that action is *prima facie* very seriously wrong, then the probability that action *A* is *very* seriously wrong, all relevant rightmaking and wrongmaking properties considered, both known and unknown, must also be greater than one half.

Of these two conclusions, it is only (C_1) that we really need for the argument set out earlier, since (C_1) is itself tantamount to the crucial, probabilistic claim that stood in need of justification, namely:

(16) For any action whatever, the logical probability that the total wrong-making properties of the action outweigh the total rightmaking properties—including ones of which we have no knowledge—given that the action has a wrongmaking property that we know of, and that there are no rightmaking properties that are known to be counterbalancing, is greater than one half.

Nevertheless, (C_2) is of interest, since it could be employed in a slightly modified and strengthened version of the evidential argument from evil. For notice that, although the action under consideration—namely, that of allowing the Lisbon earthquake—is an action that, judged by known rightmaking and wrongmaking properties, is not merely *prima facie* wrong, but *prima facie* very seriously wrong, I did not make any use of the latter fact in the argument set out above. The above argument can be modified, however, so as to make use of that information by employing (C_2), and the result will be an argument that generates an even more damaging conclusion about the likely moral character of any omnipotent and omniscient being who existed at the relevant time.

4.5.2 A comparison with William Rowe's claim

In Section 4.4, I argued that the type of inductive *inference* used by William Rowe in the formulation of the argument from evil in his article "Ruminations about Evil" (1991) does not appear to be sound. But how is my *conclusion* related to Rowe's conclusion—that is, to the claim that it is unlikely that there are unknown, relevant rightmaking properties that outweigh known wrongmaking properties? In particular, is it the case that I am trying to arrive at Rowe's conclusion by an alternative route?

The answer is that I am not. I am arguing, instead, for a number of other theses—one of which is that it is unlikely that an action that is *prima facie* wrong, as judged by known rightmaking and wrongmaking properties, is morally permissible all things considered.

But *could* one use the above line of argument to defend Rowe's claim? The answer is that one cannot. This is probably clear from the argument itself. But since an appreciation of the difference between the two arguments is crucial for an understanding of the present approach, I think that is important to show that the above line of argument cannot serve as an alternative route to Rowe's conclusion. This can be done as follows.

Rowe's conclusion, recast in terms of the terminology of rightmaking and wrongmaking properties, can be put as follows:

> Let A be the action of allowing some state of affairs S, where we know that A possesses some serious wrongmaking property W, and where there is no known, counterbalancing, rightmaking property. Then it is unlikely that there is an unknown rightmaking property R that is sufficient to outweigh the known wrongmaking property W.

To establish the compatibility of the present argument with the denial of Rowe's thesis, suppose, for concreteness, that there is a breakthrough in the field of ethical theory, and that decisive proofs are found for the following, rather surprising theorems:

(a) There are two morally significant properties that humans are not aware of, one a rightmaking property, R, and the other a wrongmaking property, W.

(b) R and W are equal weighty.

(c) R outweighs any combination of all of the morally significant properties that humans are aware of, and similarly for W.

(d) If S is any state of affairs whatsoever, and A is the action of allowing S to come about, then the probability that A possesses the unknown rightmaking property, R, is 0.9, and the probability that A possesses the unknown wrongmaking property, W, is also 0.9. Moreover, these possibilities are statistically independent of each other, so that the probability that A possesses R, given that it possesses W, is equal to the probability that A possesses R, given that it does not possess W, and conversely.

Given these theorems, consider a situation in which, judged by the rightmaking and wrongmaking properties of which we have knowledge, allowing S to occur would be *prima facie* very wrong. Then there is a 90% chance that the unknown rightmaking property, R, is present, and thus that there is a property that outweighs the *known* wrongmaking properties. So Rowe's thesis would be false, if propositions (a) through (d) were true.

By contrast, my inductive argument would be totally unaffected by the above, imaginary theorems. For the arguments used to establish conclusions (C_1) and (C_2) still go through, and so it is still more likely than not that allowing S to occur is both morally wrong, and morally very wrong, all things considered. The reason is that although, given the imagined ethical theorems stated above at (a) through (d), there is a very high probability that there is an unknown rightmaking property that is very likely to be present, and that will defeat the *known* wrongmaking properties, there is an equally high probability that an unknown and equally weighty wrongmaking property is present in the case of the action of allowing S. In most cases—specifically, $(0.9 \times 0.9) = 81\%$ of the time—this unknown wrongmaking property will be present along with the unknown rightmaking property, and when this occurs, it will defeat the defeater of the *known* wrongmaking properties. In some cases, of course—and this will happen $(0.9 \times 0.1) = 9\%$ of the time—the unknown rightmaking property will be present on its own, and then the action will not be morally wrong, all things considered. But this will be balanced by the fact that 9% of the time the unknown wrongmaking property will be present unaccompanied by the unknown rightmaking property. Finally, the remaining 1% of the time, neither of the unknown morally significant properties will be present.

Figure 2.5 sums up the situation.

So the following propositions are true in this case:

(1) There is an unknown rightmaking property that is present 90% of the time, and that is sufficiently serious to outweigh the *known* wrongmaking property.

(2) The action in question is morally wrong, all things considered, 91% of the time.

Both my argument, then, and the conclusions to which it leads, are perfectly compatible with Rowe's thesis being false.

	Unknown rightmaking property is present	Unknown rightmaking property is absent
Unknown wrongmaking property is present	81% of the cases action is wrong	9% of the cases action is wrong
Unknown wrongmaking property is absent	9% of the cases action is not wrong	1% of the cases action is wrong

Figure 2.5

4.5.3 The existence of instances of rightmaking and wrongmaking properties

The argument that I have just offered focuses upon rightmaking and wrong-making properties, considered *in themselves*. A possible response to this argument is as follows:

(1) It is true that if one considers only the existence of rightmaking and wrongmaking properties in themselves, there is no *a priori* reason for thinking either that there are likely to be more unknown rightmaking properties than unknown wrongmaking properties, or that the former are likely to be more weighty than the latter.

(2) It is also true that if one considers only the existence of rightmaking and wrongmaking properties in themselves, there is no *a posteriori* reason for thinking either that there are likely to be more unknown rightmaking properties than unknown wrongmaking properties, or that the former are likely to be more weighty than the latter.

(3) By contrast, if one focuses upon *instances* of rightmaking and wrong-making properties, it is true, as a matter of fact, either that there are more instances of the former than of the latter, or that instances of the former are on average weightier than instances of the latter.

(4) This fact concerning instances of known rightmaking and wrongmaking properties provides one with reason for holding that instances of *unknown* rightmaking properties are either more numerous, or weightier, or both, than instances of *unknown* wrongmaking properties.

(5) This, in turn, undercuts the argument offered above in defense of the crucial probabilistic claim put forward in statement (16).

This possible objection certainly focuses upon a relevant issue. Rather than addressing that issue at this point, however, I shall instead return to it later, if necessary, and in response I shall argue in support of the following three claims. First, it is not true, in our world, that there are more instances of rightmak-ing properties than of wrongmaking properties. Secondly, neither is it true that instances of rightmaking properties are, on average, more weighty than instances of wrongmaking properties. Thirdly, even if either of these things were the case, that fact would not provide support for any corresponding claim about instances of unknown rightmaking properties and wrongmaking properties.

4.6 Extending the argument to encompass more than one evil

As set out up to this point, my argument has focused upon a single action—that of allowing the Lisbon earthquake. The result of the argument, so formulated, is the somewhat modest conclusion that the probability that God existed at the time of the Lisbon earthquake is less than one half. I now want to argue, however, that one can, by appealing to two or more evils, arrive at much stronger conclusions.

For reasons that will become apparent, this requires a two-step argument in which one focuses, first, upon multiple evils at a single time, and then, secondly, upon evils that exist at different times. These steps will be set out in this section and the next.

4.6.1 Multiple, simultaneously preventable evils

Consider any number of states of affairs, each of which is such that, relative to known rightmaking and wrongmaking properties, allowing that state of affairs to obtain would be *prima facie* seriously wrong, and where there is some moment at which a sufficiently powerful and knowledgeable being could have prevented all of the states of affairs in question. For brevity, let us refer to such states of affairs as 'simultaneously preventable evils.'

Suppose, then, that there are n such evils—$S_1, S_2, \ldots, S_n$ and that they could have been prevented by an omnipotent and omniscient being acting at time t. Then in view of the argument to this point, we can say that the logical probability that God existed at time t, given the occurrence of S_1, is less than one half, and, similarly, that the logical probability that God existed at time t, given the occurrence of S_2, is also less than one half, and so on for all of the remaining evils. But merely being able to point to n pieces of evidence, relative to each of which the probability that God existed at time t is less than one half, is not especially interesting. The crucial question is whether the n pieces of evidence have a cumulative impact. I shall argue that they do.

4.6.2 Inductive logic—Carnapian-style

I shall set out my argument in terms of a particular, objective, inductive logic that is, I believe, correct. But philosophers who favor a different inductive logic will be able, I believe, to recast the following argument in their own preferred terms, while readers who do not share my optimism about the existence of an objectively correct inductive logic will be able to reinterpret the argument in terms of subjective probabilities. The question, in the latter case, will then be whether the equiprobability assumptions that I make agree with one's own subjective probabilities—or, at least, whether they are sufficiently close that very similar results can be derived.

The inductive logic that I shall use is essentially that set out by Rudolf Carnap in his book *Logical Foundations of Probability* (1962). A detailed consideration of Carnap's approach will not, however, be necessary, since everything that is crucial for our present purposes can be explained in terms of three fundamental concepts: the concept of a *state-description*, the concept of a *structure-description*, and the concept of a predicate that is *maximal* with respect to a set of properties.

Consider, then, a very simple world that contains only three individuals— *a*, *b*, and *c*—and only one basic property — *P*. (The idea of basic properties is crucial, since otherwise there is, arguably, no satisfactory answer to Goodman's 'new riddle of induction.') A state-description will then be a proposition that specifies, for each of the three individuals, whether it has property *P* or not. Given that, in the case of each individual, that individual may either possess property *P* or not, there are $(2 \times 2 \times 2) = 8$ possible state-descriptions, which are as follows:

Pa & *Pb* & *Pc*

Pa & *Pb* & ~*Pc*

Pa & ~*Pb* & *Pc*

~*Pa* & *Pb* & *Pc*

Pa & ~*Pb* & ~*Pc*

~*Pa* & *Pb* & ~*Pc*

~*Pa* & ~*Pb* & *Pc*

~*Pa* & ~*Pb* & ~*Pc*

To define the logical probability that one proposition has, given another, one needs to settle upon the weights to be assigned to the propositions belonging to some fundamental set of propositions. One idea is to assign equal weight to all state-descriptions, so that each of the above eight state-descriptions would be assigned the weight 1/8. But that idea—which was accepted by C. S. Pierce, John Maynard Keynes, and Ludwig Wittgenstein—is, Carnap argues (1962, pp. 564–5), unsatisfactory. For suppose that one does that, and that one knows that *Pa* and *Pb* are the case. What is the probability, then, that *Pc*?

If *Pa* and *Pb* are the case, only two of the above eight state-descriptions can obtain, namely:

Pa & *Pb* & *Pc*

Pa & *Pb* & ~*Pc*

In the first of these, *Pc* is the case, while in the second it is not. If both of these state-descriptions are assigned the same weight—namely, 1/8—it follows that the probability that *Pc*, given *Pa* and *Pb*, is equal to $(1/8)/(1/8 + 1/8)$—that is, to 1/2. But this is precisely the probability that *Pc* initially has, before one learns that *Pa* and *Pb* are the case. Moreover, this would be so regardless of whether there were three individuals, or a million: the probability that the next individual would have property *P* would still be equal to 1/2, regardless of how many individuals had been examined and found to have property *P*.

Assigning equal weight to state-descriptions would have, therefore, the rather unhappy consequence that one could never learn from experience! To avoid this problem, Carnap proposed that equal weight should be assigned, not to state-descriptions, but to structure-descriptions—where structure-descriptions are sets of state-descriptions that are structurally the same, i.e., that differ only with respect to a permutation of the individuals involved. So in the case of the mini-universe considered above, there are the following four structure-descriptions:

Structure-description 1:	*Pa & Pb & Pc*
Structure-description 2:	*Pa & Pb & ~Pc*
	Pa & ~Pb & Pc
	~Pa & Pb & Pc
Structure-description 3:	*Pa & ~Pb & ~Pc*
	~Pa & Pb & ~Pc
	~Pa & ~Pb & Pc
Structure-description 4:	*~Pa & ~Pb & ~Pc*

On Carnap's proposal, then, each of these four structure-descriptions is assigned the weight 1/4, and that weight is then distributed equally over the state-descriptions that belong to the structure-description in question. Thus the state-description *Pa & Pb & Pc*, since it is the only state-description that belongs to the first structure-description, is assigned the weight 1/4, whereas the state-description *Pa & Pb & ~Pc*, since it is one of three state-descriptions that belong to the second structure-description, is assigned the weight 1/12. As a consequence, given that *Pa* and *Pb* are the case, the probability that *Pc* is the case will be equal to the ratio of the weight of the one remaining state-description where *Pc* is true—namely, *Pa & Pb & Pc*—to the total weight of all of the state-descriptions where *Pa* and *Pb* are true — namely, *Pa & Pb & Pc* and *Pa & Pb & ~Pc*— so that that ratio is equal to

$$\frac{(1/4)}{(1/4+1/12)} = 3/4$$

The upshot is that when equal weight is assigned to structure-descriptions, rather than state-descriptions, the probability that the next individual has a certain property does depend upon how many previously observed individuals have had that property. One can, therefore, learn from experience.

Finally, there is the concept of predicates that are *maximal* with respect to some set, S, of properties, where these are predicates that, when applied to an individual, indicate, for every property in S, whether the individual in question has the property or not. So, for example, if S is a set of three properties, with associated predicates 'P,' 'Q,' and 'R,' the following eight predicates will be maximal with regard to that set:

'$P \& Q \& R$'	'$P \& Q \& {\sim}R$',
'$P \& {\sim}Q \& R$'	'${\sim}P \& Q \& R$',
'$P \& {\sim}Q \& {\sim}R$'	'${\sim}P \& Q \& {\sim}R$'
'${\sim}P \& {\sim}Q \& R$'	'${\sim}P \& {\sim}Q \& {\sim}R$'

4.6.3 The obstacles in the way of an exact calculation

Given these ideas, and a Carnapian-style, structure-description approach to inductive logic, let us now turn to the problem at hand. Suppose that there are n events, each such that, judged in the light of the totality of known rightmaking and wrongmaking properties, it would be morally wrong to allow that event. What is the probability that there are unknown rightmaking and wrongmaking properties such that, given the totality of rightmaking and wrongmaking properties, both known and unknown, it would not be morally wrong, all things considered, to allow *any* of the n events?

The calculation of an exact answer to this question is a complicated matter, for a number of reasons. First, there is no logical limit upon the number of unknown morally significant properties there may be, so in the absence of some substantive moral theory that can be shown to be correct and that entails such a limit, one needs a calculation that sums over an infinite number of possibilities. Secondly, unknown rightmaking and wrongmaking properties can vary in significance from ones that are quite trivial to ones whose significance is very great indeed. Thus, there might, for example, be an unknown rightmaking property that could have been possessed by an act of allowing the Lisbon earthquake, but that would not have been sufficiently weighty to make it the case that that act would not have been wrong, all things considered. So one also needs a calculation that sums over the non-denumerable number of possibilities with respect to strengths of unknown rightmaking and wrongmaking properties. Thirdly, the n events that one is focusing upon may vary enormously with regard to the extent to which, judged by known rightmaking and wrongmaking properties, it would be morally wrong to allow the event in question, so that unknown rightmaking properties that would render it morally permissible to allow one event might not suffice at all in the case of some other event. Therefore any exact calculation would also need to be geared to the specific events that one is considering.

4.6.4   Finessing the problem: calculating an upper bound

There are, then, a number of serious difficulties that stand in the way of calculating an exact answer to our question. Because of these obstacles, I shall not attempt to carry out such a calculation. My approach, instead, will be to argue that, given a set of *n* events, each of which, judged by known rightmaking and wrongmaking properties, it would be morally wrong to allow, one can place *an upper bound* upon the probability that, judged in the light of the totality of rightmaking and wrongmaking properties, both known and unknown, it is not morally wrong to allow any of those *n* events.

How can this be done? The basic idea is that the calculation of the probability that it is not morally wrong, all things considered, to allow any of the *n* events is simplified enormously if one makes some assumptions that result in an *overestimate* of the number of favorable distributions of unknown rightmaking and wrongmaking properties—where a distribution is *favorable* if it is such that, given that distribution, *none* of the *n* events on which one is focusing is such that allowing that event is morally wrong, all things considered. The formula that then results will yield probabilities that are on the high side, so that those results will place an upper bound upon the probability that none of the *n* events is such that allowing that event is morally wrong, all things considered.

What are the 'probability-increasing' assumptions that I shall make? First, I shall assume that any unknown rightmaking and wrongmaking properties that exist are so significant that any single unknown rightmaking property on its own is sufficiently weighty to make it morally permissible to allow even the most morally problematic of the *n* events. This will generate an overestimate of the probability because some unknown rightmaking properties whose presence would not be sufficient to render it morally permissible to allow a certain event will be treated as if they were sufficient, so that some unfavorable distributions of morally significant properties will be classified as favorable ones.

Secondly, in addition to assignments of unknown morally significant properties to a given event that make it morally permissible to allow that event, and assignments that make it even more impermissible to do so, there are also assignments that make no difference. These can be divided into, on the one hand, cases where both unknown rightmaking and unknown wrongmaking properties are present, but cancel out, and, on the other hand, cases where neither unknown rightmaking properties nor unknown wrongmaking properties are present. Such neutral assignments are unfavorable cases, since the moral status of any event that it would be morally wrong to allow, given only information about known rightmaking and wrongmaking properties, will be unchanged given such an assignment of the unknown, morally significant properties. My method of calculation, however, treats half of those assignments as if they were positive, and so it generates a further overestimate of the likelihood that none of the n events is such that it is wrong to allow that event, all things considered.

4.6.5   The calculation

Let M be the set of all rightmaking and wrongmaking properties, K the set of all known rightmaking and wrongmaking properties, and U the set of all unknown rightmaking and wrongmaking properties. Let Q be the set of predicates that are maximal with respect to U, and let us refer to such predicates as 'Q-predicates.' In addition, let us say that a Q-predicate, P, is *positive* if and only if, considering only the properties in U, any action to which P applies is neither morally neutral nor morally impermissible. Similarly, let us say that a Q-predicate, P, is *negative* if and only if, considering only the properties in U, any action to which P applies is morally impermissible. Finally, let us say that a Q-predicate, P, is *neutral* if and only if, considering only the properties in U, any action to which P applies is morally neutral.

Next, let us introduce the idea of *a justifying predicate*, relative to some action, A, where P is a justifying predicate relative to A if and only if P belongs to the set of predicates that are maximal with respect to the set, U, of all unknown rightmaking and wrongmaking properties, and P is such that if it applies to action A, then action A will be morally permissible, all things considered.

A predicate that is maximal with respect to U cannot be a justifying predicate with respect to the actions we are considering unless it is a positive predicate, since all of those actions, judged only in terms of known rightmaking and wrongmaking properties, are morally wrong. But, in general, not all positive predicates will be justifying predicates with respect to any particular action, since some positive predicates will be insufficiently weighty to overcome the known wrongmaking properties of the action in question. Hence the set of predicates that are justifying predicates with respect to some action A will usually be a proper subset of the positive predicates.

The goal is now to work out how likely it is that, given n events, each of which is such that, judged simply by known rightmaking and wrongmaking properties, it would be morally wrong to allow, *none* of those n events is such that it is morally wrong to allow that event, given the totality, M, of all rightmaking and wrongmaking properties, known and unknown. Doing this will involve two main steps. First, we need to derive a formula that places an upper bound upon the probability that this is so, given the assumption that there are precisely k unknown morally significant properties. This upper bound will be equal to the number of structure-descriptions involving the n events together with the positive maximal predicates corresponding to the k properties, divided by the number of structure-descriptions involving the n events together with the totality of the maximal predicates corresponding to the k properties. Then, given that formula, the second step will involve considering how this upper bound varies for different values of k—the number of unknown, morally significant properties. The result will be an upper bound on the upper bounds associated with different values of k.

Let us use the expression '$P(k,n)$' to refer to the relevant upper bound upon the probability that none of the *prima-facie* evils is really evil, all things considered. Then, as is shown in the appendix, it turns out that this is equal to

$$\frac{(2k-1)(2k-2)\cdots(k+1)(k)}{(n+2k-1)(n+2k-2)\cdots(n+k)}$$

Next, one needs to consider how the value of $P(k,n)$ depends upon k and n, and here there are two important results:

(1) $P(k,n)$ **is a monotonically decreasing function of** n.

(2) $P(k,n)$ **is a monotonically decreasing function of** k, **except where** n **is equal to one, when the value of** $P(k,n)$ **is the same for all values of** k.

Of these, the second is especially important, since it allows us to place an upper bound upon the probability that, given n states of affairs, each of which it would be morally wrong to allow if the only rightmaking and wrongmaking properties that existed were the ones that we are aware of, *none* of those n states of affairs is such that it would be wrong to allow that state of affairs to exist, given the totality of rightmaking and wrongmaking properties, both known and unknown. For we know that, for any n, $P(k,n)$ is a maximum when k is equal to one. But when we set k equal to one, the result can be shown to be as follows:

$$P(1,n) = \frac{1}{n+1}$$

We have arrived, then, at the following conclusion:

The maximum value of $P(k,n)$ **is equal to or less than** $1/(n+1)$

How large is n—the number of states of affairs each of which, judged by known rightmaking and wrongmaking properties, it would be morally wrong to allow? One way of arguing that it must be very large, and thus that $P(1,n)$ must be very low, is as follows. The present population of the world is about six billion people. What proportion of those people will be allowed, at some point in their lives, to undergo something that, judged by the rightmaking and wrongmaking properties of which we have knowledge, they should not have to suffer? The answer, it would seem, is very high. For one thing, everyone undergoes the evil of death, and a high proportion of people undergo the evil of aging, and given the rightmaking and wrongmaking properties of which we are aware, allowing either is surely unjustified, except in a small proportion of cases. Taking n to be in excess of a billion would seem, therefore, to be a very conservative estimate. So n is very high indeed, and the value of $P(1,n)$, consequently, is very, very low.

4.6.6 Summing up: the case of multiple, simultaneously preventible evils

We have arrived, then, at the following result:

> (C₃) If $S_1, S_2, S_3, S_4, \ldots, S_i, \ldots, S_n$ are states of affairs, all of which are preventable at some time, t, and such that, for each S_i, choosing not to prevent S_i is an action that, judged by known rightmaking and wrongmaking properties, is *prima facie* wrong, then the probability, all things considered—including relevant, *unknown* rightmaking and wrongmaking properties—that none of $S_1, S_2, S_3, S_4, \ldots, S_i, \ldots, S_n$ is such that it is morally wrong to allow that state of affairs to obtain is less than $1/(n+1)$.

Moreover, as we have also seen, in virtue of the derivation of (C₃), no additional information simply about *the number* of unknown morally significant properties that exist could serve to make the probability greater than $1/(n+1)$. Finally, we have also seen that there is good reason for supposing that the value of n is very high, and therefore that the value of $1/(n+1)$ is very low.

The upshot is, then, that by appealing to n evils that could have been prevented at some time t by any omnipotent and omniscient person who existed at that time, and by paralleling, for each of the n evils, the reasoning in the first part of the argument set out earlier in section 4.3, one can use (C₃) to construct a deductive argument that leads to the following conclusion:

> (G₁) If $S_1, S_2, S_3, S_4, \ldots, S_i, \ldots, S_n$ are states of affairs, all of which are preventable at some time, t, and such that, for each S_i, choosing not to prevent S_i is an action that, judged by known rightmaking and wrongmaking properties, is *prima facie* wrong, then the probability, all things considered—including relevant, *unknown* rightmaking and wrongmaking properties—that there is

an omnipotent, omniscient, and morally perfect person at time t is less than $1/(n+1)$.

4.7 Multiple, not simultaneously preventable evils, and the present non-existence of God

The conclusion for which I have just argued focuses upon the case of evils, all of which are preventable at some single time, and it assigns an upper bound to the probability that God exists at *that* time. But in setting out the argument from evil, one wants to appeal to evils that may be preventable only at different times. In addition, one is interested in the probability that God exists now. So the question is how one can move from the above result—(G_1)—to a conclusion about the probability that God exists now, given information about the occurrence of evils at many different times.

4.7.1 Evils that are not simultaneously preventable

Let us first consider what happens when one shifts to a consideration of evils that are not simultaneously preventable. What conclusion can one establish with regard to such evils? To answer this question, notice, first, that since the *argument* for (C_3) makes no use of the fact that the evils are simultaneously preventable, that argument also establishes the following, slightly more general conclusion:

(C_4) If S_1, S_2, S_3, S_4, . . ., S_i, . . ., S_n are states of affairs that are preventable, respectively, at times $t_1, t_2, t_3, t_4, \ldots, t_i, \ldots, t_n$, and that are such that, for each S_i, choosing not to prevent S_i is an action that, judged by known rightmaking and wrongmaking properties, is *prima facie* wrong, then the probability, all things considered—including relevant, unknown rightmaking and wrongmaking properties—that none of S_1, S_2, S_3, S_4, . . . S_i, . . . S_n is such that it is morally wrong to allow that state of affairs to obtain is less than $1/(n+1)$.

Then, secondly, given (C_4), it is a straightforward matter to set out a deductive argument for the following conclusion:

(G_2) If S_1, S_2, S_3, S_4, . . ., S_i, . . ., S_n are states of affairs that are preventable, respectively, at times $t_1, t_2, t_3, t_4, \ldots, t_i, \ldots, t_n$, and that are such that, for each S_i, choosing not to prevent S_i is an action that, judged by known rightmaking and wrongmaking properties, is *prima facie* wrong, then the probability, all things considered—including relevant, unknown rightmaking and wrongmaking properties—that there is an omnipotent, omniscient, and morally perfect person at *all* of the n times in question—that is, at t_1, t_2, t_3, t_4, . . ., t_i, . . ., t_n—is less than $1/(n+1)$.

4.7.2   The present non-existence of God

We have arrived at the conclusion that, given n evils that are preventable at n different times, the probability that God exists at all of those times is less than $1/(n+1)$. How do we move from that conclusion to a conclusion concerning the probability that God exists now? It turns out—perhaps surprisingly—that the length of the journey that is needed at this point very much depends upon whether one defines God, as I have done, simply as an omnipotent, omniscient, and morally perfect person, or whether, instead, one also makes it part of the concept of God either that he exists at all times, or that he is the creator of the physical universe.

If one makes it part of the concept of God that he is omnitemporal, the argument is straightforward. Things are slightly more complex if, instead, one defines God as an omnipotent, omniscient, and morally perfect creator of the physical universe. For then one has to forge a connection with the property of being omnitemporal by arguing that if such a being exists at any time, he will also exist at all later times. Finally, the argument is much more complicated if one defines God simply as an omnipotent, omniscient, and morally perfect person, for then it does not appear possible to show that such a being can exist at one time only if he exists at all times. Consequently, what one has to do in this case is to show that a probability can be assigned to the rather bizarre possibility that such a being has recently popped into existence!

For our present purposes, however, I think that we can ignore such possibilities, and simply focus upon the case of an omnipotent, omniscient, morally perfect, and omnitemporal person. When this is done, the argument is very simple. For if God, by definition, exists at all times, then his non-existence at any time entails his non-existence at every time, and therefore one has, in virtue of (G_2), the following conclusion:

(G_3) If S_1, S_2, S_3, S_4, . . ., S_i, . . ., S_n are states of affairs that are preventable, respectively, at times t_1, t_2, t_3, t_4, . . ., t_i, . . ., t_n, and that are such that, for each S_i, choosing not to prevent S_i is an action that, judged by known rightmaking and wrongmaking properties, is *prima facie* wrong, then the probability, all things considered—including relevant, unknown rightmaking and wrongmaking properties—that there is an omnipotent, omniscient, morally perfect, and *omnitemporal* person is less than $1/(n+1)$.

4.8   Carnap's λ-continuum of inductive methods

In arriving at the above conclusion, I have used a method based upon structure-descriptions. Might this result be undermined if one adopted a different approach to logical probability? I think that there is good reason for holding that it would not.

In the first place, suppose that one used, instead, the method based on state-descriptions. Then, as is shown in the appendix, (G_3) would be replaced by

$(G_3{}^*)$ If S_1, S_2, S_3, S_4, . . ., S_i, . . ., S_n are states of affairs that are preventable, respectively, at times t_1, t_2, t_3, t_4, . . ., t_i, . . ., t_n, and that are such that, for each S_i, choosing not to prevent S_i is an action that, judged by known rightmaking and wrongmaking properties, is *prima facie* wrong, then the probability, all things considered—including relevant, unknown rightmaking and wrongmaking properties—that there is an omnipotent, omniscient, morally perfect, and *omnitemporal* person is less than $1/2^n$.

The probability that God exists would, accordingly, turn out to be even lower.

Now the method based on state-descriptions seems, as I have indicated above, to be clearly unsound. But that method, together with the method of structure-descriptions, stands in an important relation to a very general approach to inductive logic—namely, that set out by Rudolf Carnap in his monograph *The Continuum of Inductive Methods* (1952)—and that relation provides a reason for thinking that it will be true, given any sound approach to inductive logic, that the probability that God exists tends to zero as the number of apparent evils increases.

What Carnap showed in that monograph is that certain plausible axioms for logical probability entail that the probability that the next thing observed will have a certain property, given that n out of the first s things have had that property, must be equal to $(n + \lambda/k)/(s + \lambda)$—where k may be viewed as the number of properties in some family of properties, and λ is a parameter that may take any non-negative integral value. (A more general result that covers families whose properties may differ in logical width is set out in section 19 of Carnap's "A Basic System of Inductive Logic, Part 2" (1980).)

The relation between Carnap's λ-continuum of inductive methods and the two methods used here is as follows. First, if one considers the probability function that results as λ tends to infinity, it is equivalent to that generated by the method of state-descriptions. On the other hand, if λ is set equal to k, then the resulting confirmation function is equivalent to the confirmation function that results via the method of structure-descriptions. The two methods that I have used, therefore, correspond more or less to opposite ends of the λ-continuum, and this, together with the fact that $(n + \lambda/k)/(s + \lambda)$ is a monotonic function of λ means that any intermediate λ-system approach to logical probability will yield a probability for the existence of God that lies between those generated by the method of state-descriptions and the method of structure-descriptions.

Summing Up

The argument from evil is a very natural argument, since in everyday life we constantly draw conclusions concerning the moral character of a given individual from information both about what the individual in question does, and about what the individual intentionally refrains from doing. But when one attempts to extend this type of reasoning to the case of an omnipotent and omniscient being, a crucial question arises concerning what exactly the logical form of the central inductive step is. Moreover, when this question is carefully examined, it turns out to be more difficult than one might have expected to provide an account that withstands critical scrutiny. I have argued, however, that a satisfactory account can be offered. Consequently, unless there is countervailing positive evidence in support of the existence of God, or unless belief in the existence of God can be shown to be non-inferentially justified, and in a way that is not easily defeasible, the argument from evil establishes not only that one cannot know that God exists, but also, and even more unhappily, that it is unlikely—indeed, extremely unlikely—that God exists.

Appendix: The Structure-Description Approach to Inductive Logic

If one adopts the view that probabilities are based upon assigning equal weights to structure-descriptions, then to arrive at an upper bound for a fixed value of k, one needs a formula that specifies the number of structure-descriptions there are involving n individuals and m that maximal predicates. It turns out that the number of such structure-descriptions is equal to the number of ways of choosing $(m - 1)$ things from a set of $(n + m - 1)$ things, as can be shown by the following simple, but elegant argument, from Carnap's *Logical Foundations of Probability*:

> The distributions in question may be represented by serial patterns consisting of n dots and $m - 1$ strokes, as follows: the number of individuals which have the first property is indicated by the number of dots preceding the first stroke; that of the second property by the dots between the first and second stroke, etc.; finally, that of the mth property by the dots following the last stroke. (For example, the pattern '...//./' indicates the numbers 3, 0, 1, 0 for the four properties.)

Therefore the number sought is equal to the number of possible patterns with n dots and $m - 1$ strokes. These patterns may be produced by starting with a series of $n + m - 1$ dots and then replacing a subclass of $m - 1$ of them by strokes. The number of these subclasses is $[n + m - 1^C m - 1]...$; therefore this is also the number of possible patterns. (1962, pp. 159–60)

So the number of structure-descriptions that involve m maximal predicates, together with n events, is equal to $n + m - 1^C m - 1$, which in turn is equal to

$$\frac{(n+m-1)!}{n!(m-1)!}$$

What we want to determine is how likely it is that, given n events, each of which is such that, judged simply by known rightmaking and wrongmaking properties, it would be morally wrong to allow that event, *none* of those n events is such that it is morally wrong to allow that event, given the totality, M, of all rightmaking and wrongmaking properties, known and unknown. To do this, we need to derive a formula that places an upper bound upon the probability that this is so given the assumption that there are precisely k unknown morally significant properties.

Consider, then, the set of all possible Q-predicates of actions—that is, predicates that are maximal with respect to U, the set of all unknown rightmaking and wrongmaking properties. By symmetry considerations, the number of positive Q-predicates cannot be greater than the number of negative Q-predicates. In addition, since some Q-predicates will be neutral, less than half of the Q-predicates will be positive.

Since the number of Q-predicates is always a power of 2, we can set that number equal to $2k$. Then, since the number of positive Q-predicates must be less than k, we can divide the Q-predicates into two sets, S and T, each containing k Q-predicates, such that all of the positive Q-predicates are in S, along with some neutral Q-predicates, while all of the negative Q-predicates, together with the remaining neutral ones, are in T.

The number of structure-descriptions that contain only Q-predicates in set S (or only predicates in set T) is then given by the formula $_{n+k-1}C_{k-1}$. So it is

$$_{n+k-1}C_{k-1} = (n+k-1)!/n!(k-1)!$$
$$= (n+k-1)(n+k-2)\cdots(n+1)(n)\cdots(2)(1)/(n)(n-1)\cdots$$
$$(2)(1)(k-1)(k-2)\cdots(2)(1)$$
$$= (n+k-1)(n+k-2)\cdots(n+1)/(k-1)(k-2)\cdots(2)(1)$$

Similarly, the number of structure-descriptions that contain Q-predicates in the union of set S and set T is given by the formula $_{n+2k-1}C_{2k-1}$. So it is

$$
\begin{aligned}
_{n+2k-1}C_{2k-1} &= (n+2k-1)!/n!(2k-1)! \\
&= (n+2k-1)(n+2k-2)\cdots(n+1)(n)\cdots(2)(1)/(n)(n-1)\cdots \\
&\quad (2)(1)(2k-1)(2k-2)\cdots(2)(1) \\
&= (n+2k-1)(n+2k-2)\cdots(n+1)/(2k-1)(2k-2)\cdots(2)(1)
\end{aligned}
$$

Let us now introduce the expression '$P(k,n)$' to represent the probability that a structure-description involving Q-predicates in the union of the sets S and T will be a structure-description involving only Q-predicates in set S. In view of the above, we have that

$$
\begin{aligned}
P(k,n) &= {}_{n+k-1}C_{k-1} / {}_{n+2k-1}C_{2k-1} \\
&= \frac{(n+k-1)(n+k-2)\cdots(n+1)}{(k-1)(k-2)\cdots(2)(1)} \bigg/ \frac{(n+2k-1)(n+2k-2)\cdots(n+1)}{(2k-1)(2k-2)\cdots(2)(1)} \\
&= \frac{(n+k-1)(n+k-2)\cdots(n+1)}{(k-1)(k-2)\cdots(2)(1)} \times \frac{(2k-1)(2k-2)\cdots(2)(1)}{(n+2k-1)(n+2k-2)\cdots(n+1)} \\
&= \frac{(2k-1)(2k-2)\cdots(k+1)(k)}{(n+2k-1)(n+2k-2)\cdots(n+k)}
\end{aligned}
$$

Let us now consider how the value of $P(k,n)$ depends upon k and n. First, then, how does the value of $P(k,n)$ depend upon n, the number of relevant evils? We can answer this question by dividing $P(k,n+1)$ by $P(k,n)$, and examining the result:

$$
\begin{aligned}
&P(k,n+1)/P(k,n) \\
&= \frac{(2k-1)(2k-2)\cdots(k+1)(k)}{(n+2k)(n+2k-1)\cdots(n+k+1)} \bigg/ \frac{(2k-1)(2k-2)\cdots(k+1)(k)}{(n+2k-1)(n+2k-2)\cdots(n+k)} \\
&= \frac{(2k-1)(2k-2)\cdots(k+1)(k)}{(n+2k)(n+2k-1)\cdots(n+k+1)} \times \frac{(n+2k-1)(n+2k-2)\cdots(n+k)}{(2k-1)(2k-2)\cdots(k+1)(k)} \\
&= \frac{(n+2k-1)(n+2k-2)\cdots(n+k)}{(n+2k)(n+2k-1)\cdots(n+k+1)} \\
&= \frac{n+k}{n+2k}
\end{aligned}
$$

Since k is greater than zero, and n is positive, this ratio must always be less than one. So $P(k,n+1)$ is always less than $P(k,n)$. This gives us our first, important conclusion:

Theorem 1: *P(k,n)* is a monotonically decreasing function of *n*.

Secondly, how does the value of $P(k,n)$ depend upon the number of unknown, morally significant properties? This question can be answered by dividing $P(k+1,n)$ by $P(k,n)$, and examining the result:

$$P(k+1,n)/P(k,n)$$

$$= \frac{(2k+1)(2k)\cdots(k+1)}{(n+2k+1)(n+2k)\cdots(n+k+1)} \bigg/ \frac{(2k-1)(2k-2)\cdots(k+1)(k)}{(n+2k-1)(n+2k-2)\cdots(n+k)}$$

$$= \frac{(2k+1)(2k)\cdots(k+1)}{(n+2k+1)(n+2k)\cdots(n+k+1)} \times \frac{(n+2k-1)(n+2k-2)\cdots(n+k)}{(2k-1)(2k-2)\cdots(k+1)(k)}$$

$$= \frac{(2k+1)(2k)(n+k)}{(n+2k+1)(n+2k)(k)}$$

$$= \frac{(2)(2k+1)(n+k)}{(n+2k+1)(n+2k)}$$

$$= \frac{4k^2 + 2k + 4nk + 2n}{n^2 + 2nk + n + 2nk + 4k + 2k}$$

$$= \frac{4k^2 + 2k + 4nk + 2n}{n^2 + 4k^2 + 2k + 4nk + n}$$

How does the numerator of this fraction compare with the denominator? To answer this question, subtract the numerator from the denominator. The result is

$$n^2 - n = n(n-1)$$

From this one can see that the result is positive, except when *n*, the number of relevant evils, is equal to one. So the denominator is always larger than the numerator, except when *n* is equal to one, in which case the numerator is equal to the denominator.

The conclusion, accordingly, is that $P(k+1,n)$ is always less than $P(k,n)$, except when *n* is equal to one. We have, then, the following, crucial result:

Theorem 2: *P(k,n)* is a monotonically decreasing function of *k*, except where *n* is equal to one, when the value of *P(k,n)* is the same for all values of *k*.

This second result allows us to place an upper bound upon the probability that, given *n* states of affairs, each of which it would be morally wrong to allow if the only rightmaking and wrongmaking properties that existed were the ones that we are aware of, *none* of those *n* states of affairs is such that it would be wrong to allow that state of affairs to exist, given the totality of rightmaking and wrongmaking properties, both known and unknown. For we know that, for any n, $P(k,n)$ is a maximum when k is equal to one. But when we set k equal to one, $P(k,n)$ becomes

$$
\begin{aligned}
P(1,n) &= {}_{n+1-1}C_{1-1} / {}_{n+2-1}C_{2-1} \\
&= {}_{n}C_0 / {}_{n+1}C_1 \\
&= \frac{1}{n+1}
\end{aligned}
$$

The state-description approach to inductive logic

The argument that Carnap offered against basing logical probabilities upon relevant numbers of state-descriptions, and which was set out earlier, seems to me sound. Nevertheless, it is worth considering the state-description approach, since the two different approaches are closely related to the extreme ends of Carnap's 'λ-continuum' of inductive methods (Carnap, 1952).

If one adopts the view that logical probabilities are based upon the ratios of the numbers of state-descriptions associated with the two propositions, then to arrive at an upper bound for a fixed value of k, one needs a formula that specifies the number of state-descriptions formed from n individuals and m maximal predicates. Since for each of the n individuals there are m possible maximal predicates, the total number of state-descriptions is equal to m^n.

As before, we can divide the Q-predicates of actions into two sets, S and T, each containing k Q-predicates, such that all of the positive Q-predicates are in S, along with some neutral Q-predicates, while all of the negative Q-predicates, together with the remaining neutral ones, are in T.

The number of state-descriptions that contain only predicates in set S (or only predicates in set T) is given by the formula k^n Similarly, the number of state-descriptions that contain predicates in the union of set S and set T is given by the formula $(2k)^n$.

The probability $P(k,n)$ in which we are interested is therefore given by the ratio $k^n/(2k)^n$, which is equal to $1/2^n$.

3
Reply to Tooley's Opening Statement

Alvin Plantinga

We are very much in Michael Tooley's debt for his clear, rigorous, and detailed statement of a version of the atheistic argument from evil.[1] His version is *probabilistic*; he aims to show that the existence of God is improbable, unlikely, given the existence of evil. Prior to thirty years ago, or so, those who offered an atheistic argument from evil—'atheologians,' as we may call them—ordinarily offered *deductive* arguments from evil to the non-existence of God. The proposition

(G) There is an omnipotent, omniscient, wholly good person

they said, is inconsistent, in the metaphysical or broadly logical sense,[2] with the proposition

(E) There is evil;[3]

there is no possible world in which both G and E are true. But since it is wholly obvious that there is evil, it follows that G is false. About thirty years or so ago, however, most people came to see that there is no contradiction here, that

---

[1] The term 'evil' is best applied to wrong-doing on the part of free creatures, and in particular the way in which we human beings abuse and mistreat each other. Some evil of the latter sort—the Holocaust, the appalling seventy-year Marxist/Communist experiment—is horrifying both in extent and in intensity; much evil, however, is trite, quotidian, banal, but none the better for that. Following Tooley and common custom, I'll also use 'evil' to refer to suffering of all kinds.

[2] For comment on necessity in the broadly logical sense, see my *The Nature of Necessity* (Oxford: Clarendon Press, 1974), pp. 2–9.

[3] Henry David Aiken, "God and Evil," *Ethics*, 68 (1957–8): 79, H.J. McCloskey, "God and Evil," *Philosophical Quarterly*, 10 (1960): 97, J.L. Mackie, "Evil and Omnipotence," *Mind*, 64 (1955): 200.

in fact the conjunction of (1) and (2) is possible (in the broadly logical sense). One factor leading to this change was the 'Free Will Defense,' a thought going all the way back at least to Augustine in the fifth century. The basic idea of the Free Will Defense is that even if God is omnipotent, it is not the case that he can create or actualize just any possible world. If he creates free creatures (and leaves them free), for example, he can't guarantee that they will do only what is right; what they do is up to them, if they are free, not up to him.[4]

The atheologians, of course, did not silently fold their tents and fade away. Instead, they turned to various *evidential*, or *inductive*, or *probabilistic* arguments from evil for the non-existence of God. The basic idea is something like this. Perhaps there is no contradiction involved in the joint affirmation of God and evil; nevertheless, the existence of evil, or of certain kinds of evil, or of the amount and varieties of evil we find, makes it improbable, unlikely, that there is such a person as God.

In a way, this was something of a comedown for atheologians. That is because probabilistic or evidential arguments are much messier and more problematic than deductive arguments. The deductive argument is short and sweet: if the existence of evil (or of some of the evils the world displays) is logically inconsistent with the existence of God, then either there isn't any evil, or else straightforward belief in God[5] is straightforwardly false. But it is extremely hard to deny the existence of evil; indeed, the central Christian message is that Christ, the second person of the Trinity, came into the world to make salvation from sin available to us human beings; Christian belief, therefore, entails that there is evil in the world.

But now suppose the atheologian could persuasively argue that the existence of God is unlikely with respect to the existence of evil, or of a certain kind of evil. That would be hard enough, but suppose he succeeded: what follows from that? How much does that show? Even if G is improbable with respect to evil, there is a great deal we know in addition to evil; G might still be more likely than not on our total evidence. Our total evidence, furthermore, is a vast and variegated affair; many different arguments for the existence of God— theistic arguments—have been proposed;[6] the atheologian bent on showing

---

[4] See my *God, Freedom, and Evil* (New York: Harper and Row, 1974), chapter 9, *The Nature of Necessity*, and *Alvin Plantinga* (Profiles V. 5), ed. James E. Tomberlin and Peter Van Inwagen (Dordrecht: D. Reidel Pub. Co., 1985), pp. 36–55.

[5] 'Straightforward theistic belief'—of course it would be possible to amend, revise belief in God by retrenching in various ways. Perhaps you hold that God is good, but in a way having little to do with goodness as we are familiar with it, or perhaps, as with contemporary 'open theists,' you hold that God is extremely powerful, but not omnipotent, or magnificently knowledgeable, but not omniscient.

[6] See my "Two Dozen (Or So) Theistic Arguments" (unpublished, but available on the web at *http://philofreligion.homestead.com/files/Theisticarguments.html*).

that theism is unlikely with respect to our total evidence must presumably show that none of these arguments have any force, or that if some do, their combined force doesn't equal that of evidence on the other side from evil. And even if G is not more likely than not on our total evidence—even if it is unlikely on that evidence—how does it follow that it is unjustified or irrational or in some other way intellectually improper or second-rate to believe G? Most Christian thinkers have held that there are other sources of justification for belief in God: religious experience, for example, or something like Calvin's *Sensus divinitatis*, or Thomas Aquinas's internal instigation of the Holy Spirit.[7] All of these questions and more would have to be examined.

Nevertheless, as attested to by believers over the centuries (going back at least to the book of Job and Psalms in the Old Testament), the extent and appalling character of evil have often perplexed believers. The probabilistic argument from evil, furthermore, is centrally important in this context. Prior to thirty years ago, as I said, nearly all who offered atheological arguments from evil proposed that the joint assertion of G and E is logically inconsistent. There was one important exception, however. In 1935, John Wisdom argued that the existence of God is logically consistent with the existence of evil; but he said it is unlikely, given the *amount* of evil, that there is such a person as God.[8] That's about all he had to say on the topic, but it is more than what most writers on evil said on it. The distance between Wisdom's simple statement and Tooley's rigorous formulation is impressive; we have certainly come a long way from the former's offhand comment. Tooley's statement of the argument gives us believers in God a wonderful target; if we can show that this formulation of the argument doesn't succeed, it seems unlikely, for the moment, at any rate, that any formulation will.

Does Tooley's formulation succeed? I think it does not, and that is what I propose to argue (below, section 2). But first, how, exactly, does Tooley's version of the argument go? What, exactly, is he arguing for?

Tooley proposes that the subject of discussion be G, the proposition there is an omniscient, omnipotent, and perfectly good person. Classical Christians and classical theists of other sorts do indeed affirm G, and they use the term 'God' (or some cognate) as a name of that being. But they typically go further; they add that God has created the world. And while they say that God is omniscient, omnipotent, and perfectly good, those who have thought about it usually[9] go on to add that God has these properties *essentially*. This means that he could not

---

[7] See my Opening Statement p. 8ff; and my *Warranted Christian Belief* (New York: Oxford University Press, 2000), chapters 5, 6, and 8 (hereafter WCB).
[8] "God and Evil," *Mind*, V. 44 (1935): 1–20.
[9] But not always: see, for example, Richard Swinburne, *The Existence of God* (Oxford: Clarendon Press, 1979), p. 93.

have existed and lacked those properties. There are no possible worlds where God exists but is epistemically challenged; he is omniscient, knows everything, in every possible world in which he exists. The same goes for omnipotence and moral perfection; there is no world in which God exists but is relatively power-less, and no world in which he is less than perfectly good, no world in which he does something morally wrong.

Still further, on the classical conception, God is a necessary being; he exists in every possible world; he could not have failed to exist. Thus Thomas Aquinas, the premier medieval philosopher/theologian, says that the existence of God is "self-evident in itself" though not self-evident to us.[10] What he means is that God is a necessary being, a being who exists in every possible world. Now many necessary propositions are self-evident to us: they are such that we can see that they are true and necessary just by considering them, holding them before our mind. Simple mathematical and logical propositions, for example

$$(1)\ 2 + 1 = 3$$

and

(2) If all men are mortal and Socrates is a man, then Socrates is mortal

are like that; one can simply see that they couldn't be false. Other necessary propositions, however, are not such that we can see them to be true just by considering them. For example,

$$(3)\ 2381 \times 9782 = 23{,}290{,}942$$

is true and necessarily true, but we can't tell that just by considering the propo-sition (most of us, anyway; there is the occasional idiot savant). We have to calculate it. And Aquinas's thought is that G is like that: it is indeed necessarily true, but it isn't self-evident to us. Of course there might be other beings for whom G *is* self-evident: for example, God himself.

Second, Tooley proposes that the existence of God is unlikely, perhaps very unlikely, with respect to the existence of certain evils in the world. This by itself isn't all that impressive. Even if the probability of G, given evil, is low, belief in God might still be perfectly acceptable; even if the probability of G given evil is low, believers in God could be perfectly justified in this belief. For there might be other propositional evidence, other evidence from things we know,

---

[10] Thomas Aquinas, *Summa Theologiae*, Pt. 1. Q. 2, A. 1.

with respect to which the probability of G was very high; and it might be that on balance, with respect to the totality of our evidence, G is much more likely than not. Example: you tell me that you saw Paul at the mall yesterday; with respect to that bit of evidence it is more likely than not that Paul was at the mall yesterday. But then I learn that you suffer from prospagnosia and have a really hard time recognizing people; furthermore, Eleonore, Paul's wife, tells me that she and Paul spent the whole day, yesterday, skiing. If the rest of your evidence is more or less evenly balanced with respect to Paul's whereabouts yesterday, then on balance it is more likely than not that Paul wasn't at the mall yesterday.

It could also be that on our total propositional evidence G is improbable, but nonetheless G is justified and is the right thing to believe. Thus, for example, suppose you are accused of stealing my Frisian flag. You have always wanted a Frisian flag to add to your extensive flag collection; you have been known to acquire flags and other valuable items by shady means; my neighbor next door, a man of impeccable rectitude, claims to have seen you lurking around the back door of my house at about the time the flag was stolen; the jury convicts you. You, however, know perfectly well that you didn't steal the flag, in fact you know that you spent the entire afternoon at home alone, thinking about the probabilistic argument from evil. Then with respect to the available propositional evidence, it is very likely that you stole the flag. That propositional evidence is also *your* total propositional evidence; you know that the neighbor reported you lurking around the door, that you have a bad record along these lines, etc. So with respect to your propositional evidence, it is more likely than not, perhaps very much more likely than not, that you stole the flag; still, you are eminently justified in believing that you didn't, and indeed you know you didn't. The reason, of course, is that you have powerful *non*-propositional evidence: you *remember* where you were, and that you didn't steal that flag.

Things could stand the same way with respect to G. It could be that G is improbable with respect to the totality of our propositional evidence, but nonetheless such that many of us are justified in believing G, and indeed know that G is true. This would be the case if there were, in accord with my suggestions in my opening statement, a cognitive faculty or process, like memory or sense perception, by virtue of which G can be known and is known. Tooley is aware of these possibilities—i.e., (1) that even if the probability of G on E is low, the probability of G on our total propositional evidence might be as high as you please, and (2) even if the probability of G on our total evidence is low, it might still be that many people know G to be true; however he doesn't address them in his opening statement. I'll argue that the really crucial question here is just whether *there is* a cognitive faculty or process that is the source of belief in God. If there is, then, presumably, such belief is justifiable and rational. I'll also argue that if theism or Christian belief is in fact true, then very likely many believers in God are justified in believing as they do, and indeed know that G is true.

I Justification

Now Tooley proposes (p. 116) to argue that G is unlikely on E—more exactly, he proposes to argue that G is improbable given such states of affairs as the Lisbon earthquake. We'll take a careful look at his argument below. For now, note that he doesn't mean to argue this just for its own sake; what Tooley really wants to argue is that theistic belief is not *epistemically justified*. But what is epistemic justification? Under what conditions is a belief epistemically justified? Justification, says Tooley, "is a function of the epistemic probability of the relevant proposition: the latter fixes, non-epistemic factors aside, what degree of assent to the proposition in question is appropriate . . ." (p. 77). So the first basic idea is that justification of my belief that p is a function of, depends upon, the epistemic probability of p; presumably the greater the epistemic probability of p, the greater the degree of its justification.[11] As Tooley is thinking of it, the same proposition can have different degrees of epistemic probability for different people; the epistemic probability of a proposition for me will depend on what else I know and on my current experience. You have just looked up the population of Novosibirsk, Siberia; according to the atlas it is 1,500,000. For you, therefore, the proposition *the population of Novosibirsk is 1,500,000* is epistemically very probable. I haven't looked it up, and have only a vague idea as to how populous Novosibirsk is; for me that same proposition is epistemically much less probable than it is for you.

So justification is a function of epistemic probability; what, then, is epistemic probability? Here Tooley is a bit indecisive. "One answer", he says, "is that it is logical probability relative to one's total evidence" (p. 77). Here he finds a problem: shall we take my total evidence to be all the propositions I am justified in believing? But my justification for some beliefs is greater than my justification for other beliefs; presumably, then, my justified beliefs shouldn't all count equally as parts of my total evidence. There is another problem with this suggestion as well, a problem Tooley doesn't mention. We are presumably trying to explain what justification is; justification, he says, is a function

---

[11] Alternatively, one could hold that justification doesn't come in degrees (although epistemic probability does), and there is a certain degree of epistemic probability such that any proposition having more than that degree of epistemic probability, for me, is justified for me.

of the epistemic probability of *p* for me; but then it won't help to explain epistemic probability in terms of logical probability with respect to my total evidence, and then explain *total evidence* in terms of propositions I am justified in believing.

A natural response to the first of these problems, says Tooley, "is to say that the epistemic probability of a proposition, rather than being equal to its logical probability relative to one's total evidence, is equal instead to its logical probability relative to the propositions that one is non-inferentially justified in accepting" (p. 77). This suggestion, of course, suffers from the same kind of explanatory circularity as the first: if I don't know what justification is, it won't help me to be told that it is logical probability with respect to propositions one is non-inferentially justified in believing.

Apart from this problem of explanatory circularity here, there is another: if we explain epistemic probability in terms of logical probability with respect to propositions one is non-inferentially justified in believing, should those propositions all be accepted to the same degree, and if so, should that degree be one? Tooley isn't quite sure here: "If one is an indirect realist with regard to both perception and memory, one *may* be able to maintain that both of these things are the case" (p. 77, Tooley's emphasis). (I should think the answer is that some of these beliefs should be accepted more firmly than others. If I have a grasp of what Tooley means when he speaks of non-inferential justification, I should think I am justified in accepting non-inferentially both the proposition *2 + 1 = 3* and the proposition *5 + 4 = 9*; but presumably I should accept the first more firmly than the second.)

Alternatively, says Tooley, if I am an indirect realist I "may be able to hold that the epistemic probability of a proposition is its logical probability relative to the propositions describing one's 'basis' states—that is, those states in virtue of which various beliefs are non-inferentially justified" (p. 77). Here the idea, I take it, is that I may be in such states as *being appeared to redly* (in such and such circumstances), or *seeming to see that 4 + 5 = 9*; these would be basis states, and the epistemic probability of my belief that I see something red or that 4 + 5 = 9 will be the logical probability of the proposition in question with respect to the propositions that say what basis states I am in. On the other hand, he says, if I am a direct realist, things go somewhat differently: here I will need the idea of "'foundational' probability" (p. 77).

It is therefore not entirely easy to see what Tooley has in mind when he speaks of epistemic probability, and hence not easy to see what he has in mind when he speaks of epistemic justification. But in the present context, this doesn't really matter. That's because, so it seems to me, none of the above will be an adequate explanation of epistemic justification. Why not? Because all of these proposed accounts involve the notion of logical probability; in each case the epistemic probability of a proposition, for me, is the logical probability of that

proposition with respect to some set of propositions—the set of propositions
I am justified in believing, or non-inferentially justified in believing, or the
set of propositions that describe my total basis state. And this causes serious
problems.

First, the notion of logical probability is itself a bit problematic. According
to this idea, every proposition has an intrinsic probability, a probability, as they
say, on tautological evidence; and for any pair of propositions A and B, there
is the probability of A on B (provided that the intrinsic probability of B is not
zero). This relationship is a necessary, objective, quasi logical fact about A and
B. If we like, we can think of this relation among propositions as *partial entailment*. Entailment is the limiting case of the relation; if we think in terms of
possible worlds, A entails B just if B is true in every world in which A is true.
We can also think of $P(A/B)$ as something like the proportion of worlds in
which both A and B are true among B worlds. If there were only finitely many
possible worlds, we could think of $P(A/B)$ as the quotient of the number of
$A\&B$ worlds by the number of B worlds. But of course it seems unlikely that
there are only finitely many possible worlds; presumably, for example, for any
number N there is a possible world in which there are exactly N donkeys. If so,
there will be at least as many worlds as there are natural numbers; the number
of worlds will be at least countably infinite. No doubt, however, there are even
more worlds than that. Suppose you are exactly six feet tall; presumably you
could have been a bit taller or shorter. (For example, if you hadn't carefully
followed your mother's admonitions to eat your spinach, you might have been
a bit shorter.) Indeed, for each real number in the unit interval centered on
72, you could have been precisely r inches tall. But there are uncountably
many real numbers in that interval; hence there are uncountably many possible worlds.

And this produces problems. The main problem is that there doesn't seem to
be a measure on the space of possible worlds of the right kind. Formally, probability theory is a branch of measure theory. The latter grew out of our attempts
to understand our everyday notions of length, volume, and area. We think of this
in terms of points: a line contains or is composed of uncountably many points.
Unfortunately, the cardinal number of points in a long line is no greater than
the number of points in a short line; and even if line A is a proper part of line B,
A will have the same (cardinal) number of points as B. The history of measure
theory is the history of attempts to come to an understanding of a measure that
deals properly with sets of infinite magnitude and is also intuitively satisfactory.[12]

[12] See Bas van Fraassen's *Laws and Symmetries* (Oxford: Oxford University Press, 1989), pp. 325–31
for an instructive account of this history.

As it turns out, no wholly satisfactory account is possible.[13] Analogues of the geometrical problems afflict logical probability as ordinarily construed. For example, suppose propositions form a set,[14] a countable set.[15] Then it won't be possible that logical probability be both connected in the set of propositions and also countably additive (i.e., such that for a countable family of propositions mutually exclusive in pairs, the probability that a member of that set is true is the sum of the probabilities of the members of the set.) Consider, for example, the number of donkeys in the world. It would seem on the face of it that it is as likely, given only necessary truths, that there be five donkeys as that there be ten—or twenty, or any other number you like. Here, one supposes, all numbers have been created equal. It seems plausible to think, therefore, that for any numbers n and m, the logical probability that there are n donkeys is equal to that of their being m donkeys. If probability is a real valued function, however, this won't be possible: obviously there is no way to assign the same non-zero probability to infinitely many propositions mutually exclusive in pairs. The only way to assign the same probability to each of these propositions, then, is to assign each a probability of zero: the logical probability of there being just n donkeys is zero. But if the logical probability that there are n donkeys is zero for any n, it follows that the logical probability that there is at least one donkey (or for that matter at least a million donkeys) will be 1; and the same goes for Siberian cheesehounds, left-handed Frenchmen, Cartesian evil demons, goblins, and any other nasties you can think of. If the probability of there being witches or goblins (or omniscient beings), furthermore, is 1, then the conditional probability of there being such things will be 1 on any further evidence; no matter what evidence we come up with, the probability of there beings witches or demons, given that evidence, is 1. Rudolf Carnap (see Tooley's Opening Statement, p. 135), perhaps the foremost probabilist

---

[13]Thus H. L. Royden in *Real Analysis* (New York: Macmillan, 1968), pp. 53–4: "Ideally, we should like *m* (the measure) to have the following properties": that *m* is defined for every set of real numbers, that the measure of an interval is its length, that the measure is countably additive, and that it is translation-invariant. "Unfortunately," he goes on to say, "as we shall see . . . , it is impossible to construct a set function having all of these properties . . . ."

[14]That they do so is far from obvious: for any set *S* of propositions, there is presumably the proposition that *S* is distinct from the Taj Mahal; but then the set of propositions (supposing there is one) will be as large in cardinality as its power set; and this conflicts with the theorem of ordinary set theories to the effect that the power set of a set *S* always exceeds *S* in cardinality.

[15]This isn't at all obvious either: for presumably for each distinct positive real number *r* there is a distinct proposition *r is greater than 0* and for each real number *r* between 71 and 73 it is possible that I should be *r* inches tall. If so, there will be at least continuum many propositions.

of the twentieth century, was prepared to put up with this consequence and others; but it certainly seems awkward. We might think to improve matters by supposing that each of these propositions gets an *infinitesimal* intrinsic probability—a probability greater than zero but closer to zero than any real number; for then the intrinsic probability of the proposition that there are at least *n* donkeys, say, for any number *n* you please, will not be zero. Still, however, this probability will be closer to 1 than any real number is; and that's an improvement hardly worth mentioning. Further, now we get the original problem with uncountable sets of mutually exclusive and jointly exhaustive propositions. For any real number *r* in the interval centered on 72, for example, presumably you could have been precisely *r* inches tall. But then even if we resort to infinitesimals, we can't assign all of the relevant propositions the same intrinsic probability.

As a result of these and other problems, many reject the whole notion of logical probability; Frank Ramsey said, for example, that "A more fundamental criticism of Mr. Keynes' views [according to which there is such a thing as logical probability] . . . is the obvious one that there really do not seem to be any such things as the probability relations he describes."[16]

I'm inclined to think that the extent and seriousness of these problems can be overestimated.[17] There is such a thing as logical probability, even if we run into difficulties involving infinite sets of propositions, and even if our grasp of this relation among propositions is often tenuous in the extreme. Even so, however, there are serious problems in Tooley's attempt to explain epistemic probability and justification in terms of logical probability. I take it Tooley means to use the term 'justification' in the way it is ordinarily used, so that it is a good thing to believe propositions that are justified (for one), and not a good thing to believe propositions that are not justified. *Being justified* is a good thing for a belief; a belief that is justified has a positive epistemic status. Furthermore, the idea, I take it, is that this property of being justified is a property of which we have an initial grasp. Tooley then proposes to say more exactly what this property of being justified is; he proposes a partial account or partial analysis of it.

As we saw, the account goes as follows: justification is a function of epistemic probability. The idea, presumably, is that the greater epistemic probability a proposition has for me, the greater is its degree of justification for me.

---

[16] "Truth and Probability," in *The Foundations of Mathematics and Other Logical Essays*, ed. R.B. Braithwaite (New York: Humanities Press, 1950), p. 161. (The essay was written in 1926.)

[17] As I did in "The Probabilistic Argument from Evil," *Philosophical Studies*, 35:1 (1979), p. 14, 18ff (1979). See my *Warrant and Proper Function* (New York: Oxford University Press, 1993) pp. 149ff (hereafter WPF).

Epistemic probability, furthermore, is the logical probability of the proposition in question on some body of other propositions—perhaps those that are justified for me, or those that are non-inferentially justified for me, or perhaps propositions describing my basis states. No matter which of these we choose, however, we run into real problems.

The *intrinsic* logical probability of any *necessary* proposition—one true in all possible worlds—is, of course, 1. But the same goes for the *conditional* (logical) probability of a necessary proposition on any body of propositions; it too will be 1. If a proposition A is true in every possible world, then $A\&B$ will be true in the very same worlds as B no matter what proposition B is; hence $P(A\&B)$ will equal $P(B)$; and hence $P(A/B)$ will be 1. That means, then, according to Tooley's proposals, that the epistemic probability of any necessary proposition, for me, will be 1; hence every necessary proposition will have maximal justification for me. But that can't be correct. Consider some difficult logical truth—Gödel's theorem, for example—or some reasonably complicated arithmetical proposition—$3927 \times 812 = 3{,}188{,}724$. These propositions, on Tooley's proposals, have an epistemic probability of 1 for me, and hence enjoy maximal justification for me. This is entirely independent, furthermore, of whether I know or have heard of a proof of Gödel's theorem (or have read or heard something about it), or whether I have calculated that product. I may have come, perversely, to believe Gödel's theorem just because my favorite comic book character, who usually asserts falsehoods, asserts it. In fact I may have come to believe it, perversely, just *because* it is asserted by someone most of whose assertions I know to be false. I may have come to believe it just because I am superstitious, and found on the sidewalk a piece of paper on which the theorem was written. Even so, the epistemic probability of this belief will be 1, and it will be maximally justified for me. This can't be right.

A second problem here: on this account all necessary propositions have the *same* degree of epistemic probability for me, and are justified to the same degree. But again, that can't be right. Consider what we may call existentialism: the view that necessarily, if Paul had not existed, the same would have held for propositions like *Paul is happy*, propositions directly about Paul, as we may put it. I believe existentialism is false. But existentialism is a non-contingent proposition: if it is true, it is necessarily true, and if false, necessarily false. I believe it is false; if I am right, therefore, it is necessarily false, and its denial is necessarily true. But then the proposition that existentialism is false has an epistemic probability of 1 for me; hence it is as epistemically probable for me as is the proposition $2 + 1 = 3$. Still further, the former proposition is justified, for me, to the same degree as the latter. But surely it isn't. The denial of existentialism is a contentious philosophical claim; it is not nearly as justified as a simply and self-evident arithmetical truth like *2 + 1 = 3*.

More generally, most philosophical claims are non-contingent—either necessarily true or necessarily false. This means that any such philosophical claim will have an epistemic probability of 1 or 0—1 if it is true and 0 if it is false. But again, that can't be right. Most philosophical propositions aren't just obvious, and even if they are, they aren't nearly as obvious as $2 + 1 = 3$. It isn't ordinarily the case that, when there is philosophical argument or dispute, the true proposition has an epistemic probability of 1 and is maximally justified, while the false proposition has an epistemic probability of 0 and is maximally unjustified. If that were so, philosophy would be a whole lot easier than it is. A correct conception of epistemic probability or justification will allow different necessary falsehoods to have different degrees of epistemic probability and of justification. Existentialism is false, so I say; but wouldn't it be insufferably arrogant for me to claim that those who accept it believe something that has no more justification than $2 + 1 = 17$? The existentialist holds false beliefs; but those beliefs are certainly not maximally unjustified.

This same problem is particularly bothersome in the context of our present discussion of the problem of evil. As I pointed out above, very many, perhaps most, Christian theists who have thought about the matter have thought that God is a necessary being: one that exists in every possible world. They have also thought that God is *essentially* omniscient, omnipotent, and perfectly good: that is, omniscient, omnipotent, and perfectly good in every world in which he exists. Therefore, since he exists in every possible world, there is a being who is omnipotent, omniscient, and perfectly good in every possible world. On this account, the proposition G is necessarily true, and its denial is necessarily false. G, therefore, has a probability of 1 on any evidence. If the theist is right, then, G has an intrinsic probability of 1 and therefore a conditional probability of 1 on any evidence, including the evidence provided by evil, whatever that evidence is. But if so, then on Tooley's conception of justification, G has the maximal degree of justification. If the theist is wrong, however—i.e., if she thinks that there is a necessary being who is essentially omniscient, omnipotent, and morally perfect, and in fact there isn't any such person, then G has an epistemic probability of 0 and hence has minimum justification. Again, this can't be right. Even if the theist is right, as I think she is, G presumably doesn't have absolutely maximal epistemic probability for everyone; and even if the theist is wrong, as I think she isn't, G isn't nearly as epistemically improbable as $2 + 1 = 14$.

Now of course the classical theist may be mistaken in holding that G is non-contingent. Tooley says that he will argue later on that it is not logically necessary that God exists; I'm eager to see that argument. As far as I can see, the proposition that God is a necessary being who is essentially omniscient, omnipotent, and morally perfect is perfectly coherent, and I don't believe that there are any good arguments against it; further, I am myself strongly inclined to think it is true. But if so, G is necessary. And if G is necessary, then it is hard to see how Tooley's evidential argument is relevant. It appears to be relevant only if G is contingent. Tooley's conception of justification, therefore, means that his argument must presuppose that G is contingent.

But of course this result holds only on Tooley's construal of justification and epistemic probability. As I've argued, that construal has real problems; perhaps with a more satisfactory account of justification his argument wouldn't need the presupposition that G is contingent. On a proper construal of justification and epistemic probability, it ought to be the case that non-contingent propositions can have an intrinsic epistemic probability other than 1 or 0, and can have a conditional probability on evidence other than 1 or 0. My mathematically inclined friend tells me that Gödel's theorem is true; with respect to this bit of evidence, the epistemic probability of the theorem will be greater than 1/2, but less than 1. It's clearly less than 1, because there is some chance that Paul is mistaken, or teasing, or has misspoken himself. It is clearly greater than 1/2: Paul is usually reliable, on these matters, and claims he has seen and understood a proof of the theorem.[18]

Is there a better way to think of epistemic probability and justification here? Perhaps the central idea of justification is that a proposition is justified for me if it is the (or a) right thing to believe in the circumstances—in particular, circumstances having to do with my evidence. It may be hard to explain in greater detail what this 'rightness' is; here there will be different theories, different ways of thinking about this rightness. I would take it to be rightness with respect to our cognitive design plan;[19] but perhaps we don't need to settle on a particular theory here. The basic idea is just that a belief is justified for me if with respect to my evidence it is the or a right thing to believe. And here *evidence* will include propositional evidence—the rest of what I know or believe— but also *non-propositional* evidence. I look into my backyard; I am appeared

---

[18] Of course epistemic probability so construed will not conform to the probability calculus. As we've already seen, the epistemic probability of a necessary proposition need not be 1. Another important theorem of the probability calculus is that the logical consequences of a proposition are as least as probable as the proposition itself; this too fails for epistemic probability. For example, some axiomatic formulation of arithmetic might be such that it has a high degree of epistemic probability for me: each of the axioms appears to be self-evident. These axioms, however, will entail theorems that have little by way of epistemic probability for me; perhaps Paul playfully (and falsely) tells me they really aren't theorems, or perhaps there is no proof of them simple enough for me to follow.

[19] See WPF, chapter 1 and see chapter 9 for further details, and also for an explanation of epistemic probability.

to in a certain way; I form the belief that there is a foot or more of snow on the ground. Here part of my evidence is the way things look to me. With respect to non-contingent propositions, what will be relevant will be whether the proposition in question has that peculiar and hard to explain quality of self-evidence—whether it has that "luminous glow," that obvious appearance of truth Locke thought a self-evident proposition has when held before an attentive mind. But a non-contingent proposition could also be justified for me if I could see that it followed from other propositions that are justified for me. We could spend more time here trying to get a fuller and better characterization of justification in this sense; but perhaps that's not necessary for consideration of Tooley's evidential argument. Perhaps we can work with our more intuitive grasp of justification.

II   Tooley's Arguments

Tooley's argument is complex and many-sided. I'll consider, first, his argument for the conclusion that the default position is atheism, second his argument for the conclusion that it is more likely than not that there is a state of affairs—the Lisbon earthquake—with respect to which it is likely—more probable than not—that G is false, and finally his attempt to go beyond this to the conclusion that it is very unlikely that G is true.

A.   Is atheism the default position?

Tooley argues that the default position here is atheism; in the absence of any evidence for or against theism (G), the right or rational position is atheism. His conclusion is that "in the absence of a satisfactory defense of either of these possibilities [i.e., that there is positive evidence for G, or that G is non-inferentially justified], the conclusion of the present argument will stand, and atheism will be the epistemically rational position" (p. 93). In my opening statement, I argued that the proper position here, for the theist, is that belief in God *is* non-inferentially justified—i.e., that there is powerful non-propositional evidence or grounds for the existence of God. The sensible thing for a theist to think is that there is what Aquinas calls a natural knowledge of God, or something like what John Calvin called a "*Sensus divinitatis.*" This would be a cognitive faculty or process, built into us by God, that delivers beliefs about God under a wide variety of circumstances. The natural thing for a Christian to think is that there is also something like what Aquinas calls the "internal instigation of the Holy Spirit" or what Calvin calls the "Internal Testimony of the Holy Spirit." This would be a cognitive faculty or process whereby

God gets us to see the truth of the great things of the gospel, the central tenets of Christianity.[20] So of course I believe that there is positive evidence—non-propositional evidence—for the existence of God, just as there is for external objects, other minds, and the past.

The present question, however, is this: setting aside such non-propositional evidence or grounds (pretending for the moment it doesn't exist), and also setting aside any evidence, propositional or non-propositional, against G, what would be the probability of G? We are presumably thinking of logical probability here; and since we are abstracting from all evidence (propositional or non-propositional), we are thinking of *intrinsic* probability. The question is: what is the intrinsic probability of G? In what proportion of the space of possible worlds is G true? Here Tooley reasons as follows: the intrinsic probability of

(4) There is an omniscient, omnipotent, and wholly evil being

is as high as that of

(5) There is an omniscient, omnipotent, and morally indifferent being;

and each of these is at least as intrinsically probable as G. But then, assuming as he does that there couldn't be two omnipotent beings, at most one of these propositions can be true, in which case the probability of G can't be more than one third.

Tooley toys with the idea that the intrinsic probability of G is much lower: for any degree *d* of goodness (or badness), couldn't there be an omnipotent and omniscient being who displays that degree of goodness (badness)? But he doesn't endorse this conclusion. And he thinks the fact, as he sees it, that the intrinsic probability of G is no more than a third is sufficient for his conclusion—i.e., that *atheism*, not theism or agnosticism, is the rational position, given that there is no evidence, propositional or otherwise, for belief in God. But why think a thing like that? Why wouldn't agnosticism be perfectly rational? There are many propositions *P*, and many existential propositions *P*, where we have no positive evidence for *P* and where the intrinsic probability of *P* is no greater than one third, and where we don't believe not-*P*: we just fail to believe *P*. To turn to one of Tooley's examples, I suppose most of us would think the intrinsic probability of there being living creatures on a planet circling Alpha Centauri is less than one third; we have no positive evidence that

---

[20] See WCB, chapters 8 and 9.

there are living creatures there. But surely agnosticism with respect to such creatures is perfectly rational and appropriate; we aren't obliged by rationality to believe that there *aren't* any such creatures. Why think it's atheism, rather than agnosticism, that is in this sense the default position?

But the real problem here lies in a different direction. First, the classical theist thinks G is necessarily true, because she thinks it's necessary that God exists, and necessary that he is omniscient, omnipotent, and perfectly good. But the intrinsic probability of any necessary proposition is 1; hence the intrinsic probability of G is 1. (4) and (5), however, are incompatible with G; hence there is no possible world in which they are true, so that their intrinsic probability is 0. So the classical theist won't agree for a moment that (4) and (5) are as intrinsically probable as G. Tooley's argument presupposes what the theist denies, namely, that G is contingent.

Tooley may have an effective reply here. For *why* does the theist think G is necessarily true? Perhaps she thinks as follows. What the *sensus divinitatis* delivers is the proposition that there is a being who is the creator of the world, to whom we owe obedience, worship, and adoration. This being, furthermore, is wholly good. Further, this being is unimaginably great, the greatest being in the universe. Still further: not only is he the greatest being there *is*, he is such that there *couldn't be* a greater being; he is therefore a being than which it isn't possible that there be a greater. But such a being would have the properties of goodness, omniscience, and omnipotence *essentially*: this being could not have turned out evil, or stupid, or powerless. And finally, such a being would be necessarily existent; maximal greatness requires that this being doesn't, so to speak, *just happen* to exist, but rather *could not have failed* to exist. Maximal greatness requires maximal excellence in every possible world, which requires existence in every possible world.

Suppose this is the epistemic route the theist takes to the proposition that God is a necessary being who has these properties essentially; it is important to see that this epistemic route depends essentially on the *sensus divinitatis*. But the *sensus divinitatis* is (non-propositional) evidence for the existence of God. Therefore the theistic claim that the intrinsic probability of G is 1 is not really independent of the evidence; it depends on the deliverances of the *sensus divinitatis*. But Tooley has been arguing for a certain conclusion about the probability of G, bracketing or setting aside *all* evidence, propositional or otherwise, for G. So the fact that the theist thinks G is necessary isn't really relevant to Tooley's claim here.

Right; let's accept that, at least for present purposes. But let's look more carefully at (4), (5), and G. Why does Tooley think the logical probability of G is no greater than that of either (4) or (5)? This is a quite substantial claim. We are thinking about the space of possible worlds; Tooley's claim is that the space occupied by worlds in which (4) is true, and the space occupied by worlds in which (5) is true, are each at least as large as the space occupied by worlds in which G is true. But what is the source of our information here? Tooley puts it like this: "the basic strategy involves finding possible entities whose existence is logically incompatible with the existence of an omnipotent, omniscient and morally perfect person, and whose *a priori* probability of existing can plausibly be equated with the *a priori* probability of an omnipotent, omniscient, and morally perfect person" (p. 89). "*A priori* probability," I take it, is intrinsic probability. And Tooley's strategy is to find possible entities whose existence is logically incompatible with G, and such that their intrinsic probability, the intrinsic probability of the existence of such a being, "can plausibly be equated" with that of G.

Well, I suppose it isn't particularly *im*plausible to equate the intrinsic probability of (4) (or (5)) with that of G. But that's about all, it seems to me, we can sensibly say here. Many propositions are such that we have a pretty good grasp of their modal status.

(6) All equilateral triangles are equiangular,

for example, is clearly necessary, true in all possible worlds; and we can see that this is so just by thinking about it. There are many other propositions, however, which are such that we have *some* grasp of their modal status, but not nearly as strong a grasp as we do of the modal status of (6); an example would be the proposition that existentialism (above, p. 161) is false. And still others are such that we can't really tell much about their modal status at all just by thinking about or entertaining them. Many propositions involving intrinsic probability are like this. What is the intrinsic probability that Paul is jogging right now? What proportion of logical space is occupied by worlds in which that proposition is true? What is the intrinsic probability that there is life on a planet revolving around Arcturus? Is the former probability greater than the latter? Or equal to the latter, or smaller? It's not at all easy to say.

The same goes, I think, for (4) and (5), on the one hand, and G, on the other. Perhaps G is necessarily true, as theists think; then its intrinsic probability is 1 and that of (4) and (5) is 0. Perhaps, on the other hand (setting aside the deliverances of the *Sensus Divinitatis*), G is contingent, but still enjoys more by way of intrinsic probability than either (4) or (5). Or perhaps they all enjoy the same intrinsic probability. How can we possibly tell? How can we possibly tell that these intrinsic probabilities are equal? The most one can say here, I think, is that, just by this sort of reflection, and setting aside any sort of evidence, including non-propositional evidence for the existence of God, *we can't see any difference* with respect to the intrinsic probabilities of G and (4) (or (5)). Hence, perhaps, it is not implausible to claim that these probabilities are the same.

But *failing to see a difference* here is a far cry from *seeing that there is no difference*. Consider propositions

(6) All equilateral triangles are equiangular

and

(7) If all men are mortal and Socrates is a man, then Socrates is mortal.

Here we fail to see a difference between their intrinsic probabilities; in addition, however, we see that there is no difference, because we see that these probabilities are both equal to 1. But the same doesn't go, I suggest, for

(8) The population of China is greater that one billion

and

(9) The population of the United States is less than one billion.

Perhaps we can't see a difference in the intrinsic probabilities of these two propositions, but it doesn't follow at all that we see that they are equiprobable. And the fact is, I think, we don't see that they *are* equiprobable; the most we can say is that we *don't* see that they *aren't*.

The same holds, I suggest, for G and (4) (and (5)). True; we can't see a difference between their intrinsic probabilities; but it doesn't follow that we do see that they are equiprobable. I say we don't; we only fail to see that they aren't.

Tooley's argument here can be paralleled, I think, by another argument with a conclusion inconsistent with his. Consider the propositions

(10) There is no omniscient, omnipotent, and perfectly good person.
(11) There is an omniscient, omnipotent and perfectly good person who has created fewer than 1000 persons,

and

(12) There is an omniscient, omnipotent, and perfectly good person who has created more than 1000 persons.

As far as I can see, the relation among (10), (11), and (12) is just like that between G, (4), and (5). Setting aside any evidence dependent on the *Sensus Divinitatis*, one can't see, I submit, any difference between the intrinsic probabilities of (10) and (11); (11) looks as probable as (10). Now as far as I can see, the only reason for thinking that (4) is as probable, intrinsically, as G is just that one can't see a difference in their probabilities. But then we have the same reason for thinking (11) as probable as (10); here too we can't see any difference in their probabilities. And the same goes for (12) and (10); once again, we can't see any difference in their probabilities, and hence have the same reason for thinking (12) as likely as (10), as we have for thinking (5) as likely as G. But of course if each of (11) and (12) is as probable, intrinsically, as (10), then the intrinsic probability of (10) can't exceed 1/3, in which case G, its denial, has an intrinsic probability at least as great as 2/3. But then we've got as good reason for thinking that the default position is theism as for thinking that it is atheism.

Now I don't mean to argue that the default position is in fact theism; I mean to argue only that there is as good a reason to think it is theism as to think it is atheism: in which case there isn't good reason to think it's atheism. Hence I have a two-fold response to Tooley's argument for the conclusion that the default position with respect to the question of the truth of G is atheism. First, even if this conclusion is true, it isn't very significant; the real question here is whether there is non-propositional evidence for G. And second, there isn't any reason to think that conclusion *is* true; we don't really have *a priori* insight into the relevant intrinsic probabilities, and there is just as good an argument for the claim that G is the default position here as for the claim that atheism is. The most we can sensibly say is that we can't see that the intrinsic probability of G exceeds that of either (4) or (5); but that's nowhere near having a reason for believing that the intrinsic probability of G does not exceed that of (4) and (5).

B. *Tooley's argument for the improbability of G on evil*

How exactly does this argument go? Tooley first presents a long and detailed catalogue of the ills the world contains. Some of these are perhaps a bit strained—is it really a problem that intense pleasure is associated with sexual activity, or that we aren't supermen and -women, created out of some more durable material? Still, it's undeniable that the world certainly contains a great deal of pain, misery, and suffering. Now Tooley thinks a concrete formulation of the argument will be better than an abstract formulation. In presenting his argument (p. 116ff.), therefore, he narrows his focus to one particular example of evil: the Lisbon earthquake. He aims to show that, probably, an omniscient, omnipotent, and perfectly good being could not permit the Lisbon earthquake to occur; since it *did* occur, it is unlikely that G is true.

Tooley's argument is complex and detailed. It contains some nine premises, together with inferences from those premises; I'll concentrate my comments on just two of the nine premises. He proposes that the action of permitting the Lisbon earthquake, an action that God has performed if there is such a person as God, "has a very serious wrongmaking property"; he then adds, as a premise of his argument:

(15) No rightmaking properties that we know of are such that we are justified in believing both that an action of choosing not to prevent the Lisbon earthquake would have had those rightmaking properties, and that those properties are sufficiently serious to counterbalance the relevant wrongmaking property. (p. 119)

The next step of the argument is to claim that

(16) For any action whatever, the logical probability that the total wrongmaking properties of the action outweigh the total rightmaking properties—including ones of which we have no knowledge—given that the action has a wrongmaking property that we know of, and there are no rightmaking properties that are known to be counterbalancing, is greater than one half. (p. 120)

(Here Tooley uses the phrase "there are no rightmaking properties that are known to be counterbalancing" as an abbreviation for "there are no rightmaking properties that we know of such that we are justified in believing both that the action in question has those rightmaking properties, and those properties are sufficiently serious to counterbalance any relevant, known, wrongmaking property (or properties)"). These are the two premises of the argument on which I wish to comment.

Consider (15). As Tooley says, "Statement (15) makes a claim that would be challenged by philosophers who respond to the evidential argument from evil by offering a theodicy" (p. 122). Right. It would also be challenged by philosophers (and others) who don't offer a theodicy, but think those who do are justified in so doing. And it would also be challenged by those who don't offer a theodicy, but believe that in fact God has a good reason for permitting this state of affairs, even if we don't know what this good reason is. Still further, Christians and other theists believe that God exists and is a perfectly good being. If this is true, then any action God has in fact performed has the property of having been performed by a perfectly good being. Furthermore, Christians and other theists believe that God performed the action of permitting the Lisbon earthquake. They therefore believe that the action of permitting the Lisbon earthquake has the property of having been performed by God, who is a perfectly good person. This is a rightmaking property that clearly outweighs and counterbalances any wrongmaking properties that action has. But then there is a rightmaking property we know of (i.e., *being performed by a perfectly good person*) such that Christians and other theists believe both (1) that the action of permitting the Lisbon earthquake had that property, and (2) that the property in question is sufficiently serious to counterbalance the relevant wrongmaking property. Still further, Christians believe (or would believe if they thought about it) that they are *justified* in believing these things. One who thinks like this (as I do) will therefore think (15) is false.

You may be inclined to object that in objecting to (15) in this way I am just *assuming* that belief in God is justified; hence in this context my objection begs the question at issue. But is this really true? I'm not proposing an argument at all; I'm simply saying why I and others don't believe (15). It's rather Tooley who is presenting an argument, and presenting (15) as a premise of that argument. The fact is that Tooley's premise presupposes that belief in God is *not* justified. So is there any good reason to believe (15)? If there are good arguments for the existence of God, arguments that justify theists in believing in God, then (15) is false. But there may also be a non-argumentative route to justified belief in God: for example, perhaps one can be non-inferentially justified in believing in God by way of religious experience. If so, then too (15) will be false. Another possibility: if we human beings have been created by God with a faculty or cognitive process by virtue of which we can be justified in believing G, then, once more, (15) will be false. The real question here is whether there are these sources of justification for theistic belief; Tooley's (15) presupposes that there aren't any such sources of justification for belief in God.

But perhaps Tooley will reply that he proposes, at present, to abstract from any other sources of justification, inferential or non-inferential, for G or its denial. We are setting aside any such sources of justification; the aim is to show that *if* there aren't any such sources of justification, then G is not justified; and Tooley will argue later that in fact there aren't any such sources of justification. So suppose we bracket any inferential or non-inferential sources of justification for G: will (15) be true from that perspective? If there weren't any such sources of justification for G, would (15) be true? I'm inclined to think so (of course I also believe that there *are* some sources of justification for theistic belief). In the present context, then, we can concede (15) to Tooley: if there aren't any inferential or non-inferential sources of justification for belief in God, then probably (15) is true.

Suppose we turn, therefore, to the second crucial premise: (16) (above, p. 120). Is it true, as (16) asserts, that for any action whatever, the logical probability that the total wrongmaking properties of the action outweigh the total rightmaking properties—including ones of which we have no knowledge—given that the action has a wrongmaking property that we know of, and there are no rightmaking properties that are known[21] to be counterbalancing, is greater than one half? As Tooley says (p. 120), this premise is very controversial. For example, anyone who thinks that belief in God is justified—either properly basic, or such that there are justifying arguments for it—will deny that the action of choosing to permit the Lisbon earthquake has a wrongmaking property we know of such that there are no rightmaking properties known (or justifiedly believed) to be counterbalancing. But we are for the moment abstracting away from any other sources of justification, inferential or non-inferential, for G or its denial. So from that perspective: what should we say about (16)? Is it true?

I certainly can't see that it is; let me explain why. In arguing for (16), Tooley makes several claims, claims that are premises in his arguments for (16) (p. 120). Here is the second such claim:

> (2) Judged from a purely *a priori* point of view, the *likelihood* that there exists a rightmaking property with a moral weight whose absolute value is equal to M is no greater than the likelihood that there exists a wrongmaking property whose absolute value is equal to M. (p. 127)

(16) speaks of logical probability; the likelihood (2) speaks of, therefore, must be presumably logical probability. Further, the logical probability in question is presumably *intrinsic* probability. Another way to put (2), therefore, is:

> (2*) Judged from a purely *a priori* point of view, for any moral weight M, the intrinsic logical probability of the existence of a wrongmaking property with moral weight $-M$ is as great as the intrinsic probability of the existence of a rightmaking property whose moral weight is M.

But is there any reason to believe that? Why couldn't there be moral weights M such that there are rightmaking properties that have M but no wrongmaking properties that have $-M$? Why couldn't there be moral weights M^* such that there are wrongmaking properties that have $-M^*$ but no rightmaking properties that have M^*? I can't see the slightest reason to think there aren't such moral weights. Of course I also can't see the slightest reason to think there *are* such weights; here, it seems to me, we simply don't have anything to go on. I would therefore suggest that the right epistemic attitude to take to (2) is agnosticism. Since we have no way to tell whether it is true, we shouldn't believe it, and also shouldn't believe its denial. But then an argument that employs (2) as a premise

---

[21] Or (from Tooley's perspective somewhat better) *justifiedly believed.*

won't be a good argument; (2) has about the same degree of epistemic probability as its denial. And the same considerations apply, I think, to (1) and (3).

In (4), Tooley presents still another premise in his argument for (16). He begins by asking whether we

> know, for example, that there are more rightmaking *properties* (not: instances of rightmaking properties) than wrongmaking properties? Or do we know that rightmaking properties are typically more weighty than wrongmaking properties? Or do we know that wrongmaking properties are more likely to be connected to rightmaking properties than to other wrongmaking properties? (p. 128, Tooley's emphasis).

He replies, rightly, in my opinion, that we don't know any of these things: "I do not believe that the moral knowledge that we have supports affirmative answers to any of these three questions." Fair enough. But then he goes on to say, "*So* I suggest that, judged from an *a posteriori* point of view, first the existence of wrongmaking properties is no less likely than the existence of rightmaking properties, secondly, wrongmaking properties are not likely to have less moral weight than rightmaking properties; and, thirdly . . ." (p. 128, my emphasis). But why the "*So*"? As he suggests, the moral knowledge that we have doesn't support affirmative answers to any of these three questions; but of course it doesn't follow for a moment that it supports *negative* answers to them. I'd say that it doesn't support either affirmative *or* negative answers to these questions: we really don't have any way of telling whether the right answer to these questions is affirmative or negative.

Tooley goes on to propose what he calls *The Symmetry Principle with Respect to Unknown, Rightmaking and Wrongmaking Properties* (p. 129) and says that it seems plausible. Well, I'd certainly concede that it doesn't seem particularly *im*plausible; but of course that's not at all the same as its seeming plausible. I can't see how we could have any reason at all for thinking it true—or, for that matter, for thinking it false. How would we know?

In short, when Tooley affirms his conclusion

> (C₁) If *A* is an action that, judged by known rightmaking and wrongmaking properties, is *prima facie* very seriously wrong, then the probability that action *A* is morally wrong, all relevant rightmaking and wrongmaking properties considered, both known and unknown, is greater than one half (p. 130),

the right answer, I think, is that (abstracting from any evidence, inferential or noninferential, for G) C_1 might be true and it might be false; we don't have any way of telling. The right attitude, here, is abstention, withholding belief.

But this means that Tooley's argument from evil doesn't succeed. It doesn't succeed in showing that (abstracting from whatever justifying evidence there is for G) the logical probability of G on the occurrence of the Lisbon earthquake is less than 1/2.

III   The Justification of Theistic Belief

But suppose Tooley's argument were successful; suppose the probability of G on E is in fact low, very low. As I argued above, that wouldn't show for a moment that belief in God is unjustified. What it would show is that we believe some-thing—E—such that the probability of G on that belief is low—perhaps as low as 1 out of a billion, as Tooley suggests (pp. 141–2). But of course there are many pairs of propositions P and Q, such that we (justifiably) believe P, the probability of Q on P is very low—less than 1 out of a billion, say—but are still perfectly justified in believing Q. We play a hand of bridge: the probability that the four of us should be dealt just the hands we *are* dealt is very low—in the neighbor-hood of 1 out of 10 to the 28th. This is vastly less than one out of a billion—it is about 1 out of 10 billion billion billion. Yet when we lay out the cards and take a look at them, we are entirely justified in thinking that this deal did in fact occur. And of course the reason is that we *perceive* that it occurred. Probabilities get swamped by the deliverances of a faculty-like perception. And the same goes for belief in God; if there is a faculty like Calvin's *sensus divinitatis* or Aquinas's internal instigation of the Holy Spirit, then belief in God may be perfectly justi-fied even if it is very improbable on E. So is belief in God justified?

First, a bit about justification. As I said (above, p. 161), we can't sensibly tie justification to logical probability in the way Tooley does; for then all neces-sary propositions are automatically justified for those who believe them, even if their beliefs are acquired in totally inappropriate and pathological ways and involve a totally inappropriate response to their evidence. So how should we think about justification? What does it amount to?

Most contemporary philosophers who think about justification locate it in the neighborhood of *evidence* and *epistemic responsibility*.[22] A belief is justified if it is appropriately related to the believer's evidence—where the appropriate relation involves something like one's belief's being formed responsibly in the light of the available evidence. Justfication has to do with believing responsibly, given one's evidence. Thus a belief may be justified, even if it is false, and in fact overwhelmingly false. Suppose I believe the universe is only 8000 years old. If I have been taught this since birth, and never encountered any reason to doubt it, then I am justified in that belief, even if the universe is in fact some 4 billion years old (or, for that matter, infinitely old). I believe the earth is flat; again, if I have been taught this since birth and encountered no reason to doubt

[22] See my *Warrant: the Current Debate* (New York: Oxford University Press, 1993).

it, I am justified in so believing, even if the earth is in fact the shape of an oblate spheroid. Suppose I am a brain in a vat or a victim of a Cartesian evil demon, and my beliefs are for the most part wildly false; I may still be justified in holding them. The reason, of course, is that in each of these cases my belief fits, is appropriate to, my evidence—even though that evidence may be monumentally misleading, so that I believe what is false. My memory suddenly and unbeknownst to me starts malfunctioning; I 'remember' things that never happened. Still, I am justified in thinking those things did happen, if I have no reason to think my memory is malfunctioning, and no reason to think those things didn't happen. And again, the reason is that my belief is appropriate to my evidence, even though my evidence is seriously misleading. In this way justification has an 'internal' aspect; what determines my degree of justification in believing *p* is not first of all whether *p* is true, or produced by reliable or properly functioning cognitive faculties, but whether it fits my evidence; and my evidence is something internal to me, something about my own cognitive condition.

What, more exactly, is 'my evidence'? Evidence comes in several varieties. Suppose I believe that the grass in my backyard is covered with snow. My evidence could be that you, who are house-sitting while I am lolling on the beach in Hawaii, tell me so. Or perhaps my evidence just is that it's the third week in January, and my backyard is always covered with snow then. Or perhaps I am looking out the window and see that it's covered with snow. What is common to all these forms of evidence, I suggest, is *an inclination to believe* the proposition in question: that proposition just seems true, appropriate, the right thing to believe. This holds for *a posteriori* beliefs like the one in question; it also holds for such *a priori* beliefs as *2 + 1 = 3*, or *25 × 5 = 125*, or *there aren't any things that don't exist*, or *justification has to do with appropriate responses to evidence*. We can appropriately call this seeming right, this inclination to believe, 'doxastic evidence.'

But responsible reaction to doxastic evidence isn't the relevant sense of 'justification' in this context. That is because it is entirely clear that belief in God does indeed seem right, true, appropriate, to very many people, evil or no evil. For many believers in God, the doxastic evidence for belief in God is very strong. And if the doxastic evidence for a certain proposition *is* very strong—if that proposition seems wholly obvious to me even after extensive reflection—could I sensibly be accused of epistemic irresponsibility in believing it? I might be seriously misled; I might even be a brain in a vat or a victim of a Cartesian demon; but can I be irresponsible in believing what seems obviously true, even after extensive reflection? It's hard to see how. It's also hard to see how Tooley's argument from evil could show that belief in God is unjustified, in this sense of justification. For again, if someone's doxastic evidence strongly supports belief in God, even after reflection on evil, then it seems that person is justified in that belief, whatever be the facts about God and evil. (Of course Tooley's argument might be relevant by way of *changing* someone's doxastic evidence, getting them to be inclined to believe, perhaps, that G is false.) The fact is this sense of justification is too internalistic for Tooley's purposes. He needs a conception of justification that is more attuned to truth and falsehood, or to the probability of truth or falsehood. What's needed is a conception of justification that implies, not just that a justified belief has been formed appropriately in response to the doxastic evidence, but also that the doxastic evidence itself is not seriously misleading.

There are several possibilities for such a conception; I would myself try to explain it in terms of proper function.[23] What is clear, here, I think, is this: any appropriate conception of justification (any conception appropriate for Tooley's project) will have to be such that the deliverances of properly functioning, truth-aimed cognitive faculties will be justified. Thus, for example, the deliverances of perception will be justified. This will mean more than just that those who form perceptual beliefs are not being irresponsible in forming those beliefs, given the doxastic evidence (i.e., given that these perceptual beliefs have that property of seeming to be true, of being the right thing to believe); some other condition will have to be met as well.

What condition? Perhaps here we can make use of something Tooley says about epistemic probability. He proposes that a direct realist will need to incorporate the "idea of 'foundational' probability—where the probability that a proposition that one is non-inferentially justified in believing is independent of its relations to any other propositions" (p. 77). Perhaps we could put this idea (or one in the near neighborhood) as follows. We can think of the underlying experiential basis states as involving the ways in which one is appeared to—in perception, that familiar perceptual imagery. But it will also include the doxastic evidence I mentioned above—those *seemings*: for example, its seeming to me, upon being appeared to in the relevant way, that my backyard is covered with snow. Now we can't say that a non-inferential belief is justified if and only if it is sufficiently probable with respect to experience (taking that to include both the phenomenal imagery and the doxastic evidence); for then, once more, necessary beliefs will all be automatically justified. But we can instead speak of the probability that a belief should be true, *given that it is produced by this process*. What is the probability that a belief is true, given that I have such and such doxastic evidence for it? We can also make this a bit more general: what is the probability that a belief is true, given that it is produced by a particular member of my array of cognitive faculties or processes? For example, what is the probability that a belief is true, given that it is produced by my perceptual faculties, or a more specific such faculty such as vision, or hearing? Perhaps we can say that a belief is justified, for me, if (1) it is a responsible and appropriate response to my evidence, and (2) it is produced by a cognitive faculty or process that is reliable—i.e., one that produces a sufficient preponderance of true over false beliefs in this and nearby possible worlds.

---

[23] Perhaps by equating justification with rationality, and explaining that as in *Warrant and Proper Function*.

The important question, for the justification of G, therefore, is whether there are in fact one or more reliable faculties or epistemic processes that yields belief in God. For if there is, then even if G is improbable on E in the way Tooley suggests, belief in God can be completely justified. In my initial statement I argued that if Christian belief is true, then very likely it has warrant, that property or quantity enough of which is sufficient, together with truth, for a belief's constituting knowledge. But I think we can see in the very same way that if Christian belief is true, then very likely it is justified in the current sense.

Justification, as we are presently thinking of it, involves two elements. First, a belief is justified only if it is a responsible and appropriate response to the evidence—in particular the doxastic evidence. And second, to be justified, the belief must be produced by one or more reliable faculties or belief-producing processes. The first condition, as I've argued, is often met. But if the main elements of Christian belief are true, then so, in all probability, is the second. For if such belief is true, then, first, there is such a person as God; second, we human beings have fallen into sin and need to be restored to a condition of fellowship with God, to be reconciled with him; the means to such a reconciliation has been provided by the incarnation, suffering, death, and resurrection of the Son of God, the second person of the Trinity. Furthermore, the typical or favored way of appropriating this reconciliation, of coming to have it, is by way of faith, which involves belief in the great things of the gospel. But then of course God would intend that we human beings can be aware of these things. There are cognitive faculties or processes that produce belief in these things in those who hold them; the natural thing to think, therefore, is that these faculties or processes have been created in us by God in order for us to be able to know these things. Furthermore, these processes, presumably, would be reliable: they produce belief in the great things of the gospel, which are in fact true, and do so in nearby possible worlds as well as the actual world.

If Christian belief is true, therefore, both of the conditions for its justification are (in all likelihood) easily met. And the important thing to see here, I think, is that there is no way to answer this question—the question whether belief in God is justified—without first answering the question whether Christian belief is true. If it is, then in all probability belief in God is often justified.

IV   Is Evil a Defeater for Belief in God?[24]

I've argued so far that if Christian belief is true, then theistic belief is probably justified for many who hold it. Perhaps the thing to say is that if Christian belief is true, then it is *prima facie* justified for many who hold it—justified in

[24]This section substantially follows but abbreviates WCB, pp. 481–9; for a fuller presentation see those pages.

the absence of *defeaters*. But of course there can be defeaters for justification, just as for rationality and warrant. We needn't spend a lot of time figuring out precisely what a justification defeater is; roughly speaking, a belief *B* of mine has its justification defeated when I acquire a new belief *B** such that as long as I hold *B**, I am not justified in accepting *B*. We must therefore ask the following question: does the existence of the Lisbon earthquake, or other evils that I know of, constitute a defeater for my belief in God? Is it the case that as long as I believe that these evils occur, I'm not justified in also believing G? I don't have the space to go into this question in the depth and detail it deserves;[25] I believe that the answer is *No*; evil does not constitute a defeater for theistic belief. But what sort of argument could be developed for the claim that evil really was a defeater for Christian or theistic belief?

First, I think it is fairly clear that atheological arguments from evil don't provide such defeaters. Tooley's argument is subtle, detailed, and sophisticated; nevertheless, if my argument above is correct, it fails. The same goes for other atheological evidential arguments: William Rowe's, for example, and Paul Draper's.[26] Is there a better way to put the atheological argument from suffering and evil? I believe there is, although I don't have the space here to lay it out in detail.[27] I've argued that if theism is true, if there is such a person as God, then belief in God will probably be justified by virtue of some such epistemic process as Calvin's *sensus divinitatis*, or Thomas Aquinas's internal instigation of the Holy Spirit. But why can't the atheologian turn the tables here? Maybe no formulation of an evidential argument against theism carries much force or conviction; but perhaps no such argument is needed; perhaps atheism is non-inferentially justified. Knowledge and appreciation of some of the horrifying evils the world displays will defeat the *prima-facie* justification (if any) enjoyed by theism for any appropriately sensitive and sympathetic person—not by way of an argument, but non-inferentially.

Dostoevsky's classic depiction in *The Brothers Karamazov* is fictional, but no less convincing and no less disturbing:

> "A Bulgarian I met lately in Moscow," Ivan went on, seeming not to hear his brothers words, "told me about the crimes committed by Turks and Circassians in all parts of Bulgaria through fear of a general rising of the Slavs. They burn villages, murder, outrage women and children, they nail their prisoners by the ears to the fences, leave them so till morning, and in the morning they hang them—all sorts of things you can't imagine. People talk sometimes of bestial cruelty, but that's a great injustice and insult to the beasts: a beast can never be so cruel as

---

[25] For a much fuller treatment, see WCB, chapter 14.
[26] See WCB, pp. 465-81.
[27] For that, see WCB, Chapter 14, section II "Nonargumentative Defeaters" pp. 481-484,

a man, so artistically cruel. The tiger only tears and gnaws, that's all he can do. He would never think of nailing people by the ears, even if he were able to do it. These Turks took a pleasure in torturing children, too; cutting the unborn child from the mother's womb, and tossing babies up in the air and catching them on the points of their bayonets before their mother's eyes. Doing it before the mother's eyes was what gave zest to the amusement."[28]

The list of atrocities human beings commit against others is horrifying; it is also so long, so repetitious, that it ends in being wearying. Occasionally, however, new depths are reached:

> A young Muslim mother in Bosnia was repeatedly raped in front of her husband and father, with her baby screaming on the floor beside her. When her tormentors seemed finally tired of her, she begged permission to nurse the child. In response, one of the rapists swiftly decapitated the baby and threw the head in the mother's lap.[29]

These things are absolutely horrifying; it is painful even to consider them, to bring them squarely before the mind. And our question, says the atheologian, is this: wouldn't a rational and sensitive person think, in the face of this kind of appalling evil, that there simply couldn't be a perfect being, an omnipotent, omniscient, and wholly good person, superintending our world? Perhaps we can't give a demonstration that no perfect person could permit these things; perhaps, also, there isn't a good probabilistic or evidential atheological argument either: but so what? Isn't it just apparent, just evident, that a perfect being couldn't permit things like that? Don't I have a defeater here even if there is no good antitheistic argument from evil? The claim, fundamentally, is that one who is properly sensitive and properly aware of the sheer horror and extent of suffering and evil our somber and unhappy world displays will simply see that no perfect being could possibly permit it. This would be a sort of inverse *sensus divinitatis*, so to speak: once you come to a real appreciation of the evils around us, the proper, rational response is to give up theistic belief. This kind of appeal will proceed, not by way of an argument, but by way of putting a person into the sort of situation where she can see the true horror of some of the world's evils. (And hence it has a certain consonance with Tooley's suggestion that a concrete, rather than abstract, formulation of the argument from evil is the proper way to go.) Indeed, from this perspective, an *argument* might be counterproductive, enabling the believer in God to turn his attention away from

---

[28] *The Brothers Karamazov*, trans. Constance Garnett (New York: Random House, 1933), pp. 245–6.
[29] Eleonore Stump, "The Mirror of Evil," in Thomas Morris (ed.) *God and the Philosophers* (New York: Oxford University Press, 1994), p. 239.

these evils, taking refuge in abstract discussion of probability functions, logical vs. epistemic probability, the nature of justification, etc. It diverts attention from the phenomena that in fact constitute defeaters for theistic belief.

This seems to me to be the strongest version of the atheological appeal to evil. Notice, of course, that defeat and defeaters are relative to noetic struc- ture, to the whole set of beliefs you have and the relations among them: what might be a defeater for a belief *B* for me need not be a defeater for *B* for you. And perhaps it is possible that under some conditions for some particu- lar distribution of belief (including belief in G) knowledge of these horrify- ing cases of evil would in fact constitute a defeater for G. Suppose someone believes in God in a sort of weak and perfunctory way; her belief is left over from childhood belief in God as a result of parental teaching, for example, but doesn't have (apart from what is involved in the childhood teaching) any sup- port, propositional or non-propositional. For such a person, perhaps a serious appreciation of the facts of evil will indeed constitute a defeater for her belief in God.[30] But of course there are other sorts of cases. Suppose we consider, on the other hand, someone whose cognitive faculties are functioning properly (from a Christian perspective); she believes in God by way of *sensus divinitatis*; this belief is supported and made more specific by the internal instigation of the Holy Spirit of which both Calvin and Aquinas speak. Her belief is for the most part firm and stable. Although, like other believers in God, she sometimes suffers through periods of dryness, when Christian belief seems lifeless, dull, etc., at other times it seems as obvious to her as that there are sun, moon, and stars. Will knowledge of the extent, duration, and distribution of suffering and evil constitute a defeater, for her, for theistic belief?

I should think not. She will certainly find herself appalled at some of the hor- rifying evils this world contains; she may also be deeply perplexed about God's role in permitting these evils. Faced with particularly dreadful suffering or evil in her own case or in the case of someone close to her, she may become angry with God, even furious. She realizes that God has good reasons for permitting these things to happen—after all, being God, he would, wouldn't he? But she may nonetheless deeply resent what she sees God as doing, hate what he's doing, and resent him as well. She realizes that all of this is for some wonderful end, some end God has in mind, an end probably beyond her ken; this need not put her at ease and she may remain angry and resentful. But she needn't even enter- tain for a moment the belief that there is no such person as God. As far as she's concerned, there certainly is such a person, and she's angry with him, or at the least deeply perplexed by what he is doing. But she's not at all inclined to give up belief in God. For such a person, the existence of evil, and of horrifying instances of it, doesn't even begin to provide her with a defeater for belief in God.

---

[30] But also perhaps not: see WCB, pp. 475–86.

Alternatively, she may initially suffer confusion and perplexity, perhaps grow angry with God; but then she reflects on the marvelous and overwhelming divine love revealed in the incarnation and atonement; she reflects on the fact, as she sees it, that God himself was willing to suffer and die on our behalf. This doesn't explain why God permits her suffering; it is crucially important nonetheless. She reads of one more horrifying atrocity; she is perhaps shaken. But then she calls to mind the inconceivably great love displayed in Christ's suffering and death, his willingness to empty himself and take on the nature of a servant, and his willingness to do this in order to make it possible for us, mired in sin as we are, to be reunited with God. She still can't imagine why God permits gigantic and horrifying upheavals such as Communism or the Third Reich with their many millions of victims; but she sees that God is willing to share in our suffering, and willing to undergo enormous suffering on our behalf. She isn't at all inclined to suspect that there isn't any such person as God; her response to her doxastic evidence is perfectly proper; if in addition Christian belief is true, so that her belief is produced by a reliable and properly functioning cognitive process, she doesn't have a defeater for her belief in God.

Some of these themes receive splendid expression in the book of Job. As the book opens, Satan challenges God to let him afflict Job; the latter, he says, is a sycophantic timeserver who will turn against God the minute he's made to suffer a bit. God then permits Satan to afflict Job. His friends Bildad the Shuhite, Eliphaz the Temanite, and Zophar the Naamathite come to comfort and console him. They tell him at great length and with considerable eloquence that the righteous always prosper and the wicked always come to grief; they conclude that Job must be wicked indeed to deserve such great suffering:

> Is it for your piety that he rebukes you and brings charges against you? Is not your wickedness great? Are not your sins endless? . . . you stripped men of their clothing, leaving them naked. You gave no water to the weary and you withheld food from the hungry, though you were a powerful man, owning land, an honored man, living on it. And you sent widows away empty-handed and broke the strength of the fatherless. That is why snares are all around you, why sudden peril terrifies you, why it is so dark you cannot see and why a flood of water covers you. (22:4–11)

They insist that Job must repent and mend his ways. Job himself knows that he isn't being singled out because he is especially sinful (and in the Prologue he is described as "blameless and upright") and is understandably annoyed:

> Doubtless you are the people, and wisdom will die with you! But I have a mind as well as you . . . . (12:1–3)
> Miserable comforters are you all! Will your long-winded speeches never end? (16:2, 3)

Job doesn't fear to speak his mind: he believes that he is innocent and undeserving of this suffering, and wants to go to court with God:

> Oh that I had someone to hear me! I sign now my defense [after a lengthy recital of his virtues]—let the Almighty answer me; let my accuser put his indictment in writing. Surely I would wear it on my shoulder, I would put it on like a crown. (31:35)

But when he realizes that God would be prosecuting attorney, judge, and jury all rolled up into one, he loses hope:

> If I say, "I will forget my complaint, I will change my expression, and smile," I still dread all my sufferings, for I know you will not hold me innocent. (9:27)

There are at least two ways to understand Job. On the one hand, it seems that his problem is intellectual: he can't see what reason God could have for permitting this suffering (or visiting it upon him); he infers that probably God doesn't *have* a reason. But the point is that Job's suffering comes to him for reasons entirely beyond his ken, reasons having to do with the relation between God and creatures he knows nothing about. When God replies to Job, he doesn't explain his reasons for permitting Job's suffering. Instead he attacks Job's unthinking assumption that if he, Job, can't see what God's reasons might be, then probably God doesn't have any reasons. He does this by pointing to the vast gulf between Job's knowledge and God's:

> Then the Lord answered Job out of the tempest: Who is this whose ignorant words darken counsel? Brace yourself and stand up like a man; I will ask questions and you shall answer. Where were you when I laid the earth's foundations? Tell me, if you know and understand! Who settled its dimensions? Surely you should know! Who stretched his measuring-line over it? On what do its supporting pillars rest? Who set its cornerstone in place, when the morning stars sang together and all the sons of God shouted for joy? . . . . Have you descended to the springs of the sea or walked in the unfathomable deep? Have the gates of death been revealed to you? Have you ever seen the doorkeepers of the place of darkness? Have you comprehended the vast expanse of the world? Come, tell me all this, if you know! Which is the way to the home of light and where does darkness dwell? And can you then take each to its appointed bound and escort it on its homeward path? Doubtless you know all this; for you were born already, so long is the span of your life! (38:1–7, 16–21)

Job can't see what God's reasons might be; he infers that probably God doesn't have any. God's reply, in essence, is that Job knows far too little to draw such a conclusion:

> All right, Job, if you're so smart, if you know so much, tell me about it! Tell me how the universe was created; tell me about the sons of God who shouted with

joy upon its creation! Of course you were there!" And then Job sees the point: "...
I have spoken of great things which I have not understood, things too wonderful
for me to know." (42:3)

Alternatively, we could understand Job like this. He doesn't really doubt that
God has good reasons for what he does or permits; after all, being omnipotent
and omniscient and all that great stuff, he would have good reasons, wouldn't
he? But Job simply hates what God is doing (or permitting) and becomes furious with God: "why do I have to suffer for those no doubt dandy ends of yours?
I detest and abhor it! These alleged 'reasons' of yours, whatever they are, are
completely inscrutable; why should I have to suffer for them? I don't give a
fig for your reasons, and I loathe what you are doing!" Here Job doesn't really
doubt that God has good reasons, but he doesn't care; he mistrusts God, is
wary of him and his no doubt magnificent aims and ends. He hates what these
aims and ends require of him; he feels like rebelling against God, telling him
off, telling him to go fly a (no doubt splendidly magnificent) kite. And then
when God comes to him in the whirlwind, the point is not really to convince
him that God has his reasons, but to quiet him, to still the storm in his soul, to
restore his trust in God. God does this by giving Job a glimpse of his greatness,
glory, beauty, and splendid goodness; the doubts and turmoil abate and once
more Job loves and trusts the Lord.

4

Reply to Plantinga's Opening Statement

Michael Tooley

In his opening statement, Professor Alvin Plantinga did not offer a direct defense of theism. Thus, although he has elsewhere defended the ontological argument in a very detailed way (1974b, chapter 10), and although he suggests, in a paper he refers to in his opening statement, that there are about two dozen or so "good arguments" for the existence of God, Plantinga did not advance any of those arguments here. In addition, although he mentioned the idea that belief in God is properly basic, he did not set out any defense of that claim. Plantinga's approach, instead, was to offer an indirect defense of theism by advancing three main arguments to show that naturalism is untenable. I shall attempt to show that all three arguments are open to decisive objections.

1. Plantinga's First Objection: Naturalism and the Concept of Function

Plantinga's first objection to naturalism turns upon the idea that naturalism cannot provide a satisfactory analysis of the concept of what it is to function properly, as applied to organisms, and he appeals to this contention, first, in connection with such concepts as health, sanity, and disease, and, secondly, in connection with the concept of knowledge. This gives rise to two arguments, the first of which is as follows:

(1) Naturalism cannot offer a satisfactory analysis of what it is for an organism to function properly.

(2) The concept of an organism's functioning properly cannot be analytically basic.

(3) The concepts of health, sanity, sickness, disease, and the like, involve the idea of an organism's functioning properly, since to be healthy is just to be functioning properly.

Therefore:

(4) If naturalism were true, concepts such as health, sanity, sickness, disease, and the like, would not apply to organisms at all.

In setting out this argument, Plantinga focuses almost entirely upon the first premise, and he attempts to show that no satisfactory naturalistic analysis has been found, either of the idea of the function of an organ or a system within an organism, or of the closely related idea of what it is for such things to be functioning properly. To show this, Plantinga's approach, both in his opening statement and in his book *Warrant and Proper Function* (1993b, chapter 11), is to examine a number of accounts that have been offered of what it is for something to have a function, or for something to function properly, and among the accounts that he considers are the following. First, there is an account mentioned by John Pollock (1987), where the key idea is how something performs most frequently.[1] Secondly, there are accounts, advanced, for example, by Karen Neander (1991) and Ruth Millikan (1984, pp. 17–18), where the function of an organ is analyzed in terms of the evolutionary history of the organism. Thirdly, there is the type of account advanced by John Bigelow and Robert Pargetter (1987), according to which the function of an organ is a matter of the properties that contribute to the likelihood that the organism will survive.[2]

1.1 Response to argument 1

Plantinga's criticisms of many of the above accounts are incisive, and seem to me correct. I am not convinced, however, that the Bigelow/Pargetter account cannot be modified to avoid Plantinga's objections. But this is a complex matter that I shall not consider here, since I believe that the clearest error in Plantinga's argument lies in the third premise.

Imagine, then, a world where a deity has created intelligent beings very similar to humans, both physically and mentally, and where aging and a rather short life span are part of that deity's original design plan. Let John be such a being. Then parts of John will have functions in Plantinga's sense, specified by the design plan. Moreover, if the third premise of Plantinga's argument is correct,

---

[1] For Plantinga's criticisms of this approach, see 1993b, pp. 199–201.
[2] For Plantinga's criticisms of this type of account, see 1993b, pp. 204–9.

for John to be healthy will simply be for his parts to be functioning properly—that is, in accordance with the design plan—while if some of his parts are not thus functioning, John will be, to that extent, sick or injured.

A virus appears, and enters John's body, destroying a certain mechanism in the cells. If Plantinga's analysis of concepts such as health and sickness were correct, it would follow that John was now sick or injured. But suppose that what the virus has done is permanently to disable the cell mechanism responsible for aging, so that although John may die in many ways, he will never grow old and will never suffer the mental and physical deterioration involved in aging. Or suppose that the virus blocks the existence of brain states that give rise to intense and continuous pain associated with nerve damage, or unpleasant terminal illnesses. If the virus causes *these* changes, is John less healthy than he was? Is he now sick, or has he suffered an injury? The answer, surely, is that none of these things is the case. John is, on the contrary, much healthier than before. But parts of his body are not functioning properly—that is, in accordance with the divine design plan. The third premise of Plantinga's argument is, therefore, false: health cannot be analyzed as proper functioning, nor disease and injury as the absence of such functioning.

Another way of seeing that the concept of health is not to be analyzed in terms of an organism's functioning in accordance with a design plan is to consider organisms with a design plan that is, from the organism's point of view, a very unwelcome one. A variant on an example that Plantinga himself uses in criticizing accounts of the concept of function offered by Ruth Millikan and Michael Levin will serve to make the point quite effectively. Plantinga imagines that a "Hitler-like madman" changes some individuals so that "their visual field is a uniform shade of light green with little more than a few shadowy shapes projected on it," and that when they open their eyes to use them, "the result is constant pain." Plantinga contends that it would be "wrong (not to mention crazy)" to say that such an individual's visual system is functioning properly (p. 26) This is rather puzzling, because his own account seems to entail that such a visual system is functioning properly, since it is functioning in accordance with a design plan—albeit one that is a modification of an earlier and better one. But waiving that point, one can simply shift to a case of a deity who was a Hitler-like madman, and who created a plan for the human race that involved precisely this sort of visual system, along with other painful features. Then it would certainly be the case, on Plantinga's account, that such individuals were functioning *properly*, even though we surely would not describe them as *healthy*.

The moral is that terms such as "healthy" and "diseased" and "injured" are evaluative: a state of health is a state that is intrinsically *good* for the individual, while states of being diseased or injured are states that are intrinsically *bad* for the individual. Given a bad design plan, an individual can be functioning in accordance with that plan, but not be functioning in a way that is good for him, or he can be failing to function in accordance with the plan, and that may be good for him. The concepts of health and disease cannot be analyzed, accordingly, in terms of the notion of functioning in accordance with a design plan.

1.2   A brief response to argument 2

Plantinga's other argument here focuses on the concept of knowledge:

(1) Naturalism cannot offer a satisfactory analysis of what it is for an organism to function properly.

(2) The concept of an organism's functioning properly cannot be analytically basic.

(3) The concept of knowledge involves the idea of an organism's functioning properly.

Therefore:

(4) "[I]f naturalism were true, there would be no such thing as knowledge." (p. 19)

As with the first argument, I shall focus upon the third premise. A thorough consideration of that premise is not possible here, since Plantinga has, elsewhere, argued for his "proper function" analysis of the concept of knowledge at great length, and that, in turn, has led to a very extensive literature.[3] But I do want to set out, very briefly, reasons for rejecting his account.

Approaches to the concept of knowledge are either internalist accounts, which claim that a person who knows some proposition must have access to states of affairs, including other justified beliefs, that serve to justify the belief, or externalist accounts, which deny that access to justifying states of affairs is necessary for knowledge. Plantinga's account is an externalist account. To defend it, therefore, he needs to show that competing externalist accounts, and also internalist accounts, are unsound. He has not, I believe, done either of these things.

---

[3] For Plantinga's exposition and defense of his account of knowledge, see his books *Warrant: the Current Debate* (1993a) and *Warrant and Proper Function* (1993b); and for a number of first-rate critical essays on his approach, along with Plantinga's responses, see *Warrant in Contemporary Epistemology*, edited by Jonathan L. Kvanvig (1996).

First of all, and as Laurence BonJour (1996, p. 61) has argued, Plantinga's "proper function" account of warrant and knowledge has a deeply counterintuitive consequence. For consider three individuals—one created by God, another produced by evolution, and the third the product of an enormous accident in which molecules come together to produce a single cell that is structurally identical to a zygote. Those three individuals could be indistinguishable with respect to their intrinsic properties and also their external surroundings, at every point in their lives. On Plantinga's account of warrant and knowledge, it follows that while the first individual could know many things, the second and third could have *no knowledge at all*. No other version of externalism has this extremely implausible consequence.

Secondly, with regard to internalist accounts, and as a number of philosophers have argued in detail—including Richard Feldman (1996) and Laurence BonJour (1996)—although Plantinga criticizes internalist approaches to knowledge at great length in *Warrant: the Current Debate* (1993a), devoting almost all the book to this, his critique of internalism is not successful.

In the first place, Plantinga's whole framework, which centers on a concept that he introduces—namely, that of *warrant*, defined as whatever it is that distinguishes knowledge from mere true belief—is unsatisfactory. The reason is that the concept of warrant, as Plantinga defines it, is an amalgam of at least two *very* different factors that need to be clearly distinguished, the one a matter of the extent to which a belief is justified, regardless of whether it is true or false, and the other a matter of whatever must be added to justified true belief to generate an analysis of knowledge that avoids Gettier-type objections (Bonjour, 1996, p. 52).

In the second place, Plantinga's criticism of internalism involves at least two crucial errors. The first reflects the framework that he has adopted, since what he proceeds to do is to attribute to internalists an internalist account of *warrant*, whereas what internalists defend is an internalist account of *justification*, and, post-Gettier, internalists were well aware both that justified true belief was not sufficient for knowledge, and that the other factor that was needed, whatever it might be, would necessarily be externalist in nature.[4]

The second way in which Plantinga's criticism of internalism is unsound is that the cases that he uses to criticize internalist views, though more dramatic than standard Gettier-style cases, are in fact simply more general cases that show, not that justification is not an internal matter, but, rather, that knowledge requires the right sort of connection between what justifies the belief, and what makes the belief true. Any adequate response to the Gettier problem will, therefore, also block Plantinga's cases. The upshot is that such

---

[4]This point is made very forcefully by Feldman (1996), pp. 200–2.

cases are no objection at all to internalism, since they do not show that *justification*, in contrast to *warrant*, is not a purely internal matter.[5]

Finally, I believe that there are good reasons for holding, not only that Plantinga's criticisms of internalism are unsound, but, also, that there are very strong arguments in favor of internalism. But this is not something I can attempt to demonstrate here.[6]

Summing up, then, Plantinga's second argument involves an account of knowledge that rests upon unsound criticisms of internalist approaches to justification, and that has a deeply counterintuitive consequence, in virtue of which it is clearly inferior to both competing externalist and internalist accounts of knowledge. Not surprisingly, then, his account of knowledge has not commended itself to other prominent philosophers working in the area of epistemology.

2. Plantinga's Third Objection: Materialism and Belief

Rather than turning at this point to Plantinga's second argument against naturalism—where he contends that naturalism is not only self-defeating, but leads to skepticism—I want to look first at his third objection, in which he attempts to show that materialism entails that humans do not have beliefs. My reason is that there is an issue—concerning the relation between beliefs, in a strict sense, and representations, broadly understood—which is relevant to both arguments, but which is best addressed in the context of Plantinga's third argument, where it is absolutely central.

As Plantinga emphasizes, his third objection is not directed against all forms of naturalism; it applies only to materialistic naturalism, understood by him as the view that humans do not have immaterial minds. Plantinga's contention, then, is that unless naturalism is combined with substance dualism, it follows that humans do not have beliefs.

As is clear from his opening statement, Plantinga also holds that materialistic naturalism entails that humans do not have *experiences* either. However, he offered no argument in support of that contention. Had he done so, I would have responded to the argument, and I would also have argued, first, that a range of animals that presumably do not have immaterial minds have experiences; secondly, that there can be psychophysical laws linking brain states with experiences, running in both directions, thereby relating experiences

---

[5] For much more detailed discussion, see BonJour (1996), pp. 48–52, and Feldman (1996), especially pp. 204–9.

[6] See, for example, the excellent article by Richard Feldman and Earl Conee (2001).

to bodies; thirdly, that awareness of experiences can be analyzed in terms of indexical beliefs and thoughts; and, fourthly, that the unity of experiences and other mental states that characterizes persons, both at a time and over time, can be explained in terms of appropriate causal relations.

Plantinga's contention concerning beliefs is a very striking claim. If he is right, then virtually all of philosophy of mind for the past half-century or so has been radically off-track. How, then, does he attempt to establish his claim? First, he appeals to an argument advanced by Leibniz. Secondly, he suggests that the claim in question is immediately evident. Thirdly, he examines present-day attempts to analyze the concept of belief, focusing, in particular, upon a sophisticated account advanced by Fred Dretske, and he argues that such attempts are unsuccessful.

2.1   Leibniz's argument

Plantinga's first argument is as follows:

> The difficulty I have in mind is not a recent invention. You can find it in Plato, but Leibniz offers a famous and particularly forceful statement of it:
>
> 17. It must be confessed, moreover, that *perception*, and that which depends on it, *are inexplicable by mechanical causes*, that is by figures and motions. And supposing there were a machine so constructed as to think, feel and have perception, we could conceive of it as enlarged and yet preserving the same proportions, so that we might enter it as into a mill. And this granted, we should only find on visiting it, pieces which push one against another, but never anything by which to explain a perception. This must be sought for, therefore, in the simple substance and not in the composite or in the machine. (p. 52)

Plantinga clearly thinks that this argument is very important, since he devotes several pages to it, and, in considering the efforts by present-day philosophers of mind to offer accounts of the nature of belief, he indicates that they have not given Leibniz's argument the attention it deserves. Thus, in discussing attempts by philosophers such as Ruth Millikan, Daniel Dennett, Jerry Fodor, Fred Dretske, and others to construct an account of belief on the basis of notions such as those of indicators, and representation, broadly understood, Plantinga says, "In so doing, they don't ordinarily try to solve Leibniz's problem—the fact that it looks as if a material thing can't think, or be a belief; they simply ignore it" (p. 61)

This criticism of present-day philosophers of mind seems to me unjustified. For suppose that one thought that something like the view advanced by David Armstrong (1968, p. 79) was at least roughly correct:

> As a first approximation we can say that what we mean when we talk about the mind, or about particular mental processes, is nothing but the effect within a man

of certain stimuli, and the cause within a man of certain responses. The intrinsic nature of these effects and causes is not something that is involved in the concept of mind or the particular mental concepts. The concept of a mental state is the concept of that, whatever it may turn out to be, which is brought about in a man by certain stimuli and which in turn brings about certain responses.

If this or some other functionalist-style account of the concepts of the mind and of particular types of mental states is correct, then Leibniz's argument has no force, since if a state is a certain type of mental state, not by virtue of its intrinsic nature, but by virtue of causal connections to stimuli, to responses, and to other mental states,[7] then mental states may perfectly well be present in the scenario that Leibniz envisages: all that is required is the rights sorts of causal connections, and they can perfectly well be present in a purely mechanical system.

Why, then, does Leibniz's argument strike Plantinga as very forceful? Here I am speculating, but I think it is because Plantinga believes that a certain type of non-functionalist account of propositional-attitude *content* is correct. But, regardless of whether I am right about this, there are three very different types of views concerning the nature of content that it is crucial to have in front of us, in order both to evaluate Plantinga's present objection, including Leibniz's argument, and to evaluate the objection that naturalism is self-defeating.[8] I shall refer to these as the intrinsic model, the purely causal (David Lewis-style) functionalist model, and the property-dualist, causal model.

2.1.1 An intrinsic model of content

(1) Simple, descriptive concepts are basic, irreducible, non-linguistic entities, with intrinsic natures.

(2) There is a basic, internal, linking relation—R—such that a descriptive concept C applies to an object by virtue of that object's having property P if and only if concept C and property P stand in the internal relation R.

(3) Propositions are complexes of concepts, both descriptive and logical.

(4) Thoughts are conscious states that involve propositions.

(5) A belief that q is a disposition to have the (assertive) thought that q.

(6) A neural state, N, is the belief that q if and only if N is a categorical basis of a disposition to have the thought that q.

---

[7] To avoid circularity at this point, one needs to set out a theory of different mental states and their relations, and then use some standard method for defining theoretical terms, such as that set out by David Lewis (1970).

[8] Other philosophers have also contended that a correct account of content is crucial here. See especially Evan Fales (2002, p. 50).

(7) The meaning of a linguistic expression is given by the concept or proposition that the person in question has chosen to associate with that expression.

According to this first type of model—of which I have set out only one possible version—the basic idea is that there are ontologically fundamental, irreducible entities—such as concepts—that are non-linguistic bearers of content, and that such things as neural states have the content that they do because, first, they are nomologically or dispositionally related to thoughts, and, secondly, those thoughts in turn involve constituents—namely, concepts—that are internally linked to properties and relations by virtue of their intrinsic natures. Finally, the meaning of a linguistic expression is a matter of the concepts and propositions to which it is related by virtue of a convention that the speaker has adopted.

The other two models are variants on a basic, causal approach. So I shall begin with the general model.

2.1.2   A neutral, causal model of content

(1) If momentary states of type N in individual H can be caused by, and only by, H's having experiences involving instances of property P, then a state of type N in H is a *proto-belief* that an instance of property P is present.

(2) If a state of type N is a proto-belief for H that an instance of property P is present, and if H's being in a state of type N disposes H, in appropriate circumstances, to produce *external* tokens of a structural type L, then such external tokens are *proto-utterances* whose *proto-meaning* is the proto-belief that an instance of property P is present.

(3) If a state of type N is a proto-belief for H that an instance of property P is present, and if H's being in a state of type N disposes H, in appropriate circumstances, to have experiences involving *internal* tokens of a structural type L, then experiences involving those internal tokens of type L are *proto-thoughts* whose *proto-content* is the proto-belief that an instance of property P is present.

The idea behind this second type of account is that there are no such *basic* entities as concepts and propositions, understood as things having intrinsic content. All bearers of content are structured entities that have the content they do because of dispositions of the relevant speakers and/or thinkers. It will then be true that structured entities of different types can, for different speakers, have the same proto-meaning, since they can, for example, express the same proto-belief. But this will not be so because those different, structured entities are related to one and the same non-linguistic, non-conventional bearer of content.

The reason will be, rather, that the different, structured entities enter into the same sort of causal network involving properties of the experiences of the speakers in question. Content, then, is not intrinsic to any type of entity. It is always fixed by relevant causal relations involving entities of that type.

I have described this as a "neutral" account. My reason is that this account leaves it open whether the stuff of physics is all there is, or whether, on the contrary, there are also irreducible qualia, or, more dramatically, immaterial minds. The causal account is supposed to be correct regardless of how the world is in this respect.

I have also spoken (constantly!) of "proto" states. The reason is that in setting out this general alternative to an intrinsic model, I do not want to beg certain questions—such as whether there could be thoughts or beliefs or content in a world without qualia, or in a world without immaterial minds.

A final point that needs to be stressed is that the above covers only proto-beliefs and proto-thoughts that are atomic, and that involve the present-tense ascription of basic descriptive properties to experiences. Accordingly, one would need, ultimately, to offer accounts of logical connectives and quantifiers, of topic-neutral, or quasi-logical, terms, of non-basic descriptive, but still observational, terms, and, finally, of theoretical terms. One also needs, as we shall see later, to give an account of indexical beliefs.

2.1.3 A property-dualist, causal model of content

This version of a causal model of content is distinguished by the fact that it combines the neutral causal model with the following three theses: first, a world without qualia is a world without states of consciousness; secondly, thoughts are states of consciousness; thirdly, a world without thoughts is a world without beliefs, or linguistic meaning, or content.

According to this approach, then, it is crucial, if the internal linguistic tokens are to be more than proto-thoughts, that those internal tokens be states of consciousness. If they are, then one has thoughts, rather than merely proto-thoughts, and this in turn converts proto-beliefs into beliefs, and proto-meanings into meanings.

The idea, in short, is that a satisfactory account of content must involve *both* qualia and causal relations.

2.1.4 A purely causal, functionalist model of content

This second version of the causal model of content denies that qualia are needed. As long as the right causal relations are present, one has beliefs, thoughts, and linguistic behavior; the intrinsic nature of the states of affairs in the causal network is irrelevant.

How does Leibniz's argument fare, under these three different models of content? First, if a purely causal, functionalist model of content is correct, Leibniz's argument has no force, since there is no reason why the necessary types of causal relations cannot be present in Leibniz's machine.

Secondly, if an intrinsic model of content is correct, then Leibniz's argument looks, initially at least, much more promising, since causal relations are irrelevant on the intrinsic model, and none of the intrinsic properties of parts or collections of parts of the machine can be identified with content, intrinsically construed. Recall, however, that naturalism, as understood here, does not involve a rejection of abstract entities—such as concepts or propositions—so, at the very least, additional argumentation is needed to show that something purely mechanical could not possibly stand in relations—or the right sorts of relations—to such abstract entities.

Finally, how does Leibniz's argument look if one adopts a property-dualist version of a causal model of content? This is a question that I shall leave for later. But what I shall argue is that, given such a model, it is logically possible, for example, for an electronic robot to have beliefs.

Does Plantinga accept an intrinsic model of content? It seems to me that he does. For first of all, in discussing naturalism, while he speaks in various places of content either as supervening upon neurophysiological states—either logically or nomologically—or as reducible to neurophysiological states, he nowhere considers the idea that content might instead supervene upon *causal relations* between qualia and neurophysiological states. (On the property-dualist causal model just mentioned, semantical content logically supervenes on causal connections of precisely that sort.)

Secondly, in discussing whether a purely material thing can have beliefs, Plantinga seems to think in terms of a possible causal relation between purely physical states and content:

> A single neuron (or quark, electron, atom, or whatever) presumably isn't a belief; but how can belief, content, arise from physical interaction among such material entities as neurons? How can such physical interaction bring it about that a group of neurons has content? (p. 54)

Perhaps "arise" and "bring it about" are not to be interpreted causally here. But if they are, then these remarks seem incompatible with a causal theory of content.

Finally, parts of Plantinga's argument that seem clearly mistaken given a causal model of content are sometimes much more plausible if one adopts an intrinsic model of content.

My basic point, in any case, is that Leibniz's argument, to have any force, needs to be combined at least with an argument against purely causal, functionalist theories of content. As a stand-alone argument, it begs the question against such theories. In addition, however, and as I shall argue later, it also fails if a property-dualist, causal model of content is correct. If this is right, then Leibniz's argument cannot possibly succeed unless it can be shown that an intrinsic model of content is correct.

2.2   The "one can just see" argument

Plantinga's second argument for the claim that a material entity cannot have beliefs is contained in the following passage:

> Well, what *is* it then that inclines me to think a proposition can't be red, or a horse be an even number? The answer, I think, is that one can just see upon reflection that these things are impossible. I can't form a mental image of a proposition's having members; but that's not why I think no proposition has members, because I also can't form a mental image of a *set's* having members. It's rather that one sees that a set is the sort of thing that has or can have members, and a proposition is not. It is the same with a physical thing's thinking. True, one can't imagine it. The reason for rejecting the idea, however, is not that one can't imagine it. It's rather that one can see that a physical object just can't do that sort of thing. This isn't as clear, perhaps, as that a proposition can't be red; some impossibilities are more clearly impossible than others. But one can see it to at least some degree. (p. 57, original emphasis)

My first comment is a general one namely, that I think that arguments of the "one can just see" variety are usually best avoided. For one thing, the vast majority of necessary truths are surely derived from more basic necessary truths, and so I think that one should always search for a derivation, rather than being content with the thought that one can just see that a certain proposition is necessarily true. In addition, however, philosophers do not have an especially impressive track record with regard to such judgments.

Secondly, a related point, albeit a more controversial one, is this. Some propositions—such as that nothing can be, at a given time, everywhere red and somewhere green—are strong candidates for the status of synthetic *a priori* truths. However, I think that one should always be reluctant to classify a proposition as a synthetic *a priori* truth: the presumption should be that if a proposition is necessarily true, then it is analytic. Accordingly, if a proposition appears to be necessarily true, the presumption should be that it either is itself a definition, or else is derivable from definitions.

Consider, for example, the claim that a cause is necessarily earlier than its effect. Many philosophers have a strong intuition that this is true. I am saying that one should neither rest content with such an intuition, nor attempt to avoid the task of searching for a supporting argument by classifying the proposition as synthetic *a priori*. One should, instead, attempt to find a derivation.

Thirdly, even if one is inclined to credit such modal intuitions, I think that one should view the conflicting intuitions of other thoughtful philosophers as defeaters, at least if such conflicting intuitions are very common—as they are in the present case, where the intuition that things other than immaterial substances can have beliefs is very widespread indeed.

Fourthly, and finally, *if* a causal model of content is correct, then it seems clear that things other than immaterial substances *can* have beliefs. Consequently, in claiming that one can just see that only immaterial substances can have beliefs, Plantinga is committed either to the claim that one can just see that a causal model of content cannot be true, or at least to the claim that the necessary falsity of a causal model of content follows very quickly indeed from things that one can just see to be true. Both of the latter claims are, I suggest, rather implausible, especially in the light of how very widespread causal theories of content are in present-day philosophy of mind.

2.3   *Plantinga's criticism of present-day philosophers of mind*

Plantinga's third line of argument consists of criticisms of attempts by current philosophers of mind to offer accounts of what it is to have a belief that will enable one to make sense of the attribution of beliefs to things other than immaterial minds. Among the philosophers whom Plantinga mentions in this connection are Ruth Millikan, Daniel Dennett, and Jerry Fodor, but the account on which he focuses in a detailed way is Fred Dretske's, in his book *Explaining Behavior* (1988).

Plantinga's central contention is that even if philosophers such as Dretske have arrived at satisfactory accounts of the ideas of indicators, and then of representation, broadly construed, the latter concept is far too inclusive to capture the idea of belief, since representation, so defined, is present in organisms and systems that do not have beliefs. The problem, accordingly, is to get from that broad concept of representation to the idea of belief, and Plantinga attempts to show that this has not been done.

It is tempting to take issue with Plantinga's claim here, but I think that might well lead to a morass, given the complexity of the accounts that have been offered. In any case, there is a different approach that is, I think, much more likely to enable one to get to the bottom of this issue.

2.3.1   My basic approach

But how can one respond to Plantinga without attempting to show either that he is wrong about the accounts offered by Dretske and others, or that some slightly modified account will provide us with a satisfactory analysis of the concept of belief? The answer, in brief, is that the relevant task that present-day philosophers of mind are almost always tackling is that of offering accounts, of belief and other mental states, that are neutral in a certain way, and my strategy, by contrast, will be to abandon that neutrality, since I think that this enables one to see, in a much more clear-cut way, that things other than immaterial minds can have beliefs.

What I have in mind is this. When most present-day philosophers of mind—with some notable exceptions, such as David Chalmers (1996)—offer analyses of the concept of the mind and of the concepts of various mental states, such as belief, they attempt to formulate analyses that are compatible with different empirical hypotheses concerning the nature of the mind—including, in particular, reductionist physicalist views. By contrast, in my response to Plantinga, I shall operate within a property-dualist framework. I shall assume, then, that there are intrinsic, qualitative properties that experiences have—qualia—that are not reducible to the properties and relations postulated by physics.

But why will this shift to a controversial view of the mind be helpful? The reason is that some philosophers do think that, whatever else beliefs may be, they are analytically related to *dispositions to have thoughts*. But, then, if one also holds both that thoughts are occurrent mental states with a qualitative nature, and that reductionist physicalism cannot account for the intrinsic, qualitative nature of experiences, one will also think that a reductionist, physicalist account of belief cannot possibly be correct. By assuming that there are qualia, I can offer an account of belief that is not open to this sort of objection.

My account of content diverges from most present-day accounts in a second way, in that I think that the idea of semantically basic concepts, understood as concepts that apply to properties or relations with which one can be directly acquainted, should play a central role. In particular, the idea is this. First, a theory of belief and of content should start with those terms or concepts that are semantically basic. Then an account should be given of logical connectives and quantifiers. This, together with the account of content for semantically basic concepts, should then automatically generate an account of content for all concepts that can be reductively defined in terms of basic concepts. Next, an account should be given of content for 'quasi-logical' or 'topic-neutral' concepts—including the general concepts of properties, relations, universals, states of affairs, events, particulars, and so on. Finally, all of the preceding should then enable one to formulate an account of content for theoretical concepts—using some familiar technique for defining theoretical terms.

Present-day approaches tend not to start out from the idea of semantically basic concepts. Thus philosophers such as Jerry Fodor, for example, usually offer accounts that, from the very beginning, are viewed as applying, for example, to beliefs about cows,[9] whereas I would argue that if an account is to have any hope of success, it must start with atomic, indexical beliefs involving semantically basic concepts that apply to things by virtue of properties and relations that can be objects of immediate awareness.

2.3.2   Motivating a causal approach to content

In his discussion of Leibniz's argument, Plantinga discusses the attribution of beliefs to immaterial minds. There he says, first, that an immaterial mind is a simple entity; secondly, that thinking is a basic activity of an immaterial mind—where a basic activity is an activity that is "not generated by the interaction of its parts"; and, thirdly, that thinking is an immediate activity of an immaterial mind—where an immediate activity is an activity that something does not do "by way of doing something else." Then, in the light of this, Plantinga concludes, "To ask 'How does a self produce thought?' is to ask an improper question. There isn't any *how* about it" (p. 58).

This conclusion is, I think, far from uncontroversial. For even if, by definition, immaterial minds cannot have spatial parts, it is not clear why they cannot be complex entities, with different, independent faculties, or why some of their faculties cannot depend upon simpler ones. But if the latter can be the case, then thinking might be such a complex faculty, in which case there would be an explanation of how an immaterial mind thinks.

Suppose, however, that there is no such explanation. It is important to notice that this does not imply that it is an improper question to ask *what it is* for an immaterial mind to think, any more than, say, the fact that having unit negative charge is a basic and immediate property of electrons entails that there is no answer to the question of what it is for something to have unit negative charge.

But are there any reasons for thinking that the concept of belief is not a semantically basic concept that neither needs nor is susceptible of any analysis? I think that there are, since the idea that the concept of belief is semantically basic has a number of very unwelcome consequences. First, there would then be no explanation of entailments between the having of different beliefs, such as that of the logical impossibility of believing that p & q without believing that p. Secondly, there would be no explanation of immediate logical incompatibilities between the having of different beliefs—such as the logical impossibility of explicitly believing that p, while also explicitly believing that $\sim p$.

---

[9] Recall the passage that Plantinga (p. [62]) quoted from Fodor (1990, p. 91): "But 'cow' means *cow* and not *cat* or *cow* or *cat* because *there being cat-caused "cow" tokens depends on there being cow-caused "cow" tokens, but not the other way around.*"

If the concept of belief is not semantically basic, how should it be analyzed? A direction in which to look emerges, I suggest, if one focuses upon the distinction between extensional, sentential contexts and intensional ones. So consider a sentence '*Fa*.' If the context following the predicate '*F*' is extensional, then the following two sorts of inferences are valid:

Fa
a = b   *Fa*
Therefore: *Fb*   Therefore: $(\exists x)Fx$

By contrast, if the context following the predicate '*F*' is intensional, then those inferences are not necessarily truth-preserving.

Extensionality is a very natural property. For if '*Fa*' functions to attribute some property of *F*-ness to an entity *a*, and if *a* and *b* are one and the same entity, then if *a* has *F*-ness, *b* must have *F*-ness as well. Similarly, if *a* has the property of *F*-ness, then there is certainly something that has the property of *F*-ness. By contrast, if the context following the predicate '*F*' is intensional, then the function of sentences of the form '*Fa*' cannot be, or cannot be simply, to attribute a property of *F*-ness to an entity. So the question arises as to how such sentences do function.

Propositional attitude sentences—including belief sentences—exhibit intensionality. First, substitution of co-extensive terms or expressions may not preserve truth, since, for example, John may believe that Mark Twain wrote *Huckleberry Finn*, but not believe that Samuel Clemens wrote *Huckleberry Finn*. Second, existential quantification may fail to be truth-preserving, since, for example, although Moses believed that Yahweh was the creator of the universe, there may very well be no actual entity such that Moses believed that that entity created the universe.

Other types of sentences, however—such as modal sentences—also exhibit intensionality. Of particular interest, here, however, are causal and nomological sentences. Thus, for example, it may be true that the candle melted because it was near the hottest object in the room, but not true that that the candle melted because it was near the reddest object in the room, even though the hottest object in the room was identical with the reddest object in the room. Similarly, it could be a law of nature that all *F*s are *G*s, without its being a law of nature that all *H*s are *G*s, even though it was true, as a matter of fact, that the predicates '*F*' and '*H*' were co-extensive.

These cases are of interest for two reasons. First, in the case of causal and nomological sentences, a plausible explanation of the intensionality is available. For as regards nomological sentences, there are very strong reasons for holding that the truthmakers for statements expressing laws of nature are states of affairs consisting of second-order relations between universals (Dretske, 1977;

Tooley, 1977 and 1987; Armstrong, 1983). But then, given that a second-order relation may hold between properties P and R, without holding between properties Q and R, even though properties P and Q are always co-instantiated, we have an explanation of the intensionality of nomological sentences.

For causal sentences, two possible explanations are available. One is that, provided that causal relations fall under causal laws, the explanation of the intensionality of nomological sentences just given also explains the intensionality of causal sentences. Alternatively, one can argue that causal relations hold between states of affairs, since the intensionality of causal sentences will then follow from the fact that, even if everything that has property P has property Q, and vice versa, the (Armstrongian) state of affairs that is a's having property P is not identical with the state of affairs that is a's having property Q.

The second reason that causal sentences are of interest here is this. Consider a very simple device—which I shall refer to as 'Robo the Robot'—that scans its environment, and, for each location, records the temperature of that location and its color—that is, the distribution of wavelengths of light coming from that location. Having recorded information for all the locations in its environment, if it is an odd-numbered day of the month, Robo either remains motionless if it has not scanned a location whose temperature is greater than 120 degrees Fahrenheit, or, if it has scanned such a location, it moves to the hottest location it has found, whereas, if it is an even-numbered day of the month, Robo either stays where it is if it has not scanned a location that is red, or, if it has scanned such a location, it moves to the reddest location it has found.

Robo enjoys states that are, in a broad sense, representational: for each location it scans, Robo stores information, understood broadly, about the color and temperature of that location. Moreover, there must be other states of Robo that, together with the stored information, determine whether Robo will remain motionless for the day, or whether it will move towards the hottest object, or the reddest object, in its vicinity. So one could speak here of 'quasi-desires' or 'quasi-preferences': on odd-numbered days of the month, Robo quasi-prefers to be near the hottest of any sufficiently hot object that it has scanned; on even-numbered days of the month, Robo quasi-prefers to be near the reddest of any red objects that it has scanned.

Plantinga would hold—and I would agree—that Robo's information-storing states are not beliefs. He would also hold—and again I would agree—that although Robo has states that one can refer to as 'quasi-desires,' those states are not really desires or preferences. Moreover, neither my judgments, nor Plantinga's, I am confident, would change if Robo were endowed with much more sophisticated sensing devices, information-storing and information-manipulating programs, along with much more complicated dispositions that, together with the stored information, determined what behavior Robo would exhibit in an enormous range of circumstances. Add as much as you want of *those* sorts of things, and the result is still something that has neither beliefs nor preferences.

In spite of this, it is worth considering what happens if we introduce sentences to describe the 'quasi-preferences' of Robo:

> Robo quasi-prefers to be near the hottest of sufficiently hot objects in its environment.
>
> Robo quasi-prefers to be near the reddest of any red objects in its environment.

Here the idea is that Robo quasi-prefers to be near the hottest of sufficiently hot objects in its environment if Robo is in a state that, in conjunction with stored information to the effect that location A has the property in question, will cause Robo to move toward location A. Similarly, Robo quasi-prefers to be near the reddest of any red objects in its environment if Robo is in a state that, in conjunction with stored information to the effect that location A has the property in question, will cause Robo to move toward location A.

Notice, now, that the above sentences are intensional. For suppose that it is an odd-numbered day of the month, and that Robo scans a location that is both sufficiently hot, and hotter than any other location that it scans. Then the following sentence will be true:

> (1) Robo quasi-prefers to be near the hottest of sufficiently hot objects in its environment.

It may happen, however, that the hottest of the sufficiently hot objects in Robo's environment on that day is also the reddest object in its environment, so that the following is also true:

> (2) The hottest of the sufficiently hot objects in Robo's environment = the reddest of any red objects in Robo's environment.

Substituting in (1) on the basis of the identity in (2) would then yield:

> (3) Robo quasi-prefers to be near the reddest of any red objects in its environment.

But (3) is false, since Robo is not in a state that would play the causal role in question.

The conclusion, in short, is that sentences about quasi-preferences involve intensional contexts. Moreover, the intensionality of such contexts is reducible to the intensionality of causal sentences.

The same point could be made about quasi-belief sentences about Robo. One could imagine, for example, that Robo's color-sensing mechanism breaks down. Then it could well be the case that sentence (2) is true, along with

(4) Robo quasi-believes that the hottest of sufficiently hot objects in its environment is at location *A*,

whereas the result of substituting in (4) on the basis of the identity in sentence (2)—namely,

(5) Robo quasi-believes that the reddest of any red objects in its environment is at location *A*

—would be false.

The upshot is that it seems to me that there is a strong reason for seriously considering accounts of belief, and of content, in which causation plays a central role. The reason is that, first, statements about beliefs, and about content, involve, as do propositional-attitude sentences generally, intensional contexts, and such contexts are inherently puzzling; secondly, intensionality also arises in connection with devices, such as Robo, that arguably do not have beliefs, but that do have information-storing, representational states; thirdly, the intensionality in the latter sorts of cases can be explained in terms of the intensionality of causal sentences, for which, in turn, we do have a satisfying explanation. Accordingly, there would appear to be a very good reason to consider whether the intensionality of genuine propositional-attitude contexts, including those of beliefs, is not to be explained in a comparable fashion.

2.3.3   From Robo to Robbie: beliefs and material entities

The preliminaries have been somewhat lengthy, but I am now in a position to argue that things other than immaterial minds can have beliefs. This requires moving from the simple-'minded' Robo to a considerably more complex robot—Robbie—that, among other things, has experiences and uses language.

The first difference that I want to introduce between Robo and Robbie, then—and the most dramatic one—is that Robbie's internal, purely physical states causally give rise to qualia. Am I entitled to make this assumption? Well, human brain states causally give rise to sensations and experiences, so it is not easy to see how it could be *logically* impossible for electronic circuitry to do the same. In addition, might it not even be that the causal laws operating in the case of humans are laws connecting electrical events as causes to qualia as effects, and ones that involve no reference to neuronal circuits in particular?

Again, this seems surely possible. But if this were the case, then, in the actual world, appropriate electronic circuitry could give rise to experiential states.

Those experiential states could then give rise to the storing of information in syntactically structured electronic states, and the causal laws connecting the qualitative properties of experiences to such electronic states might generate a one-to-one mapping between a given qualitative property and the corresponding electronic state, so that, for example, if Robbie had an experience that caused an electronic state involving a certain physical property, G, the experience would always be of the qualitative-green variety. Such syntactically structured electronic states would then be indicators of the presence of a quale of the green variety.

Those who believe that the physical world is causally closed will, of course, offer a somewhat different account at this point. But I believe—contrary to Frank Jackson (1982), David Chalmers (1996), and others—that there are very strong arguments against epiphenomenalism.

The second difference that I want to introduce is proto-linguistic behavior. Imagine, then, that Robbie can produce sequences of sounds, and that when he goes into an electronic state of type G, he is disposed, in certain circumstances, to produce a sequence of sounds corresponding to those in an utterance of "That's an instance of greenness." Such a sequences of sounds would then be a reliable indicator, first, of the presence of an electronic state of type G, and, thereby, of a quale of the green variety.

Would sequences of sounds of the form "That's an instance of greenness" then be sentences—understood as entities with meanings? Not necessarily, since one might think, first, that if electronic states of type G are not *beliefs*, then the sequences of sounds to which they give rise, on appropriate occasions, are not sentences, and, secondly, that the completely reliable neural indicators that are present in Robbie, although representations, in a broad sense, of qualia states, are not yet beliefs.

Let us now, however, introduce a third difference between Robo and Robbie. Imagine that Robbie's use of language (or proto-language), rather than being purely external, is also internal, in the following way. A syntactically structured electronic state with property G, in addition to grounding a disposition to produce, in appropriate circumstances, external sequences of sounds of the form "That's an instance of greenness," also grounds a disposition to produce, in appropriate circumstances, a sequence of experiences involving qualitative properties of an auditory sort that, though less vivid, correspond to the experiences Robbie has on hearing an utterance of "That's an instance of greenness."

There is one final property with which I need to endow Robbie. We often have, at a given time, a wide variety of experiences—visual, auditory, tactile, olfactory, and so on. Not all of these experiences give rise to corresponding beliefs at a given time: one may focus on the sounds that one is hearing, and pay no attention to one's tactile sensations; or one may focus on one part of one's visual field, while ignoring another. There are, in short, differences in the extent to which various experiences will at a given time give rise to beliefs, ranging from no beliefs at all, through beliefs about some of the qualities of the experiences, up to fully detailed beliefs. Moreover, the extent to which experiences give rise to corresponding beliefs is something that is generally responsive to one's desires: one can decide which part of one's total experience at a given time will give rise to the most detailed beliefs.

This property is crucial, I believe, to the having of indexical beliefs and thoughts, since it seems to me that it is the ability to determine which part of one's total experience is the part that gives rise to the most detailed beliefs that determines, for example, which part of one's visual field is being referred to when one has the indexical thought that *that* is a quale of the green variety. So we need to attribute this ability to Robbie.

The upshot is that we now have, in Robbie, sequences of qualia that have the following three properties. First, they are reliable indicators of electronic states of type *G*. Secondly, they are also, therefore, reliable indicators of qualia involving instances of qualitative greenness. Thirdly, they are caused by the qualia to which Robbie stands in the strongest information-accessing relation. The question, now, is whether such a structured sequence of qualia, caused in this way, is a *thought*—and, specifically, an indexical thought that *that* is an instance of qualitative greenness.

I think that this is the case, and my reason is as follows. First, I think that the correct account of content is the property-dualist, causal account set out earlier. If this is right, then electronic states of type *G*, regardless of whether they are beliefs, or merely proto-beliefs, have as their content that there exists an instance of qualitative greenness. Secondly, if one has the ability to determine the part of one's total experience to which one stands in the strongest information-accessing relation at a given time, one thereby has the power to fix the referents of indexical terms, and so one can have indexical proto-beliefs to the effect that *that* is an instance of qualitative greenness. Thirdly, if such information-storing states are also the categorical basis of a disposition to give rise, in appropriate circumstances, to sequences of sounds of the form "That's an instance of greenness," then the content of such a syntactically structured sequence of sounds coincides with the content of the categorical basis of the relevant disposition. Fourthly, it makes no difference whether the syntactically structured sequence of states involves a sequence of sounds, or, instead, a sequence of auditory images. Finally, if a syntactically structured sequence of qualia has the indexical proto-content that *that* is an instance of greenness, then such a sequence of qualia *is* the indexical thought that *that* is an instance of greenness.

My overall argument, in short, is this. First, if one attempts to offer a *purely* functionalist or causal account of content and belief—as, I think, most present-day philosophers of mind do—one is open to the objection that beliefs involve dispositions to give rise to corresponding thoughts, and that thoughts are experiential states involving qualia. But if one adopts, instead, a property-dualist, causal account of content, this objection does not arise. Secondly, and as I have illustrated by the case of Robbie, by combining the resources of qualia, syntactically structured sequences of experiences, and causal relations, it is very plausible that one can construct a satisfactory account of thoughts and beliefs. Finally, none of these things—qualia, syntactically structured sequences of experiential states, and causal connections—presupposes the presence of an immaterial mind, as the case of Robbie shows. Purely material entities, accordingly, can have beliefs and thoughts.

3. Plantinga's Second Argument: Naturalism as Self-Defeating

3.1 Plantinga's argument

We are now in a position to turn to Plantinga's most important argument against naturalism, where he attempts to show that philosophical naturalists can be given a good reason for doubting that their cognitive faculties are reliable. But, then, "if you have a defeater for the belief that your faculties are reliable, then you also have a defeater for each of the beliefs produced by those faculties; you therefore have a defeater for each of your beliefs. That means that you have a defeater for your belief in naturalism itself; hence naturalism is self-defeating" (p. 30)

Plantinga has advanced this general argument against naturalism, in slightly different versions, in a number of places (1991; 1993b, chapter 12; 1994). The present formulation reflects, I think, some criticisms directed against earlier formulations.

Plantinga's argument is, I believe, open to strong objections at more than one point. One crucial issue, for example, is whether he needs to argue that the probability that our cognitive faculties are reliable, given naturalism, is low, or only that the probability is either low *or inscrutable*. Plantinga contends that the latter is sufficient:

> Suppose, however, that this probability really is completely inscrutable: we haven't the faintest idea what it is. As far as we can tell, it could be as high as 1; it could also be zero; and it could be anything in between. We still get the same result. If this probability is inscrutable, then so will be $P(R/N)$; but *N & P(R/N) is inscrutable* is a defeater for R, just as is *N & P(R/N) is low*. (p. 47)

If, as I do, one thinks that for any hypothesis h and any evidence e, there is some number that is the logical probability of h given e, one might attempt to show that if one cannot determine what that number is, one is at least justified in believing that it is not high. But is this right? I think that it is not at all clear that it is. Consider, for example, the hypothesis that there is life elsewhere in the universe. I think that one might well think that one cannot determine what the probability of that hypothesis is, relative to what we know, without thereby thinking that the probability cannot be high.

In addition, the thesis that, for any hypothesis *h* and any evidence *e*, there is some number that is the logical probability of *h* given *e* is a highly controversial claim that many philosophers reject. But if that claim is false—and Plantinga has offered no argument to show that it is not—then the conjunction of *e* with the proposition that the probability of *h* given *e* is inscrutable is surely not a defeater for *h*.

Finally, consider an ordinary person who initially believes that his cognitive faculties are reliable, but who has no idea either what produced those faculties, or how probable it is—relative to the totality, *T*, of the other things that he is justified in believing—that his faculties are reliable. If Plantinga is right that *N&P(R/N) is inscrutable* is a defeater for *R*, then *T&P(R/T) is inscrutable* is equally a defeater for *R*, and so such a person, if he is to be rational, must suspend judgment about everything, unless and until he has a definite view about the source of his cognitive faculties, and is justified in believing that this source would be likely to produce reliable faculties. This is a very strong claim, and not, I suggest, at all plausible.[10]

The upshot is that a contention that is crucial for Plantinga's argument against naturalism is in fact very dubious–the contention, namely, that it is sufficient for his argument that the probability that our cognitive faculties are reliable, given naturalism, is inscrutable.

I shall concentrate, however, on what I take to be the most crucial part of Plantinga's argument. In the present version, that part can be set out as follows:

(1) If naturalism is true, a belief is a neural state that, in addition to its "electro-chemical or neurophysiological properties," has propositional content (pp. 33–4).

(2) If naturalism is true, then the content of a neural state that is a belief either (a) supervenes upon its electro-chemical or neurophysiological properties, or (b) is reducible to such properties (p. 35).

(3) If the content of a neural state that is a belief is reducible to its electro-chemical or neurophysiological properties, then content properties just are electro-chemical or neurophysiological properties (p. 35)

---

[10] Here I am indebted to Wes Morriston.

(4) If the content of a neural state that is a belief supervenes upon its electro-chemical or neurophysiological properties, then that neural state has electro-chemical or neurophysiological properties, "the possession of which is logically or causally sufficient for the possession of that particular content" (p. 38).

(5) If naturalism is true, then living things have come into existence via unguided, Darwinian evolution (p. 34).

(6) If Darwinian evolution is true, then natural selection has given rise in animals to neural states that are reliable indicators of important states of affairs—such as the presence of predators (p. 38).

(7) If Darwinian evolution is true, then even if it is true both that neural states of type N are, in an organism H, reliable indicators of the presence of an instance of property P, and also that states of type N have content C, there is no reason why content C need be related to property P.

Thus Plantinga says,

Indication is one thing; belief content is something else altogether, and we know of no reason why the one should be related to the other. Content simply arises upon the appearance of neural structures of sufficient complexity; there is no reason why that content need be related to what the structures indicate, if anything. The proposition constituting that content need not be so much as *about* that predator (p. 38, original emphasis).

(8) Consequently, if naturalism is true, the probability that the content C associated with any given neural state is true is no greater than the probability that a belief chosen at random is true.

(9) Therefore, if naturalism is true, the probability that any given belief is true is no greater than one half, and this means that the probability that most of one's beliefs are true—even for quite a small number of beliefs—is very small indeed (pp. 41–2).

(10) Therefore, the probability that one's cognitive faculties are reliable, if naturalism is true, is extremely low.

3.2   *Critical evaluation of Plantinga's argument*

The crucial claim in the above argument is the one advanced at step (7). Let us consider, then, whether that claim is correct, first, given an intrinsic model of content, and, secondly, given a causal model.

3.2.1   Plantinga's argument and an intrinsic model of content

How does Plantinga's argument fare if we suppose that an intrinsic model of content is correct? Given that assumption, it seems to me that the argument is sound. For let N be some electro-chemical or neurophysiological property of some neural state, and let C be the content property of that state, and consider the three alternatives that Plantinga says are open to the naturalist with regard to the relation between content properties and electro-chemical or neurophysiological properties:

> Option 1: Content property C is reducible to the electro-chemical or neurophysiological property N.
>
> Option 2: The electro-chemical or neurophysiological property N is logically sufficient for the presence of content property C.
>
> Option 3: The electro-chemical or neurophysiological property N is causally sufficient for the presence of content property C.

If an intrinsic model of content is correct, then options 1 and 2 do not appear plausible. If a content property is some sort of intrinsic property, how can such a property—which could equally be a property of a mental state in an immaterial mind—be identical with some electro-chemical or neurophysiological property? Or how could some electro-chemical or neurophysiological property logically necessitate the occurrence of such an intrinsic property?

The plausible alternative, accordingly, if an intrinsic model of content is correct, is option 3: appropriate electro-chemical or neurophysiological properties causally give rise to the presence of content properties.

Consider, then, the crucial claim:

> (7) If Darwinian evolution is true, then even if it is true both that neural states of type N are, in an organism H, reliable indicators of the presence of an instance of property P, and also that states of type N have content C, there is no reason why content C need be related to property P.

Given option 3, this claim seems very plausible. For, on the one hand, there will be certain causal laws that, given the neurophysiology of a given organism, make it the case that neural states with a neurophysiological property N are, in that organism, a reliable indicator of the presence of property P, whereas it will be in virtue of a different set of causal laws that electro-chemical or neurophysiological properties causally give rise to intrinsic content properties. So if naturalism is true, it will simply be a lucky accident if, in any give case, the intrinsic content C that is caused by a neurophysiological property N applies to that particular property P, of whose presence neural states with property N are reliable indicators.

By contrast, no lucky accident would be needed if there were an omnipotent, omniscient, and morally perfect creator, since such a friendly designer of the world could create laws such that neural states with the neurophysiological state N would causally give rise to an intrinsic content C that *was* true of property P, thereby ensuring that the relevant beliefs were true, and that the corresponding faculties were reliable.

3.2.2 Plantinga's argument and a causal model of content

But how do things stand on a causal model of content? Consider, in particular, the property-dualist version of such an account. Here the basic idea is that if qualia of a given type P stand in the relevant causal relations to neural states of a given type N, neural states of that type are indexical proto-beliefs with a specific content (or proto-content) C. Then, if a neural state of type N is also the categorical basis of a disposition to generate, in appropriate circumstances, a syntactically structured sequence of qualia of the right sort, the proto-belief becomes a belief, and the resulting syntactically structured sequence of qualia is a thought whose content is the same as the underlying belief, namely, C.

Now consider, again, the crucial claim, along with the passage from Plantinga's discussion on which my formulation is based:

(7) If Darwinian evolution is true, then even if it is true both that neural states of type N are, in an organism H, reliable indicators of the presence of an instance of property P, and also that states of type N have content C, there is no reason why content C need be related to property P.

Indication is one thing; belief content is something else altogether, and we know of no reason why the one should be related to the other. Content simply arises upon the appearance of neural structures of sufficient complexity; there is no reason why that content need be related to what the structures indicate, if anything. The proposition constituting that content need not be so much as *about* that predator. (p. 38, original emphasis)

Is it true, as Plantinga claims, that indication is one thing, and belief content something else altogether? What is true, as Plantinga argues in criticizing Dretske and some other present-day philosophers of mind, is that neural states that are indicators *need not* be beliefs. But if a property-dualist, causal theory of content is correct, and *if* a neural, indicator state does give rise to syntactically structured experiential states in an appropriate way, then that neural state *is* a belief. In addition, if the neural state is an indicator of the presence of a *basic* descriptive property of *experiences*, such as qualitative greenness, then the causal relation in question fixes the content of the neural state. Finally, given the satisfaction of a further condition related to indexicality, the content of the neural state is precisely the indexical belief that that's an instance of qualitative greenness. It is therefore false, in the case of neural states that do have content, that "there is no reason why that content need be related to what the structures indicate, if anything," since the content of any indexical belief about a *basic* observational/introspectible property of experiences *logically supervenes* upon the causal relation that makes it the case that the relevant neural state is a reliable indicator of the qualitative property in question.

3.2.3   The central conclusion

The basic picture, in short, is this. If an intrinsic model of content *were* right, then step (7) in the argument would be correct, and Plantinga's argument would go through. For it would then be plausible that the neurophysiological properties of neural states causally give rise to the intrinsic content properties of those neural states, and this, in turn, would make it extremely unlikely, in the absence of a designer, that the content, in any particular case, was such that it was true of the relevant qualitative property, instances of which give rise to the neurophysiological property in question.

I have argued, however, first of all, that causal approaches to content have the advantage over intrinsic models of content of being able to offer a promising account of the source of intensionality, and, secondly, that, in particular, a property-dualist version of a causal approach to content allows one to set out a satisfactory account of belief and thought. Given a property-dualist, causal account of content, however, step (7) in Plantinga's argument, as I have set it out above, is false, and the argument therefore collapses, since such an account entails that relevant causal relations both make it the case that certain indicator states *are* indexical, *basic* beliefs, and also logically determine the contents of those indicator states in such a way that the indexical beliefs in question must be true whenever the indicator states are accurate.

3.3   *Evolution, communication, and thought*

Basic indexical beliefs are concerned with qualitative properties of one's experiences. Survival often requires, however, much more information about the world than is provided by the totality of one's true, basic, present-tense, indexical beliefs. In particular, one needs information, first, about the external, physical objects that one is presently perceiving; secondly, about how things were; and, thirdly, about how things are likely to be. If one thinks that indirect realism is correct—as I do—the matter is especially complex, since there is a large story to be told about how one gets from beliefs about one's experiences to beliefs about the external world. To avoid this added complexity, let me skip the first step just mentioned by pretending that direct realism is true, so that one's foundational, present-tense, indexical beliefs are beliefs about basic observational properties of external objects, rather than about basic properties of experiences.

The causal model of content that I set out earlier attributed certain abilities to individuals. One was the ability of individuals to produce, in appropriate circumstances, syntactically structured tokens, either external or internal. Here two points are important. First, if that individual could form, for example, reliable present-tense indexical indicators of the presence of a tiger, but could not communicate those indicators to friends and family, the latter's chances for survival would be radically reduced, as would that individual's chances if others lacked this ability. So animals with the ability to communicate information to others will certainly be selected for.

Sounds that do not involve the use of language can, of course, serve as warnings, but language enables one to communicate much more detailed information, concerning, for example, whether there's a tiger or a snake nearby, or whether there is one tiger or two, and so on. Language-users have, then, a great survival advantage.

All of this is a matter of the production of external tokens. But, secondly, very little little is required to go from the external use of tokens to the internal use. Can one form an image of how things looked just a moment ago, or how things sounded? Then if one can produce external tokens that represent stored information, when one wants to, it would seem that one will also be able to produce internal tokens that are images of those external tokens. For compare, on the one hand, hearing music, and forming an image of the same music, with hearing the sentence "That's a tiger," and having the thought that that's a tiger. Is it not true that when one has the thought that that's a tiger, part of what is present is a series of auditory images that corresponds to hearing the spoken sentence?

The overall picture, in short, is, first, that groups of animals with the ability to communicate with each other have an enormous survival advantage; secondly, that the only thing that is required to be able to use language internally, once one can use it externally, is the ability to form images; thirdly, that the internalized use of language *is* thinking; and, fourthly, that one has beliefs once one has information states that can give rise to thoughts.

3.4   *The variety of types of information needed for survival*

Consider Paul and his tiger companions. If Paul is to have a reasonable chance of surviving, he needs to be able to go into neural states that are proto-beliefs with the indexical content that that's a tiger. His prospects for survival will be greatly enhanced, as we have just seen, if he and others in his circle can communicate such proto-beliefs to one another. The internalization of such linguistic behavior will then be the having of corresponding thoughts, and so the indexical proto-beliefs will then have become beliefs.

But if Paul's chances of survival are to be good, he has to be able to form a variety of proto-beliefs. For example, Paul forms, at one moment, the indexical beliefs that that's a tiger on the left and that that's a bush on the right. The tiger walks towards the bush, and disappears. If it is a case of out of sight, out of mind, Paul is in trouble: if the only belief he now has is that that's a bush on the right, his future is not bright. Clearly, he needs to be able to form other proto-beliefs that are about the presence, right now, of a tiger, and that are indexical, but where the indexical element does not refer to the tiger—since he needs to form, in the present case, the proto-belief that there is a tiger lurking behind that bush on the right.

In addition, his survival and that of his family and friends depends upon the ability of members of his group to communicate *that* sort of information to one another. The internalized use of that language then produces, once again, thoughts with the same content as the external utterances, thereby changing what would otherwise be merely proto-beliefs into full-fledged beliefs involving dispositions to have the relevant thoughts.

Paul's proto-belief that there is a tiger lurking behind that bush on the right is not, however, a belief that has come into being *ex nihilo*. It is, rather, a belief that Paul has inferred from other beliefs. Before the tiger moved behind the bush, Paul had the indexical proto-belief that that's a tiger on the left. As the tiger walks to the right, Paul is constantly storing information about where the tiger was. In addition, Paul has formed generalizations about the behavior of ordinary objects, to the effect that they do not pop into and out of existence. So when the tiger disappears behind the bush, Paul can infer from his memory information about the tiger and its trajectory, together with his information about the general 'conservation' of objects, that there is a tiger behind that bush. Moreover, these additional proto-beliefs, about the existence and location of a tiger in the very recent past, and about the tendency of ordinary objects to continue to exist, are ones whose communication to others will greatly enhance everyone's chances of surviving. The internalization of the language used in such communication will then give rise to the corresponding thoughts, and, again, this means that the information-storing states in question are beliefs, rather than merely proto-beliefs.

3.5   *A brief overview*

What I have offered here is a very brief sketch of an account that would require much more space to develop in a detailed way. The basic picture that I have set out, however, is this. First, a satisfactory causal account of content needs to proceed in a step-by-step fashion. The starting point should be with semantically basic items that pick out properties and relations that can be objects of immediate awareness. The basic information-storing states involved in this case will be of the direct, present-tense, indexical sort, and the proto-content of such states will be fixed by their causal relations to the qualia that give rise to them.

Given this starting point, the next step is to provide an account of the content of non-atomic beliefs involving logical terms and operators. This should be done, I suggest, in terms of causal and nomological relations between representational states that parallel in structure appropriate rules governing logical connectives and operators—including introduction and elimination rules. So, for example, just as the elimination rule for conjunction enables one to move from a conjunction of two propositions to either of the conjuncts, so a representational state that stores conjunctive information should be such that it is nomologically impossible, given the structure of the organism, to be in that state without also being in the information-storing states associated with each of the conjuncts. Similarly, if the explicit proto-content of neural state M is the proposition that p, while the explicit proto-content of neural state N is the proposition that $\sim p$, then it should be nomologically impossible, given the structure of the organism, for it to be in both states simultaneously. The idea, in short, is that logical relations between propositions get mapped into nomological relations between representational states.

An account of logical connectives and operators then allows one to move, for example, from information-storing states with the direct indexical proto-content that *that*'s an instance of greenness to information-storing states with the existentially quantified indexical proto-content that there is an instance of greenness over there, and to information-storing states with the non-indexical, existentially quantified proto-content that there exists an instance of greenness.

An account of logical connectives and operators also enables one to give an account of the proto-content of information-storing states that correspond, so to speak, to combinations of the basic descriptive properties and relations, so that one will be able to explain not only information-storing states having the proto-content that this is red and that is round, but also information-storing states having the proto-content that that is both red and round.

The next step is then to offer an account of information-storing states whose proto-content involves quasi-logical, or topic-neutral, proto-concepts—such as those of things, events, states of affairs, properties, relations, and so on. This, together with the accounts of the logical connectives and quantifiers, and of basic descriptive terms, will then enable the assignment of proto-content to information-storing states concerning theoretical states of affairs.

The second main idea—discussed in the preceding section—is that animals with the ability to communicate such information-storing states to one another through the use of language will have greatly enhanced survival chances, and so the ability to use language is something that evolution will select for. In addition, a causal theory of content is once again relevant: the proto-meanings of such utterances are fixed by the proto-content of the information-storing states that are the categorical bases of the relevant dispositions.

The third main idea is that one has thoughts when one has an internalized use of language, and here I argued that all that is required to move from the external use of language to an internalized use is the ability to form images. The proto-content of those thoughts will then be causally fixed via the proto-content of the underlying information-storing states that give rise to them.

The fourth main idea is then that once one has thoughts, one has states that have content, rather than merely proto-content: thought is the fundamental locus of content. As a result, the proto-contents of earlier states in the process also become contents: the external linguistic tokens that had proto-meaning now have meaning; the information-storing states that were proto-beliefs are now beliefs.

The final point is that I believe it is crucial to all of this that thoughts are states of consciousness. If a satisfactory functionalist account of consciousness can be found, then the above picture can be set out within the framework of a purely causal, functionalist model of content. But if, as I am very strongly inclined to think, consciousness requires irreducible, qualitative properties of experiences, then one needs to adopt, instead, the property-dualist, causal account of content that I have employed.

3.6   *Perceptual faculties and the possibility of systematic error*

Humans can reason badly. In the case of deduction, as long as one starts with true beliefs, and reasons in accordance with the introduction and elimination rules that define the logical connectives and operators, all will be well. But humans can be tempted by other moves—such as denying the antecedent—not licensed by introduction and elimination rules, and the result will then often be false beliefs.

Moreover, a human's prospects for survival will be rather bleak if he or she does not make inductive inferences. But once one starts engaging in inductive reasoning, one will often arrive at false beliefs even if one does not reason badly. In addition, however, if humans have come about via unguided evolution, one would expect that the need for speedy calculations in dangerous situations makes it very likely that evolution will, in some cases, have selected organisms that are disposed to perform fast, but inductively somewhat crude, inferences.

What do we find when we examine the types of reasoning that humans actually engage in? This is not an issue that I can pursue here, but I do think that there are very strong reasons for concluding that humans follow some deeply entrenched patterns of reasoning that are unsound, especially in making causal inferences.[11]

This is not at all surprising if evolution is true. But if humans were, instead, created by God, and had immaterial minds, as Plantinga holds, would it be likely that such rough and ready methods were present? After all, immaterial minds are not subject to the limitations that brains are with regard to storage capacity and speed of processing, so if humans had immaterial minds, they could have cognitive faculties that quickly generated the results that follow from a completely sound inductive logic: there would be no difficulty in having both speed and accuracy.

False beliefs that arise via induction or faulty deduction will tend to get rooted out as more evidence becomes available, or as humans enjoy exciting interactions with the environment. But there is also the possibility of errors of a less random sort, including systematic errors that involve deep misconceptions of a type suggested by Plantinga (1994, p. 10):

> Perhaps Paul is a sort of early Leibnizian and thinks everything is conscious (and suppose that is false); furthermore, his ways of referring to things all involve definite descriptions that entail consciousness, so that all of his beliefs are of the form *That so-and-so conscious being is such-and-such.*

What is one to say about such possibilities? First of all, on a causal theory of content, just as the introduction and elimination rules for conjunction make it the case that it is logically impossible to believe that p and q without believing that p, so they also make it the case that it is logically impossible to believe, for example, that there is a conscious F that is a G without also believing that there is an F that is a G. In this sort of case, then, although there are numerous false beliefs, almost all of those beliefs entail a related belief that is *true, and which one must have.* Any adaptiveness associated with the false beliefs, moreover, is really due to the closely related true beliefs.

Secondly, widespread systematic error is not just a possibility that could arise if evolution were true: it is, instead, a feature of some of our most basic cognitive systems—namely, those involved in the generation of basic perceptual beliefs. Thus, when I look at a well-watered fairway that I am walking along, I acquire a certain belief, which I express by saying, "The grass is very green." But it is not the belief I would have if I were now a child. Nor is it the type of belief that human beings had, with a very few exceptions—such as Democritus—before the distinction between primary and secondary qualities

---

[11] For some very interesting discussion of inferential strategies, see Fales (2002). Also especially relevant here are Nesbitt and Ross (1980) and Kahneman, Slovic, and Tversky (1982).

was set out by Robert Boyle (1666), and later made famous by Locke with the publication of his *Essay Concerning Human Understanding* in 1690. For when a scientifically educated person looks at green grass now, the belief that the person acquires—unless his or her knowledge of the scientific facts of perception is unusually detailed—will be something like the belief that there is a power in the grass to reflect wavelengths of light of such a sort as to produce experiences with the property of qualitative greenness in him or her, whereas, when one was a child, the belief one acquired was a very different one: the belief, namely, that qualitative greenness was a property of the grass itself. It is the latter sort of belief that our perceptual faculties *naturally* give rise to, and such beliefs are false.

The upshot is that our perceptual faculties are not, contrary to what Plantinga claims, reliable in his sense, since they do not generate mainly true beliefs. On the contrary, all of the beliefs that they naturally generate concerning secondary qualities are false, since they locate those properties in external, physical objects, whereas those properties are in fact properties of experiences. So systematic error reflecting a very deep misconception about the world is not only possible: it is actual.

Ultimately, of course, we have been able, by supplementing perceptual experience with scientific reasoning and theorizing, to arrive at beliefs about the objects we perceive that are true, rather than false.

Summing Up

In his opening statement, Plantinga attempted to show that theistic belief is rational by demonstrating that one very important alternative to it—namely, philosophical naturalism—is untenable, and he offered three arguments in support of that claim. In response, I have argued that none of those arguments is sound.

I have not, on the other hand, set out any argument in support of naturalism. My main reason for not doing so is that the topic we are discussing is whether theism is true, not whether naturalism is true.

In addition, however, the argument I offered for the conclusion that it is very unlikely that God exists is completely independent of the question of whether naturalism is true. As far as the argument from evil goes, some non-theistic form of supernaturalism might be true. Perhaps there is an omnipotent and omniscient deity, but he is either evil, to a greater or less extent, or morally indifferent. Or perhaps there is a rather good deity with limited power or limited knowledge. Or perhaps some form of polytheism is true.

Finally, naturalism involves very different claims, including, first, the thesis that no supernatural being intervenes in the events of this world; secondly, the claim that the natural world does not have a supernatural origin; and, thirdly, the thesis that reality contains no supernatural beings at all. Though I am inclined to think that all three theses are probably true, I also believe that they differ greatly with regard to epistemic status. The third thesis, for example, seems to me a rather speculative thesis for which I think there is probably only rather mild support, whereas the first thesis, in contrast, is one for which I think there is very strong evidence, but evidence requiring extremely detailed investigation of such things as religious experiences, and purportedly miraculous events.

A defence of the first of these theses would be an effective way of arguing that *revealed* religions—such as Christianity, Judaism, and Islam—are not true. But this would not itself show that theism is false. For that, one needs the argument from evil.

To sum up, then, in this chapter I have, first of all, examined Plantinga's arguments against naturalism in a detailed way, and argued that none of them is successful. I then concluded by making the crucial, but widely overlooked point that even if some argument against naturalism were sound, that would not serve to show that it was reasonable to believe in the existence of God.

5

Can Robots Think?

Reply to Tooley's Second Statement

Alvin Plantinga

There is much to admire in Michael Tooley's response to my opening statement, although of course I am less than wildly enthusiastic about his conclusion that my arguments against naturalism are unsound. On the contrary, I believe they are cogent, and in what follows will explain why I don't find Tooley's arguments to the contrary compelling.

Now Tooley starts more hares than I can chase, given my space. For the most part I'll focus on the most important claims he makes, but I'll begin with a brief comment on his first two responses. I proposed that the notion of health involves proper function. Tooley suggests that this notion can't be explained just in terms of proper function: "The moral is that terms such as 'healthy' and 'diseased' and 'injured' are evaluative: a state of health is a state that is intrinsically *good* for the individual . . ." (p. 186, Tooley's emphasis). Perhaps he's right. If he *is* right, then the thing to say is that the notion of health involves proper function (in such a way that the assertion that an organism is healthy entails that it is functioning properly), but also involves a normative component. This is of course entirely compatible with my main claim in this neighborhood, namely, that naturalism can't accommodate the notion of proper function.

Tooley also offers objections to my account of warrant (in *Warrant and Proper Function*); I've responded elsewhere to most of these (e.g., the suggestion that a being capable of knowledge could come to be just by way of an accident[1]) and won't repeat those responses here. Further, Tooley suggests that warrant, as

---

[1] "Warrant and Designing Agents: a Reply to James Taylor," *Philosophical Studies* 64 (1991):203–15.

I think of it, is a complex concept, involving both justification and some fourth condition. I'm not sure warrant *does* entail justification (that depends, in part, on what justification *is*), but the concept of warrant is indeed complex (involving, as I see it, the notions of an appropriate environment and a good design plan as well as proper function). What I don't see is why that's a problem. Finally, Tooley suggests that my criticism of internalist epistemologies is lacking, in that internalist epistemologists never intended to propose an account of warrant, but only of justification: "what Plantinga proceeds to do is to attribute to internalists an internalist account of *warrant*, whereas what internalists defend is an internalist account of *justification. . . .*" (p. 188, Tooley's emphasis). I took it that internalist epistemologists were proposing that justification (along with belief and truth) is the central property involved in knowledge; it is *nearly* sufficient for knowledge, and needs in addition only a fillip of some sort to mollify Gettier. I argued that justification isn't anywhere nearly sufficient, and that (depending on the specific version of justification suggested) it isn't necessary either.

I   Can a Material Thing Think?

Turning to Tooley's more crucial claims, let's first look at his attempt to explain how it is possible that a material object can think. This does double duty in the context of our discussion. On the one hand, it is a direct response to my argument that no material object *can* think; on the other, his attempt to link belief content with indication is a response to my suggestion (in part III B, pp. 30ff.) that there need be no connection between indication and belief.

So let's take a closer look. I claimed (part III C, pp. 54ff.) that we can see on reflection, just as Leibniz suggested, that thought can't arise from the interaction of the parts of a material object. So if elementary particles can't think, then the same will go for atoms composed of such particles, molecules composed of atoms, cells composed of molecules, and so on. Here Tooley is replying to this argument; he's attempting to explain how a material object *can* think. What he proposes, in brief (very brief), is that a material thing, for example a robot, can have *experiences*; but then if those experiences are causally related in the right way to behavioral or motor outputs, sequences of them can become beliefs. This proposal is what I want to examine.

A.   Intensionality relevant?

Tooley begins by pointing out that sentential *belief* contexts are *intensional* (p. 199). He proposes two marks for an intensional context: (a) interchange of co-designative singular terms doesn't always preserve truth value, and (b) existential generalization doesn't always hold (p. 199). Next, he claims that *causal* (sentential) contexts are also intensional. The fact that both these kinds of sentential contexts are intensional, he says, gives us a clue as to the source of the intensionality of belief contexts: the source is an intimate connection of belief with causality. But here already things have the look of going awry. First, it is far from clear that causal contexts *are* intensional. Note Tooley's example:

(1) The candle melted because it was near the hottest object in the room.

(2) The hottest object in the room = the reddest object in the room.

Therefore

(3) The candle melted because it was near the reddest object in the room.

Tooley claims that (1) and (2) are true and that (3) is false. But isn't (3) *true*? The candle *did* melt because it was near the reddest object in the room (that being the hottest object in the room). It is of course true that this object caused the candle to melt by virtue of its *heat*, not by virtue of its *color*; still, the above inference seems perfectly truth-preserving. Furthermore, existential generalization also seems to hold for (1): if (1) is true, then indeed there *is* something x such that the candle melted because it was close to x, namely, that thing which is both the hottest thing in the room and the reddest thing in the room.

More important, though, why think the intensionality of certain sentential contexts has anything to do with questions about the nature of mental entities or processes? Intensionality is a property of certain *linguistic* items, i.e., sentential contexts. The question we are addressing, however, is a question about *the nature of belief content* and what sorts of things can have it; what has the former to do with the latter? Notice that it is easy to construct a language in which *all* contexts are intensional. Consider an extension of English in which everything has two names, a name with an even number of letters, and a name with an odd number of letters, e.g., 'Jorge' and 'George.' On even-numbered days of the month, a context containing an even-numbered name expresses the proposition you think it does; on odd-numbered days it expresses the proposition *2 = 1*. On odd-numbered days of the month, on the other hand, a context containing an odd-numbered name expresses the proposition you think it does, while a sentence containing an even-numbered name expresses the proposition *2 = 1*. (We ignore, for the moment, complex contexts containing more than one name, etc.) All sentential contexts in this language are intensional; but does that have any implications whatever for questions about the nature of beliefs, the sorts of things that can have beliefs, or indeed any metaphysical questions at all?

B. Can Robbie think?

Of course Tooley's case doesn't depend on this alleged clue; so let's follow him further. He first introduces a robot named 'Robo,' who, he says, has *quasi*-beliefs and *quasi*-desires; and certain sentences about Robo are intensional. (As I pointed out above, we can easily extend English in such a way that all sentences about Robo—and everything else—come out intensional.) Tooley agrees that in having quasi-beliefs and -desires, Robo doesn't actually have beliefs and desires; but then why does he call these states "quasi-beliefs" and "quasi-desires"? Is he trying to soften us up for his conclusion that material objects like robots really can have beliefs and desires? In any event, he turns next to a much more impressive robot, Robbie, who, he says, has qualia, experiences: "... . Robbie's internal, purely physical states causally give rise to qualia" (p. 202). Here, I take it, the subject of these qualia, the thing that *has* these experiences, is Robbie, this material object, itself; presumably Tooley doesn't intend that there is an immaterial self connected with Robbie (in the way, say, the dualist typically thinks immaterial selves are connected with human bodies). He then asks: "Am I entitled to make this assumption?" (p. 202). Apparently he thinks the answer is yes: "Well, human brain states causally give rise to sensations and experiences, so it is not easy to see how it could be *logically* impossible for electronic circuitry to do the same" (p. 202, Tooley's emphasis).

But that's not much of a reason for supposing that a material object like a robot could have experiences. First, the dualist, one who believes that material objects can't think, won't ordinarily hold that it is logically impossible for electronic circuitry to give rise to sensations and experience (perhaps such circuitry could replace the neural processes that give rise to sensation and experience); what she thinks logically impossible is that a material thing can *have* experiences and sensations. Second, the dualist, at least the interactionist dualist, will of course agree with Tooley that human brain states can causally give rise to sensations and experiences; they do so by causing mental states in the immaterial mind or self whose body contains those brain states. (Descartes, surely, realized that a sharp rap on the head can induce certain mental states—seeing stars, for example.) So it is agreed on all sides that brain states can cause sensations and experience. But why think that so much as even slyly suggests that a *material thing* can have experiences, or qualia, or mental states? The dualist agrees that brain states can causally give rise to sensations and experiences; but why think that's a reason for thinking a material thing can *have* experiences?

Part of the dialectical structure of the debate between materialists and dualists, of course, is that according to dualists, material objects can't be the subject of such mental states as experiences, qualia, ways of being appeared to, although material processes and events can cause such mental states in immaterial selves; how does it advance the state of the debate by blandly assuming that a material robot can be the subject of those experiences?

Further, as of course Tooley realizes, Leibniz's argument is for the conclusion that *no* mental states can be generated just by the interaction of material substances or events. It's not just that, according to Leibniz, *beliefs* can't be generated in that way: mental states in general, and experiences, qualia, in particular can't. Indeed, the intuition that no merely material object can have experiences or qualia is probably even stronger than the intuition that material objects can't form beliefs and reason.[2] Thus Jerry Fodor proposes an account of how a material structure could be a belief: roughly, such a structure *S* is a cow-belief just if it is a cow concept in the belief box.[3] (Where a structure is a cow-concept if it is caused by cows and is such that if there were no cow-caused structures of that sort, there would be no non-cow-caused structure of that sort; and it is not the case that if there were no non-cow-caused structure of that sort, there would be no cow-caused structures of that sort.) So Fodor proposes an answer to the question: how can a material object think? But he despairs of giving an answer to the same question about material objects and qualia.

Now in a way Tooley anticipates this objection; earlier on he says that if in my original statement I had argued (as I just did) that material objects cannot have experiences, he would have responded

> . . . first, that a range of animals that presumably do not have immaterial minds have experiences; secondly, that there can be psychophysical laws linking brain states with experiences, running in both directions, thereby relating experiences

---

[2]Tooley suggests that materialists don't have the intuition that material objects can't think. But many, perhaps most, materialists *do* have that intuition. (Paul Churchland, Jaegwon Kim, and many others propose that dualism is the natural base-line position: merely material things can't think. There is also empirical evidence for their suggestion: see, for example, the empirical studies by Justin Barrett, "Exploring the Natural Foundations of Religion," *Trends in Cognitive Science* 4 (2000), pp. 29–34, and those referred to by Paul Bloom in "Is God an Accident?" *Atlantic Monthly* 296:5 (Dec. 2005), pp. 105–12. What's true, here, is that materialists propose positions according to which material objects *can* think; but that is far from showing that they don't also have the intuition that material objects *can't* think. Clearly they might have that intuition, but think there are stronger reasons for supposing that material objects can think—e.g., a general commitment to materialism, or fear and loathing of dualism (Daniel Dennett), or the thought that dualism is subject to insurmountable difficulties.

[3]*A Theory of Content and Other Essays* (Cambridge, MA: MIT Press, 1992), p. 91.

to bodies; thirdly, that awareness of experiences can be analyzed in terms of indexical beliefs and thought; and, fourthly, that the unity of experiences and other mental states that characterizes persons, both at a time and over time, can be explained in terms of appropriate causal relations. (p. 222)

By way of brief response: I'm in enthusiastic agreement with Tooley that some animals have experiences; but I fail to see the source of his presumption that they don't have immaterial minds. As for psychophysical laws linking brain states with experiences, perhaps (*pace* Davidson) there are such laws, but even if there are, I fail to see how their existence suggests (let alone shows) that material objects can have experiences; the existence of such laws, obviously, is perfectly compatible with the position that no material object can have experiences. (What these laws show, from the dualist perspective, is that there are causal relations between an immaterial person and her body.) As for the third suggestion, I can't quite see its relevance. Tooley analyzes belief in terms of experiences; how, then, does the fact, if it is a fact, that awareness of experiences can be analyzed in terms of certain beliefs and thoughts tend to show that a material object can have experiences? What the dualist claims is that material objects can't have either beliefs *or* experiences; it doesn't really matter whether or not awareness of experiences can be analyzed in terms of beliefs and thoughts. Finally, there is the suggestion that the unity of experience (both at a time and over time) can be explained in terms of appropriate causal relations. I very much doubt that this is so; certainly no one has so far succeeded in giving such an explanation.

An essential part of Tooley's attempt to show how a material object can think and have beliefs, therefore, is his *assumption* that such objects can have experiences. So is he entitled to this assumption? I should think not. He's certainly entitled to *argue for* this proposition (he doesn't); but he can't sensibly just *assume* it.

The next step in Tooley's project is to argue that a belief *just is* a certain sequence of experiences. First, he postulates "a considerably more complex robot—Robbie—that, among other things has experiences and uses language" (p. 202). Furthermore, he says (p. 202), Robbie is such that these experiences are caused by and cause electronic states; still further there are one-to-one correspondences between the types of experiences Robbie enjoys and certain electronic states it harbors, so that a given electronic state is an *indicator* of the robot's having a given sort of experience (for example, being appeared to greenly). Next, this robot is equipped with sound-generating devices of such a sort that when, for example, it is appeared to greenly, it tends to produce "a sequence of sounds corresponding to those in an utterance of 'That's an instance of greenness'" (p. 202). (What we have here, apparently, is an English-speaking robot.) Thus its producing those sounds, like those electronic states, is an indicator of its being appeared to greenly. But endowing this robot with these two properties isn't sufficient, says Tooley, for its having beliefs. He therefore adds two more properties. First, this electronic state G in the robot, the state caused by its being appeared to greenly, not only causes it to utter those sounds; it also causes the robot to have a sequence of auditory experiences corresponding to the experiences it has when it 'hears' an utterance of "That's an instance of greenness" (p. 203).

Finally, Tooley also attributes to this robot the ability to "focus its attention" on certain parts of its 'phenomenal field': "one can decide which part of one's total experience at a given time will give rise to the most detailed beliefs. This property is crucial, I believe, to the having of indexical beliefs and thoughts . . . . So we need to attribute this ability to Robbie" (p. 203). This robot, then, has attention (can attend to things) and is able to focus its attention; still further, it can make decisions! And the next and crowning step is to claim that the series of experiences that Robbie 'has' under these conditions just is a belief:

> The upshot is that we now have, in Robbie, sequences of qualia that have the following three properties. First they are reliable indicators of electronic states of type G. Secondly, they are also, therefore, reliable indicators of qualia involving instances of qualitative greenness. Thirdly they are caused by the qualia to which Robbie stands in the strongest information-accessing relation. The question, now, is whether such a structure sequence of qualia, caused in this way, is a *thought*—and specifically, an indexical thought that *that* is an instance of qualitative greenness.
>   I think that this is the case, . . . (p. 204, Tooley's emphasis)

All this strikes me as the sheerest phantasmagoria. You might as well claim that my new and very complex high-definition television has beliefs. Can't I just assume that it, like Robbie, has experiences, qualia, corresponding to what it displays on the screen? It also issues sounds that, when uttered by a person, express propositions appropriate to what it displays on the screen; we can add, if we like, that (like Robbie) it has the sort of experience had by a person who hears the sounds it produces. My television also seems to display the ability to 'focus its attention' on certain parts of its experience—it sometimes zooms in on part of what it displays, for example, thereby evincing its 'decision' to focus on that part. But the fact is my television doesn't have qualia, it doesn't focus its attention (or have any attention to focus), and it doesn't make decisions. Furthermore, it *can't* make decisions, just as a tree can't decide that now it's time to shed its leaves. Both a tree and Robbie are the wrong sorts of thing to make decisions—or to have experiences, or to attend to them. These are things that only a *person* can do; and Robbie isn't the right kind of thing to be a person—any more than, say, a number or a triangle or a set or a proposition. Merely assuming, as Tooley does, that this robot *can* do these things—that it is a person—doesn't touch that intuition at all. Of course if there were an *argument* for Robbie's being able to do these things, we would have to pay attention. But merely *positing* a robot with these powers goes nowhere.

That's the basic problem; there is another nearly as serious. According to Tooley, a certain sequence of qualia, a sequence of ways of being appeared to, is a thought—in particular a belief. This also seems mistaken. This idea— that a belief is a mental image or quale or a way of being appeared to, or perhaps a series of such—goes back to the British empiricists. Thus David Hume thought that mental life consisted in what he called impressions and ideas, with the ideas being something like fading copies of the impressions. He thought that a memory, for example, was a decaying impression. But a sequence of qualia, once more, isn't the sort of thing that can be true or false—more exactly, it isn't the sort of thing that constitutes the grasping of and asserting of a proposition. It's like a sequence of snap-shots. One can *use* a photo, or a sequence of them, to assert a proposition: I show you a photo and tell you this is what Mt. Ranier looks like from Paradise Inn at dawn.[4] Then I've used the photo to assert the proposition, *Mt. Rainier looks like that from Paradise Inn at dawn.* But I can use the same photo to assert the proposition that this is *not* the way it looks at dawn. A series of qualia, or mental images of any sort, just, in themselves, don't have or display the assertive *that's the way it is* element of a belief. A sequence of qualia isn't the or a grasp of a proposition, or an entertaining of a proposition, or an entertaining with assent of a proposition. So even if by some arcane magic one could get a mechanical device to have sensations or qualia, one still wouldn't get the thing to have beliefs—not even if you causally linked the qualia to other qualia and to devices that make sounds like those that a person makes when she utters a sentence that expresses a proposition.

Still further, suppose you thought you could get a machine to have sensations by constructing the right kind of electronic circuitry, and also that you could get it to have *beliefs* by constructing it in such a way that these sequences of these sensations were causally linked to the production of certain sounds. Add, if you like, that this machine 'focuses its attention' and 'makes decisions.' Why suppose it would hold the beliefs Tooley says it would?

---

[4] Perhaps in the same way one could also use a mental image to assert a proposition. Neuroscience advances to the point where you can induce a mental image in me, a mental image as of Mt. Rainier at sunset. Then you can assert a proposition by referring to that image—the one presently present in me—and saying, "*That's* what Mt. Rainer looks like at sunset."

He claims this machine, under these circumstances, would form the belief *That's an instance of greenness*. But even if by some magic you could get this machine to form a belief in this way, why think it would form *that* belief? Maybe instead it would form beliefs like *I really hate that color*, or *that's not an instance of greenness*, or, for that matter, *I wish I were in Dixie*, or any other belief.

Tooley asks himself the same question. He then gives his reasons: "First, I think that the correct account of content is the property-dualist causal account. If this is right, then electronic states of type *G*, regardless of whether they are beliefs, or merely proto-beliefs, have as their content that there exists an instance of qualitative greenness" (p. 204). This is perhaps fair enough; it could be that there be a certain very high-tech machine that goes into a certain electronic state whenever there exists an instance of qualitative greenness— i.e., whenever someone is appeared to greenly (which, one suspects, would be all the time). Then we could say that this electronic state had content: *indicator* content. It's an indicator of there being an instance of greenness. But of course indicator content isn't necessarily belief content. The height of the mercury column in your thermometer indicates the ambient temperature and thus the height of the mercury column has indicator content; neither the thermometer nor anything else in the neighborhood need belief that the temperature is thus and so. Second, says Tooley, "if one has the ability to determine the part of one's total experience to which one stands in the strongest information-accessing relation at a given time, one thereby has the power to fix the referents of indexical terms . . ." (p. 204). Perhaps this is right; but why think a *machine* can do that sort of thing—even granting, contrary to fact as I see it, that a machine could have experiences in the first place? "Finally," he says, "none of these things—qualia, syntactically structured sequences of experiential states, and causal connections—presupposes the presence of an immaterial mind, as the case of Robbie shows" (p. 205).

"As the case of Robbie *shows*"? Tooley *assumes*, he said earlier, that this robot could have experiences. He also just assumes that this machine has *attention*, can *focus its attention* on some of these experiences, and that it can *decide* which of its experiences it will *attend* to. He just assumes or announces, furthermore, that there is a causal relation such that when a sequence of such experiences is related in that way to other things (e.g., behavior), then it becomes a *thought*, a belief. But how can such a series of mere assumptions *show* anything at all, let alone that "Purely material entities, accordingly, can have beliefs and thoughts" (p. 205)? How can it be any kind of counter to an argument to the effect that material objects can't think?

Accordingly, I have two main criticisms. First, the assumption that material objects can have experience is unsupported, gratuitous, and, in this context, question-begging. And second, the claim that a mere sequence of qualia can be a *belief*, with *the entertainment with assent* that goes with belief, is clearly false.

II Tooley's Reply to the Evolutionary Argument against Naturalism

Let '*N*' stand for philosophical naturalism, the idea that there is no such person as God (no omnipotent, omniscient, and wholly good being) nor anything *like* God; and for present purposes construe naturalism as also including both (1) materialism about human beings, and (2) the proposition that our cognitive faculties have come to be by way of the processes to which contemporary evolutionary theory directs our attention (random genetic mutation and natural selection would be the leading candidates). Let '*R*' stand for the proposition that our cognitive faculties are reliable. '$P(R/N)$' is then the probability of *R* given naturalism so construed. Now I argued (Initial Statement, part B1) that if you believe *N*, and also see that this probability is low or inscrutable, then you have a defeater for *R*—a reason to give it up, to fail to believe it, to withhold assent from it. This defeater doesn't give you a reason for believing not-*R*; it rather gives you a reason for not believing *R*. (It's an undercutting defeater, not a rebutting defeater.)

Tooley, as one would expect, demurs. With respect to inscrutability, he says,

> If, as I do, one thinks that for any hypothesis *h* and any evidence *e*, there is some number that is the logical probability of *h* given *e*, one might attempt to show that if one cannot determine what that number is, one is at least justified in believing that it is not high. But is this right? I think that it is not at all clear that it is. (p. 206)

But here there is a misunderstanding. I wasn't supposing that if this probability is inscrutable for you, you are justified in believing that it isn't high; what I was thinking is that under those conditions you are *not* justified in believing that it *is* high. If it's wholly inscrutable for you, you aren't justified in forming *any* belief according to which it is located in some proper part of the whole unit interval. Perhaps Tooley assumed that I was proposing a *rebutting* defeater, where a rebutting defeater gives one a reason to believe the *denial* of the defeated belief. But what I was proposing is that the partisan of *N* gets an *undercutting* defeater—one (as I said above) that gives him a reason for withholding the defeated belief, but not a reason for believing its denial.

Second, Tooley suggests that the claim he accepts—that for any hypothesis *h* and any evidence *e*, there is some number that is the logical probability of *h* given *e*—is controversial, and that if it is false, "then the conjunction of *e* with the proposition that the probability of h given e is inscrutable is surely not a defeater for h" (p. 206). But this seems to me too strong. What I assume is that there is an objective probability here, but it needn't be the sort of *logical* probability that Tooley endorses. Furthermore, there need be no *number* such that the probability in question is equal to that number; perhaps the most that can correctly be said is that the probability of a proposition is high, or fairly high, or low, or fairly low, or about the same as the probability of its denial. Under these conditions it could still be that the conjunction of e with the proposition that the probability of h given e is inscrutable is a defeater for h.

Third, Tooley asks us to consider an ordinary person who "initially believes that his cognitive faculties are reliable, but who has no idea what produced those faculties, or how probable it is, relative to the totality, T, of the other things that he is justified in believing, that his faculties are reliable" (p. 206). Tooley claims that on my position such a person would have a defeater for his belief that R. But it sounds like this person doesn't believe N—he has no opinion there. Suppose, however, that he *does* believe N, but has never considered the probability of R on N and for that reason has no idea what that probability is. Under those conditions he doesn't have a defeater for R; he has a defeater only if he has thought about this probability, and finds himself unable to say what it is (it might be high, or it might be low, but he has no idea what it is). Then he does have a defeater. By analogy, suppose you've just purchased a new sphygmomanometer; naturally enough, you assume that it is reliable. But now you learn that your sphygmomanometer was made in a factory owned by a Luddite who aims to create as much confusion as he can in the medical community, to that end by fashioning instruments a certain proportion of which are completely unreliable. You know this much but you have no idea what that proportion is. Then the probability of your sphygmomanometer's being reliable, given its origin, is inscrutable for you—and you certainly have a defeater for your initial belief that it is reliable.

Tooley proposes to concentrate, however, on the following "most crucial" part of my argument, which, he says is this premise:

> (7) If Darwinian evolution is true, then even if it is true both that neural states of type N are, in an organism H, reliable indictors of the presence of an instance of property P, and also that states of type N have content C, there is no reason why content C need be related to property P. (p. 207)

He goes on to say that given an "intrinsic" (p. 208) model of content, (7) seems right, and the argument sound; but given a causal *model* of content—in particular, the version he accepts—premise (7), he says, is false.

Now here there is something confusing. In the previous section (p. 204) Tooley seemed to be claiming that a certain *sequence of qualia* is a thought, a belief (the belief that *this* is an instance of greenness). But here he suggests that a belief is a *neural state* or *neural structure*: "But if a property-dualist, causal theory of content is correct, and *if* a neural, indicator state does give rise to syntactically structured experiential states in an appropriate way, then that neural state *is* a belief" (p. 209, Tooley's emphasis). Well, perhaps it doesn't matter, for present purposes, which version we settle on—although a sequence of qualia might be a bit less counter-intuitive if only because such a series is a series of clearly mental events.

In any event, what I suggested (p. 35) is that, given materialism, the plausible thing to think is that such mental properties as *being a belief with such and such content* are either *identical* with neurophysiological (NP) properties or *supervene* upon them, either logically or causally. Tooley opts for the second of these possibilities: content properties causally supervene on NP properties. I argued, with respect to that possibility, that, as far as we can see, if belief content does thus supervene on (possibly complex) NP properties, *any* belief content could supervene on a given NP property; we can't see any reason for supposing *one* content as opposed to *another* should be the one to supervene on a given NP property. So consider a neural structure in a creature, a structure complex enough to give rise to belief content. This structure is also adaptive; let's suppose that in the circumstances in question it causes fleeing. (There's a tiger approaching.) We assume, therefore, that the structure is adaptive, and that it is complex enough to give rise to content: a content property supervenes upon its NP properties. But why assume, I said, that this content is in fact *true*? Couldn't it just as well be false? All we know is that it supervenes on the NP properties of an adaptive neural structure—one that causes the right behavior. But why think that content must be true? Indeed, it might have nothing at all to do with the environmental circumstances—it could be anything, as far as we can tell.[5] But then the probability that it is true will have to be rated as about the same as the probability that it is false. And then there will be a low probability that a high enough proportion of this creature's beliefs are true for its cognitive faculties to be reliable.

Tooley responds as follows:

> . . . if a property-dualist, causal theory of content is correct, and *if* a neural, indicator state does give rise to syntactically structured experiential states in an appropriate way, then that neural state *is* a belief. (p. 209)

How does Tooley respond? As we have seen from the quote at the top of the page, he proposes that a property-dualist, causal theory of content is indeed correct; hence if such an indicator state causes experiential states in

---

[5] Again, compare dreaming, where the subvening NP properties are presumably adaptive, but the supervening content has nothing to do with the dreamer's environmental circumstances.

the appropriate way, that indicator state is a belief. Furthermore, contrary to what I argued, this belief would have to be true. Why so? Why think the belief content thus supervening is in fact *true*? Couldn't it just as well be false? No, says Tooley, because

> If the neural state is an indicator of the presence of a *basic* descriptive property of *experiences*, such as qualitative greenness, then the causal relation in question fixes the content of the neural state. (pp. 209–10, original emphasis)

and

> … the content of any indexical belief about a *basic* observational/introspectible property of experiences *logically supervenes* upon the causal relation that makes it the case that the relevant neural state is a reliable indicator of the qualitative property in question. (p. 210, original emphasis)

OK, suppose so; still, why think the content in question, the belief, must be *true*? Because,

> … given the satisfaction of a further condition related to indexicality, the content of the neural state is precisely the indexical belief that that's an instance of qualitative greenness. (p. 210)

And this belief (in the circumstances in question) is of course true. But why think *that* is the content of the belief that thus arises? Why couldn't it just as well be the belief that, e.g., *that's* an ugly color, or *that's* a quale I've never had before, or *that's* my favorite quale, or *that's* a small green horse? Why, indeed, must it have anything at all to do with greenness? Maybe the belief that arises in Robbie, under those conditions, is *My programmer is really good to me*, or *7 + 5 = 12*. Tooley thinks it is *logically necessary* that if there is a "causal relation that makes it the case that the relevant neural state is a reliable indicator of the qualitative property in question", (p. 210), then a certain belief arises: the belief that *that's* an instance of greenness. But that proposition certainly doesn't *look* as if it's logically necessary; in fact it looks for all the world to be contingent, if true at all. It seems entirely possible that *no* belief should arise under those circumstances; it seems equally possible that a belief should arise, but some totally different belief, perhaps one inconsistent with the belief Tooley says would in fact arise. What reason, then, do we have for thinking that the belief Tooley *says* would arise is in fact the belief that *would* arise? Is this anything more than baseless speculation or mere assertion—even granting, contrary to fact, as I see it, that it is possible that such a material structure should be a belief?

There is even more trouble forthcoming. In Robbie's case, as far as we've been told, belief content consists in such propositions as *this is green* (where the referent of 'this' is a quale). But that's not going to be of much use to Tooley's project of refuting the Evolutionary Argument Against Naturalism (EAAN). Most of our beliefs, naturally enough, aren't beliefs about qualia, so even if our *qualia* beliefs were mostly true, it wouldn't at all follow that our cognitive faculties are reliable. How about beliefs involving tigers (not to mention such beliefs as naturalism itself)? Here Tooley's strategy involves "pretending that direct realism is true, so that one's foundational present-tense, indexical beliefs are beliefs about basic observational properties of external objects, rather than about basic properties of experiences" (p. 211). Tooley doesn't tell us *which* neural processes become beliefs about tigers, for example; but, following the analogy of his claims about qualia beliefs, presumably what would become a belief about tigers would be tiger-indicators—neural structures that were causally correlated with the presence of tigers. (Presumably, to be tiger beliefs, these structures would also have to be appropriately connected, causally, with behavior.) Finally, under these conditions, the belief formed would be the belief that *that's a tiger*—where the 'that' refers to a tiger.

There are two difficulties, one severe and the other crushing. Concede, as certainly seems plausible, that certain neural structures are caused by tigers, and suppose these neural structures in turn cause adaptive behavior. Presumably the neural structure in question can be caused by things other than tigers: a horse under conditions of poor lighting, or an elk in the distance, or a house cat much closer than one thinks, or even a cinematic or holographic tiger. If this can happen, wouldn't the resulting content have to be something like *this is a tiger or this is an elk or this is a house cat or . . . .* Indeed, couldn't this very structure arise in a dream? And be caused, perhaps, by indigestion? This "disjunction problem" was pointed out by Jerry Fodor and has attracted a lot of attention ever since.[6] Fodor's own solution is unsuccessful, at least if taken as a real solution—i.e., as giving necessary and sufficient conditions for a belief's having a certain content; and no one else has done much better.

But there is a much deeper and more difficult problem for Tooley's view— one in comparison with which the disjunction problem pales into utter insignificance. First, why think that, under these conditions, the creature (we're still talking about hypothetical creatures a lot like us on some other planet) in question would form the belief *that's a tiger*? Or any belief in that neighborhood? This belief is supposed to supervene on NP properties, including causal properties. These NP properties, we may assume, cause adaptive behavior. So let's assume that content properties supervene on adaptive NP properties: what does that tell us about the supervening content properties? What does this tell us about the content of the belief that gets formed under these conditions, assuming that some belief gets formed? As far as I can see, nothing whatever.

---

[6] *Psychosemantics: The Problem of Meaning in the Philosophy of Mind* (Cambridge: MIT Press, 1987), p. 100.

The subvening properties must be adaptive, cause adaptive behavior, but they can perfectly well do that no matter *what* the induced belief content. It could be that there is no connection between the state of affairs causing the subvening NP properties and the content of the supervening belief—those beliefs need not be so much as *about* the objects involved in the state of affairs causing the subvening properties. They could be anything. These supervening beliefs might be like dream beliefs—caused by adaptive NP properties, but having no relevance to what is happening. Or they could be about objects involved in the causally relevant states of affairs, but false—for example, the *denials* of the beliefs Tooley attributes to them.

Of course Tooley is endorsing a causal theory of content, involving, presumably, the idea that content properties supervening on NP properties will involve objects that are involved in those causally relevant states of affairs. So perhaps on this suggestion the presence of a tiger causes certain NP properties on which content properties supervene; the resultant belief will therefore be the belief *that's a tiger*. Presumably things *could* go that way; but we have no reason at all to think that's how they *would* go. That they would go the way Tooley says they would is, once more, mere assertion of baseless speculation. The upshot is that Tooley merely *assumes* that the content of belief is fixed by causal relations, and, furthermore, so fixed that most beliefs will be true. That, it seems to me, is nothing like a successful or satisfactory response to the EAAN. It would be as if the theist responded to Tooley's antitheistic argument from evil by simply postulating, assuming without argument, that God has a good reason for permitting each of the evils the world displays. This proposition might be true (and in fact I believe it is); but merely postulating it isn't much of a response to Tooley's argument. I say the same holds for Tooley's response to the EAAN. Tooley's response to this argument is no more effective than his response to the argument against materialism.

By way of summary: in my initial statement I proposed three arguments against naturalism (construed as including materialism and also the proposition that our cognitive faculties have come to be by way of Darwinian evolution). First, naturalism can't accommodate the notion of proper function: if naturalism were true, there wouldn't be a distinction between proper function and malfunction; no distinction between health and sickness. Second, one who accepts naturalism has a defeater for R and hence for whatever she believes, including naturalism itself, so that naturalism is self-defeating, and therefore irrational. And third, no material object can hold beliefs, so that if naturalism were true, no one would ever believe anything. These arguments still seem to me to be entirely cogent.

6

Closing Statement and Response to Plantinga's Comments

Michael Tooley

1 Plantinga's Responses to My Two Arguments

1.1 Atheism as the default position

Plantinga divides my argument here into two steps, the first of which is as follows:

Here Tooley reasons as follows: the intrinsic probability of

(4) There is an omniscient, omnipotent, and wholly evil being

is as great as that of

(5) There is an omniscient, omnipotent, and morally indifferent being;

and each of these is at least as intrinsically probable as G. But then, assuming as he does that there couldn't be two omnipotent beings, at most one of these propositions can be true, in which case the probability of G can't be more than one third. (p. 165)

The second step is then as follows:

And he thinks the fact, as he sees it, that the intrinsic probability of G is no more than a third is sufficient for his conclusion—i.e., that *atheism*, not theism or agnosticism, is the rational position, given that there is no evidence, propositional or otherwise, for belief in God. (p. 165)

Plantinga thinks that both steps are problematic. In the case of the second step, his objection is as follows:

> But why think a thing like that? Why wouldn't agnosticism be perfectly rational? There are many propositions *P*, and many existential propositions *P*, where we have no positive evidence for *P* and where the intrinsic probability of *P* is no greater than one third, and where we don't believe not-*P*: we just fail to believe *P*. . . . Why think it's atheism, rather than agnosticism, that is in this sense the default position? (pp. 165–6)

My response turns upon a point about the concept of belief, namely, that beliefs, and disbeliefs, as we ordinarily conceive of those states, *admit of degrees*. Thus we often say, for example, things such as that John believes that *p* more strongly than he believes that *q*.

How are such degrees of belief and disbelief to be represented? A natural approach is to interpret degrees of belief and disbelief in terms of *subjective probabilities*, and so to view them as having, together, values that range from zero to one.

Once it is recognized that belief admits of degrees, the question arises as to what degree of belief is needed before one can be said to believe something— such as that God exists, or that God does not exist. To require a subjective probability of one—complete subjective certainty—is surely not correct, since it would then follow that people have very few beliefs indeed. But once that answer is ruled out, one is faced with drawing a line along a continuous range of subjective probabilities, and here it seems to me that there is only one value that corresponds to any non-arbitrary point—namely, the value one half, which represents the dividing line between cases where one believes that a proposition is more likely to be true than to be false and cases where one believes that the reverse is the case.

Accordingly, it seems best to me to use the term 'agnostic' to cover cases where one thinks that the existence of God and the non-existence of God are equally likely, or where one has no subjective probability at all concerning the relevant proposition—no degree of assent at all.[1]

On Plantinga's view, in contrast, it seems that a person can properly be characterized as agnostic with regard to the proposition that *p* while thinking that the probability that *p* is true is as low as one third, or as high as two thirds. This seems to me to be a very wide range of degrees of belief to include under the label of 'agnosticism.' How low, or how high, then, does the subjective probability in question have to be for Plantinga to say that one is not agnostic on

---

[1] Compare the grounds that Paul Draper offers in support of agnosticism in his 2002 essay "Seeking But Not Believing: Confessions of a Practicing Agnostic."

the truth of the proposition in question? If someone believes that the probability that p is true is 0.75, is he or she still an agnostic? If so, what about 0.85? If even that is not enough, what about 0.95?

Plantinga gives no indication of his view on this matter. But whatever it is, it seems to me that the range of degrees of belief that he includes under the label of "agnosticism" is far too wide, since I do not think that a person who thinks that p is twice as likely to be true as it is to be false is accurately described as an agnostic. Perhaps, however, I am wrong about this. If so, then rather than saying that the default position is atheism, I shall have to say, instead, that the default position is that the non-existence of God is at least twice as likely as the existence of God.

Plantinga's second objection is directed against the first step in my argument, and here Plantinga argues that there is no reason to believe that the *a priori* probability of an omniscient, omnipotent, and perfectly evil person is no lower than that of an omniscient, omnipotent, and perfectly good person, and similarly for that the *a priori* probability of an omniscient, omnipotent, and morally indifferent person.

Plantinga's argument involves the following propositions:

(10) There is no omniscient, omnipotent, and perfectly good person.

(11) There is an omniscient, omnipotent, and perfectly good person who has created fewer than 1000 persons.

and

(12) There is an omniscient, omnipotent, and perfectly good person who has created more than 1000 persons.

and it runs as follows:

As far as I can see, the relation among (10), (11) and (12) is just like that between G, (4) and (5). Setting aside any evidence dependent on the *sensus divinitatis*, one can't see, I submit, any difference between the intrinsic probabilities of (10) and (11); (11) looks as probable as (10). Now as far as I can see, the only reason for thinking that (4) is as probable, intrinsically, as G, is just that one can't see a difference in their probabilities. But then we have the same reason for thinking (11) as probable as (10); here too we can't see any difference in their probabilities. And the same goes for (12) and (10); once again, we can't see any difference in their probabilities, and hence have the same reason for thinking (12) as likely as (10), as we have for thinking (5) as likely as G. But of course if each of (11) and (12) is as probable, intrinsically, as (10), then the intrinsic probability of (10) can't exceed 1/3, in which case G, its denial, has an intrinsic probability at least as great as 2/3. But then we've got as good reason for thinking that the default position is theism as for thinking that it is atheism. (pp. 168–9)

The first thing to be said here is that one has good reason for rejecting this argument for the conclusion that G has an intrinsic probability at least as great as two thirds. For we can run a parallel argument, involving the following propositions, which result when the term "good" in (10), (11), and (12) is replaced by the term "evil":

(10*) There is no omniscient, omnipotent, and perfectly evil person.

(11*) There is an omniscient, omnipotent, and perfectly evil person who has created fewer than 1000 persons.

and

(12*) There is an omniscient, omnipotent, and perfectly evil person who has created more than 1000 persons.

The conclusions of the parallel argument will then be, first, that the denial of (10*) has an intrinsic probability at least as great as two thirds, and, secondly, that G has an intrinsic probability that cannot be greater than one third. Accordingly, the argument that Plantinga bases on (10), (11), and (12) cannot be sound.

The second, and crucial point, however, is this. Plantinga says that "the only reason" that he can see for thinking that the *a priori*, or intrinsic, probability of an omniscient, omnipotent, and perfectly evil person is as great as that of an omniscient, omnipotent, and perfectly good person is "just that one can't see a difference in their probabilities" (p. 169). But this is not the only reason, nor is it mine. My grounds for holding that the *a priori* probability of an omniscient, omnipotent, and perfectly evil person is as great as the *a priori* probability of an omniscient, omnipotent, and perfectly good person is connected with my views on how a system of logical probability can capture what is correct in the classical principle of indifference, while avoiding the contradictions to which the latter gives rise. Essentially, it seems to me that there are at least two principles that are very plausible, the first of which is this:

Principle 1: State descriptions and permutations of individuals. Any two state descriptions that differ only by a permutation of individuals are equally likely.

The second, and closely related, principle deals with genuine, non-conjunctive properties. Here one needs the idea of a sparse theory of properties—as set out, for example, by David Armstrong (1978)—where properties are identified, not with concepts, but with genuine universals, and according to which there are, for example, no disjunctive or negative universals. Given that concept, a *family* of properties can be defined as a maximal set of mutually incompatible, *non-conjunctive* properties, and the second principle can then be set out as follows:

> *Principle 2: State descriptions and families of properties.* Any two state descriptions that differ only by a permutation of properties belonging to a family of properties are equally likely.

My argument is now as follows. First, the property—call it P—of always choosing to do what is right, rather than what is wrong, is a genuine property, and so a universal. Another universal—call it Q—and one that it is incompatible with P, is the property of always choosing to do what is wrong, rather than what is right. Form the largest set of mutually incompatible, non-conjunctive universals that contains those two universals. Finally, consider any state description that involves the existence of an omniscient, omnipotent, and perfectly good person. A replacement of property P by property Q will map that state description into a corresponding one that involves, instead, the existence of an omniscient, omnipotent, and perfectly evil person. By the second principle, then, those two state descriptions must be equally likely.

In short, my reason for holding that the existence of an omniscient, omnipotent, and perfectly evil person is intrinsically no less likely than the existence of an omniscient, omnipotent, and perfectly good person is not that I can see no reason why the latter should be more likely than the former. It is rather that it seems to me that there is a fundamental principle of logical probability that entails that state descriptions that differ only via a permutation of universals belonging to a maximal set of mutually exclusive, non-conjunctive universals are equally likely.

1.2   The argument from evil

Plantinga, in commenting upon my version of the argument from evil, challenges two premises in the argument, the first of which is as follows:

> (15) No rightmaking properties that we know of are such that we are justified in believing both that an action of choosing not to prevent the Lisbon earthquake would have had those rightmaking properties, and that those properties are sufficiently serious to counterbalance the relevant wrongmaking property.

To show that this premise is incorrect, Plantinga argues that any theist will believe, and think that he is justified in believing, that "the action of permitting the Lisbon earthquake has the property of having been performed by God, who is a perfectly good person" (pp. 170–1). But this, Plantinga contends, is a rightmaking property, and one that outweighs the known wrongmaking properties. So any theist will reject statement (15).

Suppose that God exists, and, thus, permitted the Lisbon earthquake. One can ask, "*What* property did the action of permitting the Lisbon earthquake have that *made* it morally permissible for God to permit it?" The response that it had the property of having been permitted by God, who is perfectly good, is not a satisfactory answer to that question: there must be some other property that made it permissible for God to permit the Lisbon earthquake. The property of having been permitted by God, while it entails that there must have been a rightmaking property, is *not itself* a rightmaking property.

Plantinga sums up the situation with regard to (15), as he sees it, as follows: "The fact is that Tooley's premise presupposes that belief in God is *not* justified" (p. 171, original emphasis). But this is not so: one might be perfectly justified in believing in God, without being justified in believing that there is some rightmaking property *that one is aware of* that made it permissible for God to allow the Lisbon earthquake.

Next, Plantinga turns to the second of the two premises that he wants to call into question, namely:

(16) For any action whatever, the logical probability that the total wrong-making properties of the action outweigh the total rightmaking properties —including ones of which we have no knowledge—given that the action has a wrongmaking property that we know of, and there are no rightmaking properties that are known to be counterbalancing, is greater than one half.

Among the claims that I advanced in arguing in support of (16) were the following:

(1) Judged from a purely *a priori* point of view, the mere existence of wrongmaking properties is *no less likely* than the existence of rightmaking properties.

(2) Judged from a purely *a priori* point of view, the *likelihood* that there exists a rightmaking property with a moral weight whose absolute value is equal to M is no greater than the likelihood that there exists a wrongmaking property whose absolute value is equal to M.

Plantinga focuses on (2), but he says that he thinks that the considerations he is advancing apply equally to (1). So let us begin with (1). Is Plantinga right in holding that there is no reason to think that (1) is true?

Whether the existentially quantified proposition expressed by the sentence "There is a rightmaking property" is true depends upon what state description obtains—where a state description is a certain conjunction of atomic propositions and their negations. Consider, then, a state description that contains, as one of its conjuncts, an atomic proposition expressed by the sentence "*a* is a rightmaking property." Can such a state description be more likely than the state description that results when the expressions "rightmaking property" "wrongmaking property" are interchanged with each other—a state description that will contain, as one of its conjuncts, the atomic proposition expressed by the sentence "*a* is a wrongmaking property"?

My answer turns, once again, upon principles that are needed to capture what is sound in the classical principle of indifference. Consider, in particular, the second principle mentioned above:

> Any two state descriptions that differ only by a permutation of properties belonging to a family of properties are equally likely.

The point is then that the following is a family of properties: being a rightmaking property, being a wrongmaking property, and being a morally neutral property. Therefore, the second of the two state descriptions mentioned above must be just as likely as the first. Consequently, for any set of state descriptions each of which would make true the existentially quantified proposition that there is a rightmaking property, there must be a mapping that takes each such state description into a corresponding, equally likely state description that would make true the existentially quantified proposition that there is a wrongmaking property. So (1), above, is correct.

A closely related argument can be used to support (2). The reason is, first, that the proposition expressed by the sentence "*a* is a rightmaking property of magnitude *M*" can be analyzed in terms of the notion of making an action right to degree *M*. So consider any state description that contains, as one of its conjuncts, an atomic proposition expressed by the sentence "*a* is a property that makes an action right to degree *M*." Can such a state description be more likely than the state description that results when the term "right" and the term "wrong" are interchanged—a state description that will contain, as one of its conjuncts, the atomic proposition expressed by the sentence "*a* is a property that makes an action wrong to degree *M*"? The answer is that, in view of Principle 2, it cannot, since the set of properties that consists of the property of being right, the property of being wrong, and the property of being morally neutral is a family of properties, and therefore the corresponding state descriptions must be equally likely, as must the existentially quantified statements about the existence of rightmaking or wrongmaking properties whose truth depends upon those state descriptions.

The situation, in short, is this. There are certain general principles that serve to capture what is correct in the classical principle of indifference. Those principles, moreover, are needed for inductive logic: if one rejects them, inductive skepticism appears inescapable. One of those principles, however, as we have just seen, entails that (1) and (2) are true. There is, then, excellent reason for accepting (1) and (2).

Finally, Plantinga concludes his discussion of (16) by focusing on my contentions that, judged from an *a posteriori* point of view,

> (4a) The existence of wrongmaking properties is no less likely than the existence of rightmaking properties.

> (4b) Wrongmaking properties are not likely to have less moral weight than rightmaking properties.

Plantinga agrees that the moral knowledge we have does not provide grounds for rejecting (4a) and (4b). He then contends that, since it is equally true that the moral knowledge we have does not provide grounds for accepting (4a) and (4b), the result is that when we judge from an *a posteriori* point of view, we are not justified in accepting (4a) and (4b): the proper attitude is one of agnosticism.

Plantinga's conclusion here may rest upon his earlier claims that one is not justified in accepting (1) and (2), above. In any case, once (1) and (2) have been shown to be correct, and if, as Plantinga grants, there is no *a posteriori* evidence *against* (4a) and (4b), it follows that (4a) and (4b) are justified, regardless of whether there is any *a posteriori* evidence in favor of them. For if there is no *a posteriori* evidence relative to which the existence of wrongmaking properties is less likely than the existence of rightmaking properties, or vice versa, and if the existence of wrongmaking properties is *a priori* no less likely than the existence of rightmaking properties, then it follows that the existence of wrongmaking properties is *a posteriori* no less likely than the existence of rightmaking properties. For when all *a posteriori* facts are evidentially neutral, the *a posteriori* probabilities cannot be unequal when the *a priori* probabilities are equal. The upshot, accordingly, is that, judged from an *a posteriori* perspective, (4a) and (4b) are justified.

Summing up, then, the overall conclusion is that, contrary to what Plantinga has attempted to show, premises (15) and (16) both appear correct. Given this, the conclusion that the existence of an omnipotent, omniscient, and morally perfect person has a logical probability of less than one half relative to the existence of a single, apparently unjustified evil follows in quite a straightforward way. That conclusion can then be generalized, using a structure description approach to inductive logic, to arrive at the more general conclusion that the existence of an omnipotent, omniscient, and morally perfect person, relative to the existence of n apparently unjustified evils, has a logical probability of less than $1/(n + 1)$.

2   Is Belief in God Non-Inferentially Justified?

2.1   *Internalist versus externalist accounts of justification*

Plantinga begins the section in which he argues that theistic belief is non-inferentially justified by discussing what the relevant sense of justification is, and he focuses initially upon a general approach to justification that he thinks is accepted by most contemporary philosophers who have thought about justification, and according to which justification is located "in the neighborhood of *evidence* and *epistemic responsibility*" (p. 174, 'original emphasis'). Now this is a general approach that I myself accept, and I would argue—and Plantinga would agree—that if justification is to be necessarily connected with epistemic *responsibility*, one needs an internalist account of justification. Plantinga argues, however, that I cannot employ such a concept in the present context, and that I need instead to embrace an approach that involves some externalist element: "any appropriate conception of justification (any conception appropriate for Tooley's project) will have to be such that the deliverances of properly functioning, truth-aimed cognitive faculties will be justified" (p. 176).

Why does Plantinga think this is so? His reason involves combining the uncontroversial observation that "belief in God does indeed seem right, true, appropriate, to very many people, evil or no evil" (p. 175), with the epistemological claim that a proposition's "seeming right," or "*an inclination to believe*" a proposition, constitutes non-propositional evidence for the proposition, and renders acceptance of the proposition non-inferentially justified in the absence of defeaters.

There are two problems with this argument. First, it is based upon one particular internalist account of when beliefs are non-inferentially justified— namely, the type of account defended by Michael Huemer in his book *Skepticism and the Veil of Perception* (2001, pp. 98–103), which involves the following "principle of phenomenal conservatism":

(PC) If it seems to S as if P, then S thereby has at least *prima facie* justification for believing that P.

But this type of internalist account is not the only possibility. A very important alternative—and the one that I accept—involves instead a principle of direct acquaintance: one is non-inferentially justified in believing that p if and only if one is directly acquainted with some state of affairs *T* that is a truthmaker for *p*. When this alternative is adopted, the fact that it seems to many people that God exists becomes irrelevant, and so, also, does Plantinga's argument.

Nor can Plantinga's argument be recast. The reason is that it is central to the concept of direct acquaintance that if *A* is a type of state of affairs with which one can be directly acquainted, it must be logically impossible for one to be in a qualitatively identical, purely internal state when one is not directly acquainted with *A*, and this implies that one cannot be directly acquainted with any external states of affairs.

The second point is this. Huemer advances the principle of phenomenal conservatism as a foundational principle that can be used to specify when a belief is non-inferentially justified: if it seems to *S* as if *p*, and if, in addition, *S* has no defeaters for the belief that *p*, then *S* is non-inferentially justified in believing that *p*. But this seems clearly unsound. Among other things, it leads to an extraordinary expansion of the class of non-inferentially justified beliefs. Sitting in my study, I neither see nor hear any cars at the moment. But it seems to me as if there are cars in the world, and I know of no defeaters. So that belief is non-inferentially justified. More interesting, it seems to me that quantum mechanics is true, and I know of no defeaters. So I am non-inferentially justified in believing that quantum mechanics is true. Still more interesting, it seems to me that there are other human minds, and that induction is justified, and I have no defeaters for those and many other exciting philosophical theses. So those beliefs are non-inferentially justified for me.

Clearly, the principle of phenomenal conservatism is far too strong. One natural response is to draw a distinction between seemings, or inclinations to believe, that are basic or underived, and those that are based upon other seemings, or inclinations to believe, and to treat only the former as grounds of non-inferentially justified beliefs. But then Plantinga's present argument is, it seems to me, once again undercut, since I think that it is very plausible that whenever it seems to someone that God exists, that seeming or inclination to believe is derived from other seemings or inclinations to believe—such as its seeming to one that the Bible is true, or its seeming to one that one has had experiences with a certain experiential content, or with a certain emotional content, or its seeming to one that one has witnessed miracles, and so on.

In short, there is no reason why I need to abandon an internalist approach to justification. I can either embrace an appropriately *restricted* version of the principle of phenomenal conservatism, or the principle of direct acquaintance, and in neither case will I run up against the objection advanced by Plantinga.

To sum up, then, the following conclusions seem plausible. First, only an internalist approach to justification connects the latter with epistemic responsibility. Secondly, while belief in God could be non-inferentially justified if Huemer's principle of phenomenal conservatism were true, there are very good reasons for rejecting that principle. Thirdly, if one shifts instead to a restricted version of that principle, or to a direct acquaintance version of internalism, then it seems unlikely that belief in God can be non-inferentially justified.

2.2   Is there a reliable belief-forming faculty in the case of religious beliefs?

How do things stand if one shifts to an externalist approach to justification? I am inclined to think that once one severs any necessary connection between justification and epistemic responsibility, the term 'justification' becomes inappropriate. In the present context, however, I think that the crucial issue is simply this: is it reasonable to believe that there is in fact a reliable belief-forming mechanism that is specifically geared to religious beliefs?

There are excellent reasons, I believe, for holding that this is not the case. First, consider the idea that there is a reliable, general, religious-belief-forming mechanism. What would one expect if that were true? To answer this question, consider cases where there are reliable belief-forming mechanisms—as with *perception*, *memory*, and *deductive reasoning*. What one finds in those cases is that there is massive intersubjective agreement. Two observers who are near one another, and looking in roughly the same direction, will offer descriptions of what they see that agree to a striking extent, and with an enormous amount of detail. Similarly, if two people have been in the same perceptual situation, and are asked what they saw or heard in the past few seconds, there will once again be a very strong correlation. Thirdly, people who are introduced to the basic ideas concerning deduction will typically agree with regard to the validity of simple deductive inferences, and where they do not, that disagreement can almost always be resolved. Finally, the level of agreement in the case of beliefs formed by such mechanisms is not dependent upon the individuals' having been raised in the same sort of society: as long as one is dealing with beliefs that are not too heavily theory-laden, one has a level of agreement that is more or less completely independent of the culture in which one was raised. Nor does any sort of indoctrination have any significant effect upon the extent to which people agree with regard to beliefs formed by such mechanisms.

In the case of religious beliefs, by contrast, things are not at all like this. First, there are today an enormous number of incompatible systems of religious beliefs that different people accept: Buddhism, Hinduism, Confucianism, Taoism, Shinto, Judaism, Christianity, Islam, and many others. Secondly, even within specific religions, such as Christianity, or Islam, adherents often disagree—sometimes about matters that are thought to be essential to salvation. Thirdly, in the past there were many other religions, associated both with rather primitive societies, and with relatively advanced ones, such as Greece and Rome. Fourthly, none of the major religions that exist today dates back to the beginning of human history. Fifthly, there is a *very* strong positive correlation between the religious beliefs that a person accepts and those of the family environment in which he or she was raised. Sixthly, discussions between people with differing religious beliefs only very rarely result in a shared conclusion concerning which of the parties was misperceiving how things really are.

In all of these respects, religious beliefs are in stark contrast to what obtains in the case of perceptual beliefs, memory beliefs, and beliefs about deductive relations, and are not at all what one expect if there were an inbuilt faculty for arriving at reliable religious beliefs. These facts therefore provide, I suggest, excellent reasons for concluding that it is very unlikely that humans have a faculty that is specifically aimed at the formation of religious beliefs that are likely to be true.

Secondly, what about the possibility of a much more limited belief-forming mechanism that gives rise to reliable beliefs about the nature and existence of God? Here, too, I would claim, there are facts that render the existence of such a belief-forming mechanism highly improbable. First, historically, it was a long time before monotheism appeared on the scene: early religions were polytheistic, and monotheism seems to have arisen in only two places—Israel and Egypt. Secondly, even today, most religions are not monotheistic. Thirdly, theists disagree about the exact nature of God. Fourthly, belief in God declines with level of education, and with immersion in scientific thinking and research (Glock and Stark, 1965). Fifthly, belief in God also declines—and very dramatically—with exposure to philosophical thinking and methods.

To hold, in the face of such facts, that there is a reliable belief-forming mechanism that gives rise to beliefs about the existence of God is to commit oneself to something like the idea that people intentionally blind themselves to God's existence. But that, surely, is an extraordinary hypothesis. For what possible state of affairs could be more welcome and desirable than the existence of an omnipotent, omniscient, and morally perfect person?

3   The Argument from Evil Versus Justifications for Believing in the Existence of God

3.1 Non-inferentially justified belief in God?

I have just argued that it is very unlikely that humans have an inbuilt, reliable faculty that gives rise to belief in the existence of God. If so, then non-inferentially justified belief in the existence of God would seem to be ruled out if one adopts an externalist approach.

I have also argued that the same is true on plausible internalist approaches. But suppose I am wrong about the latter. Suppose, in particular, that the unrestricted principle of phenomenal conservatism is correct. How would things stand then?

That principle would imply that belief in the existence of God was *prima facie* credible, and the crucial question would then be whether there are any defeaters. The first point that needs to be made, I think, is that in the case of ordinary perception there certainly can be defeaters, not only for particular perceptual beliefs, but also for a whole range of such beliefs. This is shown by the fact that, before being exposed to relevant parts of physics, virtually all humans naturally form the belief that there are sensuous, qualitative, intrinsic, non-dispositional, color properties that are out there on the surfaces of physical objects. The inclination to form such beliefs, moreover, is basic rather than derived, and it does not depend upon the culture in which one was raised. But, though objects may be colored in other senses—such as having the power to give rise to certain sorts of experiences in normal human observers, or having the power to reflect various distributions of wavelengths of light—they are not colored in the sense of having sensuous, qualitative, intrinsic, non-dispositional, color properties. So types of beliefs that one is naturally inclined to form on the basis of perception can be false, and false across the board—as contrasted with being false in particular cases where conditions are abnormal.

Secondly, however, would there be defeaters in the case of belief in God? It seems to me clear that there would be. For suppose that S is inclined to believe that p, and that p is therefore *prima facie* credible for S, by virtue of the unrestricted principle of phenomenal conservatism. Suppose further, however, that there is some other person T who is no less thoughtful, well-informed, and so on, than S, and who is inclined to believe that q, where q is logically incompatible with p. Once S is aware of this situation, he then has a defeater that undercuts his *prima facie* justification for the belief that p. Such defeaters, however, are available to the present-day theist, since there are people who are no less thoughtful, well informed, and so on, who are inclined to believe, for example, that there is an intelligent designer of the world, but a designer who is either morally indifferent, or else evil.

Thirdly, and contrary to Plantinga's view, it seems to me that evil is itself a defeater, since I think that it is plausible that the primary evidence for beliefs concerning a person's character consists of the actions he or she performs and intentionally refrains from performing. Suppose, for example, that someone formed the firm belief that Hitler was a morally outstanding person, and that he had good reasons for bringing about the Holocaust. (The person in question might suggest that there might have been a very powerful non-embodied being who showed Hitler that he had superhuman powers, and who told him that the whole human race would die in a horribly painful way unless he killed six million people.) Would that person's belief be non-inferentially justified, if the unrestricted principle of phenomenal conservatism were true? Or, on the contrary, would the evidence concerning Hitler's actions have more epistemic weight than the person's inclination to believe that Hitler was a morally outstanding person? The latter, I suggest, is a far more plausible view.

3.2   *Inferentially justified belief in God*

How does the argument from evil fare in the face of arguments for the existence of God? Had Plantinga appealed to such arguments, I would have discussed this issue at length. Here I shall have to be very brief.

The first point to be made is that most arguments for the existence of a deity do not provide grounds for thinking that the deity in question is even morally good, let alone morally perfect, and so they provide no counter at all to the argument from evil.

Some arguments, however, while not supporting the claim that there is a morally perfect god, do at least provide grounds for holding that the deity in question is morally good. This is true, for example, of some arguments from religious experience, and some arguments from miracles.

As regards arguments from religious experiences, the considerations that were set out above against the view that belief in God is non-inferentially justified also tell against most arguments from religious experience. (Arguments appealing to mystical experiences would need separate discussion because of the intersubjectivity that characterizes those experiences in contrast to other types of religious experience.)

In the case of arguments that appeal to supposed miraculous events, what I would argue is that careful studies that have been carried out by writers such as A. D. White (1896, chapter 13, part 2), D. J. West (1957), Louis Rose (1971), William Nolen (1974), James Randi (1987), and others provide excellent reasons for concluding that it is unlikely that what might be called 'candidate miracles' do in fact occur.

About the only argument that would, if successful, establish the existence of God, understood in the sense that we have been discussing here, is an argument that Plantinga himself has elsewhere, and famously, defended (1974a and 1974b)—namely, the ontological argument.

One response to the ontological argument goes back to one of Anselm's contemporaries—Gaunilo—who argued that Anselm's proof of the existence of a perfect being could be paralleled to prove the existence of, for example, a perfect island. In addition, a variant on Gaunilo's objection can be used to show, for example, that there necessarily exists both an immovable object and an irresistible force, or both an omnipotent, omniscient, and perfectly good being and an omnipotent, omniscient, and perfectly evil being. The form of argument, accordingly, is one that gives rise to contradictions.

To get to the bottom of the ontological argument, however, I think that one needs to grapple with the metaphysics of modality. My own preferred picture, which I do not have the space to defend here, is as follows. How can one be justified in believing that talking donkeys, or particles whose mass is precisely π times that of an electron, are logically possible? Obviously not by peering into David Lewis's concrete possible worlds. But are expansive possible worlds of any type really relevant? For consider a world that consists of nothing except a particle whose mass is precisely π times that of an electron. Does not the possibility of such a very austere world really just come down to some fact about the proposition in question?

But what is that fact? The answer, I suggest, is that the relevant fact is that there is no sequence of propositions that leads from the proposition in question to some formal contradiction, where each step is related to one or more earlier steps either by formally valid rules of inference, or by substitution in accordance with some definition, or via an incompatibility of universals.

Let us now apply this account to the proposition that there is a necessarily existent, omnipotent, omniscient, and perfectly good person. That proposition entails that, necessarily, there is an omnipotent, omniscient, and perfectly good person. The account of modality just sketched then implies that for that proposition to be true, a contradiction must be derivable from the proposition that there does *not* exist an omnipotent, omniscient, and perfectly good person. No one, however, has ever found such a derivation, and given this failure, I suggest that the belief that there is such a derivation cannot be justified.

Concluding Comment: Naturalism, Supernaturalism, and Theism

In his opening statement, Plantinga attempted to show that theistic belief is justified by arguing that naturalism is false—a strategy that a number of other theists are now adopting. In my response, I attempted to show that the arguments that Plantinga offered, interesting though they were, are not in the end successful. But beyond the question of the success or failure of particular arguments, there is the question of whether this whole approach is a promising one to pursue. It seems to me that it is not. The reason is that a refutation of naturalism would get one only to supernaturalism *of some sort or other*, and there is an enormous gulf between that conclusion, and the conclusion that God exists. The argument from evil shows, moreover, that that chasm cannot be bridged.

Bibliography

Alvin Plantinga

Adams, Marilyn, and Robert M. (eds.). (1990). *The Problem of Evil* (Oxford: Oxford University Press).

Aiken, Henry D. (1957–8). "God and Evil," *Ethics* 68: 9.

Aquinas, Thomas (1265–74). *Summa Theologiae*, pt. 1, Q. 2, A. 1.

Baker, Lynne Rudder (2000). *Persons and Bodies* (Cambridge: Cambridge University Press).

Barrett, Justin (2000). "Exploring the Natural Foundations of Religion," *Trends in Cognitive Science* 4(1): 29–34.

Beilby, James (2002) *Naturalism Defeated?* (Ithaca: Cornell University Press), pp. 220–25, 205–11.

Bergmann, Michael (2000). "Deontology and Defeat," *Philosophy and Phenomenological Research* 60: 87–102.

Bergmann, Michael (1997). "Internalism, Externalism and the No-Defeater Condition," *Synthese* 110: 399–417.

Bloom, Paul (2005). "Is God an Accident?" *Atlantic Monthly*, 296 (5): 105–12.

BonJour, Laurence (1985). *The Structure of Knowledge* (Cambridge, MA: Harvard University Press).

Brook, John, and Geoffrey Canton (1998). *Reconstructing Nature: the Engagement of Science and Religion* (Edinburgh: T&T Clarke).

Churchland, Paul (1995). "Eliminative Materialism and the Propositional Attitudes," in *Contemporary Materialism*, ed. Paul K. Moser and J. D. Trout (London: Routledge).

Collins, Robin (1998). "A Defense of the Probabilistic Principle of Indifference," lecture to History and Philosophy of Science Colloquium, University of Notre Dame, October 8, 1998, presently unpublished.

Collins, Robin (1999). "A Scientific Argument for the Existence of God: The Fine Tuning Argument," in *Reason for the Hope within*, ed. Michael Murray (Grand Rapids, MI: Eerdmans), 47–75.

Collins, Robin (2003). "The Evidence for Fine-Tuning," in *God and Design: the Teological Argument and Modern Science*, ed. Neil A. Manson (London: Routledge), pp 178–99.

Craig, William (1979). *The Cosmological Kaalam Argument* (London: Macmillan).

Dawkins, Richard (1998). "When Religion Steps on Science's Turf," *Free Inquiry Magazine* 18(2): 18–19.

Dear, Peter (1988). *Mersenne and the Learning of the Schools* (Ithaca: Cornell University Press).

Dennett, Daniel (1991). *Consciousness Explained* (Boston: Little, Brown and Co.).

Dennett, Daniel (1995). *Darwin's Dangerous Idea* (New York: Simon and Schuster).

Derrida, Jacques (1987). *The Postcard: from Socrates to Freud and Beyond*, trans. Alan Bass (Chicago: University of Chicago Press).

Dostoevsky, Fyodor (1933). *The Brothers Karamazov*, trans. Constance Garnett (New York: Random House).

Dretske, Fred (1988). *Explaining Behavior* (Cambridge, MA: MIT Press).

Dretske, Fred (1995). *Naturalizing the Mind* (Cambridge, MA: MIT Press).

(1979). "Evolution," in *New Encyclopedia Britannica*, vol. 7.

Fodor, Jerry (1987). *Psychosemantics: the Problem of Meaning in the Philosophy of Mind* (Cambridge, MA: MIT Press).

Fodor, Jerry (1990). *A Theory of Content and Other Essays* (Cambridge, MA: MIT Press).

Goldman, Alvin (1979). "What Is Justified Belief," in *Justification and Knowledge: New Studies in Epistemology*, ed. George Pappas (Dordrecht: D. Reidel).

Howard-Snyder, Daniel (ed.). (1996). *The Evidential Argument from Evil* (Bloomington: Indiana University Press).

Hume, David (1980). *Dialogues Concerning Natural Religion*, ed. Richard Popkin (Indianapolis: Hackett Publishing Co.).

Hume, David (1888). *A Treatise of Human Nature* (Oxford: Clarendon Press), Selby Bigge edition.

Kant, Immanuel (1790). *Critique of Judgment*, tr. with an introduction by J. H. Bernard (New York: Hafner Pub. Co., c.1951).

Levin, Michael (1997). "Plantinga on Functions and the Theory of Evolution," *Australasian Journal of Philosophy* 75.

Mackie, J. L. (1955). "Evil and Omnipotence," *Mind* 64.

McCloskey, H. J. (1960). "God and Evil," *Philosophical Quarterly* 10.

Millikan, Ruth (1989). "In Defense of Proper Functions," *Philosophy of Science* 56: 288–302.

Millikan, Ruth (1984). *Language, Thought, and Other Biological Categories* (Cambridge, MA: MIT Press).

Neander, Karen (1991). "Functions as Selected Effects: the Conceptual Analyst's Defense," *Philosophy of Science* 58: 168–84.

Nietzsche, Friedrich (2003). *Nietzsche: Writings from the Late Notebooks* (Cambridge Texts in the History of Philosophy), ed. Rüdiger Bittner, trans. Kate Sturge, Notebook 36, June–July 1885.

Plantinga, Alvin (1974). *The Nature of Necessity* (Oxford: Clarendon Press).

Plantinga, Alvin (1977). *God, Freedom, and Evil* (Grand Rapids, MI: Eerdmans).

Plantinga, Alvin (1979). "The Probabilistic Argument from Evil," in *Philosophical Studies*, 35.

Plantinga, Alvin (1985). "Self–Profile," in *Alvin Plantinga* (Profiles V. 5), ed. James E. Tomberlin and Peter van Inwagen (Dordrecht: D. Reidel), pp. 36–55.

Plantinga, Alvin (1991). "Warrant and Designing Agents: a Reply to James Taylor," *Philosophical Studies* 64(2): 203–15.

Plantinga, Alvin (1993). *Warrant: the Current Debate* (New York: Oxford University Press).

Plantinga, Alvin (1993). *Warrant and Proper Function* (Oxford: Oxford University Press).

Plantinga, Alvin (1996). "Dennett's Dangerous Idea: Darwin, Mind and Meaning," *Books and Culture* (Carol Stream, IL: Christianity Today International), pp. 16–18, 35.

Plantinga, Alvin (2000). *Warranted Christian Belief* (New York: Oxford University Press).

Plantinga, Alvin (2001). "The Twin Pillars of Christian Scholarship," in *Seeking Understanding: the Stob Lectures 1986–1998* (Grand Rapids: Eerdmans).

Plantinga, Alvin (2002). "Reply to Beilby's Cohorts," in *Naturalism Defeated? Essays on Plantinga's Evolutionary Argument Against Naturalism* (Ithaca: Cornell University Press).

Plantinga, Alvin (1986). "Two Dozen (or so) Theistic Arguments," available online at *http://philofreligion.homestead.com//files/Theisticarguments.html*.

Post, John (1998). Review of Ruth G. Millikan *White Queen Psychology and Other Essays for Alice*, in *Philosophy and Phenomenological Research* 58.

Ramsey, Frank (1950). "Truth and Probability," in *The Foundations of Mathematics and Other Logical Essays*, ed. R. B. Braithwaite (New York: Humanities Press). (The essay was written in 1926.)

Rea, Michael (2002). *World without Design* (New York: Oxford University Press).

Reid, Thomas (1983). *Essays on the Intellectual Powers of Man* in *Thomas Reid's Inquiry and Essays* ed. Ronald Beanblossom and Keith Lehrer (Indianapolis: Hackett Publishing Co.).

Rorty, Richard (1979). *Philosophy and the Mirror of Nature* (Princeton: Princeton University Press).

Royden, H. L. (1968). *Real Analysis* (New York: Macmillan).

Rowe, William (ed.). (2002). *God and the Problem of Evil* (Oxford: Blackwell).

Russell, Bertrand (1917). *Mysticism and Logic* (New York: Barnes & Noble).

Smith, Quentin (2001). "The Metaphilosophy of Naturalism," *Philo* 4(2).

Stump, Eleonore (1994). "The Mirror of Evil," in *God and the Philosophers*, ed. Thomas V. Morris (New York: Oxford University Press).

Swinburne, Richard (1979). *The Existence of God* (Oxford: Clarendon Press).

Taliaferro, Charles (1997). "Incorporeality," in *A Companion to Philosophy of Religion*, ed. Philip L. Quinn and Charles Taliaferro (Oxford: Blackwell), pp. 271–78.

Van Fraassen, Bas (2002). *The Empirical Stance* (New Haven: Yale University Press).

Van Fraassen, Bas (1989). *Laws and Symmetry* (Oxford: Clarendon Press).

Van Inwagen, Peter (1995). "Dualism and Materialism: Athens and Jerusalem?" *Faith and Philosophy* 12(4).

Van Inwagen, Peter (2002). *Metaphysics* (Boulder, CO: Westview Press).

Weatherford, Roy (1983). *Philosophical Foundations of Probability Theory* (London: Routledge).

Wisdom, John (1935). "God and Evil," *Mind* 44: 1–20.

Wright, Larry (1973). "Functions," *The Philosophical Review* 82: 139–68.

Michael Tooley

Adams, Robert M. (1977). "Middle Knowledge and the Problem of Evil," *American Philosophical Quarterly* 14: 109–17.

Adams, Robert M. (1985). "Plantinga on the Problem of Evil," in *Alvin Plantinga*, ed. James E. Tomberlin and Peter van Inwagen (Dordrecht: D. Reidel), pp. 225–55.

Armstrong, David M. (1968). *A Materialist Theory of the Mind* (New York: Humanities Press).

Armstrong, David M. (1978). *Universals and Scientific Realism*, 2 vols (Cambridge: Cambridge University Press).

Armstrong, David M. (1983). *What Is a Law of Nature?* (Cambridge: Cambridge University Press).

Ayer, A. J. (1936). *Language, Truth, and Logic* (London: Victor Gollancz).

Bigelow, John, and Robert Pargetter (1987). "Functions," *Journal of Philosophy* 84: 181–96.

BonJour, Laurence (1996). "Plantinga on Knowledge and Proper Function," in *Warrant in Contemporary Epistemology*, ed. Jonathan L. Kvaning (Lanham, MD: Rowman & Littlefield Publishers), pp. 47–71.

Boyle, Robert (1666). *The Origins of Forms and Qualities* (London).

Carnap, Rudolf (1952). *The Continuum of Inductive Methods* (Chicago: University of Chicago Press).

Carnap, Rudolf (1962). *Logical Foundations of Probability*, 2nd edition (Chicago: University of Chicago Press).

Carnap, Rudolf (1971). "A Basic System of Inductive Logic, Part 1," in *Studies in Logic and Probability—Volume I*, ed. Rudolf Carnap and Richard C. Jeffrey (Berkeley and Los Angeles: University of California Press), pp. 33–165.

Carnap, Rudolf (1980). "A Basic System of Inductive Logic, Part 2," in *Studies in Logic and Probability—Volume II*, ed. Richard C. Jeffrey (Berkeley and Los Angeles: University of California Press), pp. 7–155.

Chalmers, David (1996). *The Conscious Mind* (Oxford: Oxford University Press).

Chrzan, Keith (1987). "The Irrelevance of the No Best Possible World Defense," *Philosophia* 17: 161–7.

Chrzan, Keith (1988). "Plantinga on Atheistic Induction," *Sophia* 27: 10–14.

Conway David A. (1988). "The Philosophical Problem of Evil," *Philosophy of Religion* 24: 35–66.

Conee, Earl, and Richard Feldman (2001). "Internalism Defended", in Hilary Kornblith (ed.), *Epistemology: Internalism and Externalism* (Oxoford: Blackwell Publishing), pp. 231–60.

Draper, Paul (2002). "Seeking But Not Believing: Confessions of a Practicing Agnostic," in *Divine Hiddenness*, ed. Daniel Howard-Snyder and Paul Moser (Cambridge: Cambridge University Press), pp. 197–214.

Dretske, Fred (1977). "Laws of Nature," *Philosophy of Science*, 44: 248–68.

Dretske, Fred (1988). *Explaining Behavior* (Cambridge, MA: MIT Press).

Fales, Evan (2002). "Darwin's Doubt, Calvin's Calvary," in *Naturalism Defeated? Essays on Plantinga's Evolutionary Argument against Naturalism*, ed. James Beilby (Ithaca, NY: Cornell University Press), pp. 43–58.

Feldman, Richard (1996). "Plantinga, Gettier, and Warrant," in *Warrant in Contemporary Epistemology*, ed. Jonathan L. Kvaning (Lanham, MD: Rowman & Littlefield Publishers), pp. 199–220.

Fitzpatrick, F. J. (1981). "The Onus of Proof in Arguments about the Problem of Evil," *Religious Studies* 17: 19–38.

Fodor, Jerry (1990). *A Theory of Content and Other Essays* (Cambridge, MA: MIT Press).

Forrest, Peter (1981). "The Problem of Evil: Two Neglected Defenses," *Sophia* 20: 49–54.

Fumerton, Richard (1985). *Metaphysical and Epistemological Problems of Perception* (Lincoln and London: University of Nebraska Press).

Gettier Edmund L. (1963). "Is Justified True Belief Knowledge," *Analysis* Volume, 23: 121–23.

Glock, Charles Y., and Rodney Stark (1965). *Religion and Society in Tension* (Chicago: Rand McNally).

Hare, R. M. (1952). *The Language of Morals* (Oxford: Oxford University Press).

Hartshorne, Charles (1962). *The Logic of Perfection* (La Salle, IL: Open Court Publishing).

Hasker, William (1988). "Suffering, Soul-Making, and Salvation," *International Philosophical Quarterly* 28: 3–19.

Hick, John (1966; revised edition 1978). *Evil and the God of Love* (New York: Harper & Row).

Huemer, Michael (2001). *Skepticism and the Veil of Perception* (New York: Rowman and Littlefield Publishers).

Hume, David (1779). *Dialogues Concerning Natural Religion* (London). Reprinted and edited by Norman Kemp Smith (Indianapolis: Bobbs-Merril, 1974).

Jackson, Frank (1982). "Epiphenomenal Qualia" *The Philosophical Quarterly* 32: 127–36.

Kahneman, Daniel, Paul Slovic, and Amos Tversky (eds) (1982). *Judgment under Uncertainty: Heuristics and Biases* (Cambridge: Cambridge University Press).

Kane, G. Stanley (1975). "The Failure of Soul-Making Theodicy," *International Journal for Philosophy of Religion* 6: 1–22.

Khatchadourian, Haig (1966). "God, Happiness and Evil," *Religious Studies* 2: 109–19.

Kretzmann, Norman (1966). "Omniscience and Immutability," *Journal of Philosophy* 63: 409–20.

Kvanvig, Jonathan L. (ed.) (1996). *Warrant in Contemporary Epistemology* (Lantham, MD: Rowman and Littlefield Publishers).

La Para, Nicholas (1965). "Suffering, Happiness, Evil," *Sophia* 4: 10–16.

Langtry, Bruce (1989). "God, Evil and Probability," *Sophia* 28: 32–40.

Lewis, David (1970). "How to Define Theoretical Terms," *Journal of Philosophy* 67: 427–46.

Lewis, Delmas (1983). "The Problem with the Problem of Evil," *Sophia* 22: 26–35.

Locke, John (1690). *Essay Concerning Human Understanding* (London).

Mackie, J. L. (1977). *Ethics—Inventing Right and Wrong* (Harmondsworth: Penguin Books).

McKim, Robert (1984). "Worlds without Evil," *International Journal for Philosophy of Religion* 15: 161–70.

Malcolm, Norman (1960). "Anselm's Ontological Arguments," *The Philosophical Review* 69: 41–62.

Martin, Michael (1988). "Reichenbach on Natural Evil," *Religious Studies* 24: 91–9.

Millikan, Ruth (1984). *Language, Thought, and Other Biological Categories* (Cambridge, MA: MIT Press).

Neander, Karen (1991). "Functions as Selected Effects: the Conceptual Analyst's Defense," *Philosophy of Science* 58: 168–84.

Nesbitt, Richard E., and Lee Ross (1980). *Human Inference: Strategies and Shortcomings of Social Judgment* (Englewood Cliffs, NJ: Prentice-Hall).

Nolen, William A. (1974). *Healing—A Doctor in Search of a Miracle* (New York: Random House).

O'Connor David (1983). "Swinburne on Natural Evil," *Religious Studies* 19: 65–73.

Perkins, R. M. (1983). "An Atheistic Argument from the Improvability of the Universe," *Noûs* 17: 239–50.

Perry, John (1979). "The Problem of the Essential Indexical," *Noûs* 13: 3–21.

Plantinga, Alvin (1967). *God and Other Minds* (Ithaca, NY: Cornell University Press).

Plantinga, Alvin (1974a). *God, Freedom, and Evil* (New York: Harper & Row).

Plantinga, Alvin (1974b). *The Nature of Necessity* (Oxford: Clarendon Press).

Plantinga, Alvin (1979). "The Probabilistic Argument from Evil," *Philosophical Studies* 35: 1–53.

Plantinga, Alvin (1981). "Tooley and Evil: a Reply," *Australasian Journal of Philosophy* 60: 66–75.

Plantinga, Alvin (1985a). "Self-Profile," in *Alvin Plantinga*, ed. James E. Tomberlin and Peter van Inwagen (Dordrecht: D. Reidel), pp. 3–97.

Plantinga, Alvin (1985b). "Reply to Robert M. Adams," in *Alvin Plantinga*, ed. James E. Tomberlin and Peter van Inwagen (Dordrecht: D. Reidel), pp. 371–82.

Plantinga, Alvin. "Two Dozen (or So) Theistic Arguments," available online at *http://philofreligion.homestead.com/files/Theisticarguments.html*.

Plantinga, Alvin (1991). "An Evolutionary Argument against Naturalism," *Logos* 12.

Plantinga, Alvin (1993a). *Warrant: the Current Debate* (New York: Oxford University Press).

Plantinga, Alvin (1993b). *Warrant and Proper Function* (Oxford: Oxford University Press, 1993).

Plantinga, Alvin (1994). "Naturalism Defeated," available online at *http://www.home-stead.com/philofreligion/files/alspaper.htm.*

Plantinga, Alvin (1998). "Degenerate Evidence and Rowe's New Evidential Argument from Evil," *Noûs* 32: 531–44.

Pollock, John (1987). "How to Build a Person," in *Philosophical Perspectives, 1, Metaphysics, 1987,* ed. James Tomberlin (Atascadero, CA: Ridgeview), pp. 146–51.

Randi, James (1987). *The Faith Healers* (Amherst, NY: Prometheus Books).

Reichenbach, Bruce R. (1976). "Natural Evils and Natural Law: a Theodicy for Natural Evils," *International Philosophical Quarterly* 16: 179–96.

Reichenbach, Bruce R. (1980). "The Inductive Argument from Evil," *American Philosophical Quarterly* 17: 221–7.

Rose, Louis (1971). *Faith Healing* (Harmondsworth: Penguin Books).

Rowe, William (1979). "The Problem of Evil and Some Varieties of Atheism," *American Philosophical Quarterly* 16: 335–41.

Rowe, William (1984). "Evil and the Theistic Hypothesis: a Response to Wykstra," *International Journal for Philosophy of Religion* 16: 95–100.

Rowe, William (1986). "The Empirical Argument from Evil," in *Rationality, Religious Belief, and Moral Commitment,* ed. Robert Audi and William J. Wainwright (Ithaca, NY: Cornell University Press), pp. 227–47.

Rowe, William (1988). "Evil and Theodicy," *Philosophical Topics* 16: 119–32.

Rowe, William (1991). "Ruminations about Evil," *Philosophical Perspectives* 5: 69–88.

Rowe, William (1996). "The Evidential Argument from Evil: a Second Look," in *The Evidential Argument from Evil,* ed. Daniel Howard-Snyder (Bloomington and Indianapolis: Indiana University Press), pp. 262–85.

Rowe, William (1998). "Evil and Theodicy," *Philosophical Topics* 16: 119–32.

Russell, Bertrand (1959). *The Problems of Philosophy* (Oxford: Oxford University Press).

Schlesinger, George (1964). "The Problem of Evil and the Problem of Suffering," *American Philosophical Quarterly* 1: 244–7.

Schlesinger, George (1977). *Religion and Scientific Method* (Boston: D. Reidel).

Shoemaker, Sydney (1969). "Time without Change," *Journal of Philosophy* 66: 363–81.

Smith, Quentin (1991). "An Atheological Argument from Evil Natural Laws," *International Journal for Philosophy of Religion* 29: 159–74.

Stump, Eleonore (1983). "Knowledge, Freedom and the Problem of Evil," *International Journal for Philosophy of Religion* 14: 49–58.

Stump, Eleonore, and Norman Kretzmann (1981). "Eternity," *Journal of Philosophy* 78: 429–57.

Swinburne, Richard (1977). *The Coherence of Theism* (Oxford: Clarendon Press).

Swinburne, Richard (1979). *The Existence of God* (Oxford: Clarendon Press).

Swinburne, Richard (1988). "Does Theism Need a Theodicy?" *Canadian Journal of Philosophy* 18: 287–312.

Tomberlin, James E., and Peter van Inwagen, eds (1985). *Alvin Plantinga* (Dordrecht: D. Reidel).

Tooley, Michael (1975). "Theological Statements and the Question of an Empiricist Criterion of Cognitive Significance," in *The Logic of God—Theology and Verification*, ed. Malcolm L. Diamond and Thomas V. Litzenburg, Jr., (Indianapolis: Bobbs-Merrill), pp. 481–524.

Tooley, Michael (1977). "The Nature of Laws," *Canadian Journal of Philosophy* 7: 667–98.

Tooley, Michael (1980). "Alvin Plantinga and the Argument from Evil," *Australasian Journal of Philosophy* 58: 360–76.

Tooley, Michael (1981). "Plantinga's Defence of the Ontological Argument," *Mind* 90: 422–7.

Tooley, Michael (1987). *Causation: a Realist Approach* (Oxford: Oxford University Press).

Tooley, Michael (1997). *Time, Tense, and Causation* (Oxford: Oxford University Press).

Tooley, Michael (2000). "Freedom and Foreknowledge," *Faith and Philosophy* 17: 212–24.

Tooley, Michael (2003). "Basic Tensed Sentences and their Analysis," in *Time, Tense, and Reference*, ed. Aleksandar Jokic and Quentin Smith (Cambridge, MA: MIT Press), pp. 409–47.

Warraq, Ibn (1995). *Why I Am Not a Muslim* (Amherst, NY: Prometheus Books).

West, D. J. (1957). *Eleven Lourdes Miracles* (London: Gerald Duckworth).

White, A. D. (1896). *A History of the Warfare of Science with Theology within Christendom* (New York: Appleton).

Zagzebski, Linda (1991). *The Dilemma of Freedom and Foreknowledge* (New York: Oxford University Press).

Index